Student Solutions M

to accompany

College Mathematics for Technology

Sixth Edition

Cheryl Cleaves
Southwest Tennessee Community College

Margie Hobbs
The University of Mississippi

PEARSON
Prentice
Hall

Upper Saddle River, New Jersey
Columbus, Ohio

Editor in Chief: Stephen Helba
Senior Acquisitions Editor: Gary Bauer
Editorial Assistant: Natasha Holden
Developmental Editor: Ohlinger Publishing Services
Production Editor: Louise N. Sette
Design Coordinator: Diane Ernsberger
Cover Designer: Bryan Huber
Production Manager: Pat Tonneman
Marketing Manager: Leigh Ann Sims

Pearson Prentice Hall™ is a trademark of Pearson Education, Inc.
Pearson® is a registered trademark of Pearson plc
Prentice Hall® is a registered trademark of Pearson Education, Inc.

Pearson Education Ltd.
Pearson Education Singapore Pte. Ltd.
Pearson Education Canada, Ltd.
Pearson Education—Japan.

Pearson Education Australia Pty. Limited.
Pearson Education North Asia Ltd.
Pearson Educación de Mexico, S.A. de C.V.
Pearson Education Malaysia Pte. Ltd.

10 9 8 7 6 5 4 3
ISBN 0-13-049219-1

COLLEGE MATHEMATICS FOR TECHNOLOGY
Cheryl Cleaves and Margie Hobbs

Contents

PREFACE

TO THE STUDENT

This manual contains the step-by-step solutions for odd-numbered problems for the Assignment Exercises and Chapter Trial Test for each chapter. The purpose of this manual is to assist you with your study of *College Mathematics for Technology*. It is advisable to make several attempts to work the exercises before referring to the solutions given here. You will also want to study the examples and explanations given in the text in your process of understanding the concepts presented in the exercises.

A given problem often can be solved many different ways. Some approaches may require more steps than others. The approach presented in this manual will not necessarily be the shortest way of working the problem or the way you may have attempted to work the problem. If your approach is not exactly like the approach presented in this manual, compare your approach with the approach presented here to determine if both processes employ sound reasoning strategies. The authors have made every attempt to verify the accuracy of the solutions. However, if you should determine that a solution in this manual is incorrect or incomplete, the authors would appreciate hearing your comments which may be sent to the publishing address listed in this manual.

Mathematics skills are normally developed in a particular sequence so that new skills are reinforced and they build on previously learned skills; therefore, it is *very* important to master each skill before proceeding to the next skill.

Developing Your Study Plan

To be successful in a mathematics program, you must be sure to *practice* all required skills. The amount of practice needed varies from student to student, but the text is designed with built-in checks to determine if you have practiced sufficiently to master each skill.

Many books are available which offer suggestions for effective strategies for studying mathematics. In addition, you may work with your instructor to develop your study plan. The booklet "How to Study Mathematics" is available free of charge through Prentice Hall. Your instructor may request copies of this booklet. Your study plan should utilize the resources that are available to you such as learning centers, tutors, computer programs, video tapes, the *Study Wizard*, etc.

You will discover that working with a study partner or participating in a study group is a very successful strategy for studying mathematics. An effective study plan can prove to be as important to your success in mathematics as your mastery of specific mathematics skills.

Using Your Calculator

The text gives many opportunities for you to develop your skills in using both the scientific and graphics calculator. A calculator is most effective when you estimate or predict the answer before you make the calculation. Developing your number sense about calculations will enable you to determine when you have made errors in sequencing operations or pressing the appropriate keys. A calculator should not replace your computations of single digit number facts and other easy calculations that can be performed mentally. The calculator, when used properly, can be an enormous tool in discovering and verifying mathematical concepts. Many tests are not designed for the student to use the calculator; however, your proficiency in using the calculator will be desirable in most employment settings.

ASSIGNMENT EXERCISES

1. (a) $\dfrac{3}{10} = 0.3$

A fraction with a denominator that is a power of 10 can be written as a decimal number by writing the numerator and placing the decimal in the appropriate place to indicate the proper place value of the denominator.

   (b) $\dfrac{15}{100} = 0.15$

Since the denominator is 100, the last digit of the numerator is in the hundredths place.

   (c) $\dfrac{4}{100} = 0.04$

Since the denominator is 100, the last digit is in the hundredths place.

3. place value of 6 in 21.836
                    ↑
6 is in the thousandths place.

5. 13.7213 tenths place
         ↑
The 7 is in the tenths place.

7. (a)
```
          ┌──── tens place
          │
          ▼
    430
    units
```

   (b)
```
          ┌────ten-thousands place
          │
          ▼
    34,        789
    thousands  units
```

   (c)
```
          ┌──── millions place
          │
          ▼
    3,         456,       521
    millions   thousands  units
```

9. 56,109,110 fifty-six million, one hundred nine thousand, one hundred ten

11.
Millions	Thousands	Units
1	265	4_1
1	265	401
1,265,401		

13. 6.803

Read whole number part, read "and" for the decimal point, read the decimal part as a whole-number, and read the place value of the last digit. The number is read as "six and eight hundred three thousandths."

15. Six hundred twenty-five thousandths
Write digits, and place decimal point such that the last digit is in the thousandths place.
0.625

17. (a) $\underline{3}6$ Identify the tens place digit and examine the digit to its right. The first tens place digit is 3 and the digit to its right is 6. The 6 is greater than 5, so round to a larger approximate number by increasing the 3 to 4 and replacing the 6 with 0. The rounded answer is 40.

(b) $\underline{7}4$ The rounded answer is 70.   (c) nearest whole number 2④.237
                                                    (ones place)   24

(d) nearest dollar \$4②.98   (e) nearest tens ⑧3.052
     (ones place)   \$43   80

(f) nearest cent   \$8.9③_78   (g) nearest cent \$0.9⑨_86
                     \$8.94   \$1.00

(h) nearest hundred-thousandths   0.0970③2
                                          0.09703

19. (a) nearest hundred   ④6 8
                                     500

(b) nearest ten thousand   ④9,238
                             50,000

(c) nearest tenth   41.③78
                      41.4

3 is in the tenths place. 7 is digit to the right, so add 1 to the 3. Digits to the left remain the same, digits to the right (and to the right of the decimal point) are dropped.

(d) nearest hundredth   6.8⑨5 7   (e) nearest ten-thousandth   23.460⑨_7
                         6.90   23.4610

21. larger   4.783   4.79
                   ↑   ↑

Compare each place value, left to right, until two digits in the same place are different, and compare those digits.
4.783 < ④.79

23. smaller to larger
0.021   0.0216   0.02
  ↑   ↑   ↑
0.021   0.0216   0.020
  ↑   ↑   ↑
0.020 is smaller, now compare 0.021   0.0216
                                  ↑   ↑
                               0.0210 < 0.0216
                                  ↑   ↑
0.020 < 0.0210 < 0.0216
0.02 < 0.021 < 0.0216

25. $\dfrac{7}{8} = 0.875$ $\dfrac{6}{7} = 0.857$
                  ↑   ↑
0.875 > 0.857

$\dfrac{7}{8}$ is larger than $\dfrac{6}{7}$.

27.   (a) $6+9+3+5 = 15+3+5 = 18+5 = 23$

(b) $5+1+6+3+3 = 6+6+3+3 = 12+3+3 = 15+3 = 18$

(c) $8+5+3+6+2+4 = 28$

(d) $7+4+3+2+5+4 = 25$

29.

$$\begin{array}{r} \overset{1\ 1}{10.4} \\ 15.3 \\ 2.9 \\ +\ \ 6.3 \\ \hline 34.9 \end{array}$$

The total number of kilowatts used is 34.9.

31.   (a) Estimate   Exact

$$\begin{array}{r} \$17,000 \\ +\ 12,000 \\ \hline \$29,000 \end{array} \qquad \begin{array}{r} \overset{1}{\$16},\overset{1\ 1}{742}.83 \\ +\ \ 12,349.26 \\ \hline \$29,092.09 \end{array}$$

(b) Estimate   Exact

$$\begin{array}{r} \overset{1}{\$17},000 \\ +\ 19,000 \\ \hline \$36,000 \end{array} \qquad \begin{array}{r} \overset{1\ 1}{\$17},402 \\ +\ 18,646 \\ \hline \$36,048 \end{array}$$

33.   (a)
$$\begin{array}{r} 21.34 \\ -\ 16.73 \\ \hline 4.61 \end{array}$$
   (b)
$$\begin{array}{r} 15.934 \\ -\ 12.807 \\ \hline 3.127 \end{array}$$
   (c) $9-7 = 2$ (d) $5-0 = 5$

(e) $8-3-2-3 = 5-2-3 = 3-3 = 0$ (f)
$$\begin{array}{r} 284.730 \\ -\ \ 79.831 \\ \hline 204.899 \end{array}$$

(g)
$$\begin{array}{r} 345 \\ -\ 201 \\ \hline 144 \end{array}$$
   (h)
$$\begin{array}{r} 13,342 \\ -\ 1,202 \\ \hline 12,140 \end{array}$$

35.
$$\begin{array}{r} 8.296 \\ -\ 0.005 \\ \hline 8.291 \text{ in.} \end{array} \text{ to } \begin{array}{r} 8.296 \\ +\ 0.005 \\ \hline 8.301 \text{ in.} \end{array}$$

37.   Estimate   Exact   Check

$$\begin{array}{r} 700 \\ -500 \\ \hline 200 \text{ miles} \end{array} \quad \begin{array}{r} \overset{5\ 15}{6\cancel{5}3} \\ -463 \\ \hline 190 \text{ miles} \end{array} \quad \begin{array}{r} \overset{1}{4}63 \\ +190 \\ \hline 653 \end{array}$$

The difference in the routes is 190 miles.

39.
$$\begin{array}{ll} \text{B} & \overset{1\ 1}{1.861} \\ \text{C+} & 1.946 \\ \hline & 3.807 \end{array} \qquad \begin{array}{ll} \text{D} & \overset{3\ 12}{\cancel{4}.\cancel{2}37} \\ & -3.807 \\ \hline \text{A} & 0.430 \end{array}$$

The length of A is 0.43 in.

41.
$$\begin{array}{r} \overset{1}{8.935} \\ +\ 0.005 \\ \hline 8.940 \text{ in.} \end{array} \qquad \begin{array}{r} 8.935 \\ -\ 0.005 \\ \hline 8.930 \text{ in.} \end{array}$$

The limit dimensions of D are 8.940 in. and 8.930 in.

43. $2\times6\times7=12\times7=84$

$$\overset{1}{12}$$
$$\underline{\times\ 7}$$
$$84$$

45.
$$\overset{2\ 6}{127}$$
$$\underline{\times\quad 9}$$
$$1{,}143$$

47.
$$\overset{2}{\overset{\cancel{2}}{305}}$$
$$\underline{\times\ 45}$$
$$1525$$
$$1220$$
$$\overline{13{,}725}$$

49.
$$\overset{\cancel{12}\ \ \overset{4}{\cancel{1}}\ \ 1}{12{,}407}\ |$$
$$\underline{\times\quad 27}\ |0$$
$$\overset{1\ 1}{86849}$$
$$24814$$
$$\overline{3{,}349{,}890}$$

51.
$$\overset{4\ \ 1}{\overset{\cancel{2}}{\cancel{2}}\ \ 56{,}002}\ |$$
$$\underline{\times\quad\ 704}\ |0$$
$$224008$$
$$392014$$
$$\overline{394{,}254080}$$

53.
$$\overset{1}{67}$$
$$\underline{\times 21}$$
$$\overset{1}{67}$$
$$134$$
$$\overline{1{,}407}$$

A business would pay $1,407 for the keyboards.

55.
$$\overset{2}{\overset{\cancel{2}}{\cancel{2}}\ 305}$$
$$\underline{\times\ 144}$$
$$1220$$
$$1220$$
$$305$$
$$\overline{43{,}920}$$

The dealer paid $43,920 for the order.

57. Multiplying first gives:
$$5(6-2)=$$
$$5(6)-5(2)=$$
$$30-10=$$
$$20$$

Adding first gives:
$$5(6-2)=$$
$$5(4)=$$
$$20$$

59.
$$6(3+7)=$$
$$6(3)+6(7)=$$
$$18+42=$$
$$60$$

$$6(3+7)=$$
$$6(10)=$$
$$60$$

61.
$$8(7+3)=$$
$$8(7)+8(3)=$$
$$56+24=$$
$$80$$

$$8(7+3)=$$
$$8(10)=$$
$$80$$

63.
$$2(687-523)=$$
$$1{,}374-1{,}046=$$
$$328$$

$$\overset{1\ 1}{687}$$
$$\underline{\times\quad 2}$$
$$1{,}374$$

$$523$$
$$\underline{\times\ \ 2}$$
$$1{,}046$$

$$523$$
$$\underline{\times\ \ 2}$$
$$1{,}046$$

An RGB monitor costs $328.

65. 365×36

Estimate
$$370\times40=\ \$14{,}800$$

Exact
$$\overset{1\ 1}{\overset{\cancel{3}\ \cancel{3}}{365}}$$
$$\underline{\times\quad 36}$$
$$\overset{1\ 1}{2190}$$
$$1095$$
$$\overline{\$13{,}140}$$

Check
$$\overset{1}{\overset{\cancel{3}}{\overset{\cancel{3}}{36}}}$$
$$\underline{\times\ 365}$$
$$\overset{1\ 1}{180}$$
$$216$$
$$108$$
$$\overline{13{,}140}$$

The worker will earn $13,140.

67. Estimate
$$A=l\times w$$
$$=1{,}900\times600$$
$$=1{,}140{,}000\ \text{ft}^2$$

Exact
$$A=l\times w$$
$$=1{,}940.7\times620.4$$
$$=1{,}204{,}010.28\ \text{ft}^2$$

Check
$$1{,}940.7$$
$$\underline{\times\quad 620.4}$$
$$77628$$
$$0$$
$$38814$$
$$116442$$
$$\overline{1{,}204{,}010.28}$$

$$\overset{1}{620.4}$$
$$\underline{\times\ 1{,}940.7}$$
$$43428$$
$$0$$
$$24816$$
$$55836$$
$$6204$$
$$\overline{1{,}204{,}010.28}$$

The area of the land is 1,204,010.28 square feet.

69.

$$
\begin{array}{r}
0.00014 \\
\times\ \ \ \ 864 \\
\hline
56 \\
84 \\
112 \\
\hline
0.12096
\end{array}
$$

The tape will expand 0.12096 in.

71. (a) $5 \div 3$

(b) $3\overline{)5}$

(c) $\dfrac{5}{3}$

73. $1 \div 1 = 1$

75. $7 \div 0 =$ undefined or impossible

77. $84.3 \div 1.6$

$$
\begin{array}{r}
5.26875 \\
1.6\overline{)84.3} \\
\underline{80}\ \ \ \ \\
43\ \ \ \\
\underline{32}\ \ \ \\
110\ \ \\
\underline{96}\ \ \\
140\ \\
\underline{128}\ \\
120 \\
\underline{112} \\
80 \\
\underline{80}
\end{array}
$$

79. $352 \div 25$

$$
\begin{array}{r}
13 \\
25\overline{)325} \\
\underline{25}\ \ \\
75 \\
\underline{75} \\
0
\end{array}
$$

81. $30,126 \div 15$

$$
\begin{array}{r}
2,008.4 \\
15\overline{)30,126.0} \\
\underline{30}\ \ \ \ \ \ \ \\
1\ \ \ \ \ \ \\
\underline{0}\ \ \ \ \ \ \\
12\ \ \ \ \\
\underline{0}\ \ \ \ \\
126\ \ \\
\underline{120}\ \ \\
60 \\
\underline{60}
\end{array}
$$

83.

$$
\begin{array}{r}
23\ R\ 11 \\
27\overline{)632} \\
\underline{54}\ \ \\
92 \\
\underline{81} \\
11
\end{array}
$$

Each volunteer will receive 23 envelopes and 11 will be left ov

85.

$$
\begin{array}{r}
58.375 \\
0.8\overline{)46.7000}
\end{array}
$$

87.

Estimate

$$
\begin{array}{r}
5 \\
90\overline{)500}
\end{array}
$$

Exact

$5.523 = 5.52$ rounded

$$
\begin{array}{r}
86\overline{)475.000} \\
\underline{430}\ \ \ \ \ \\
450\ \ \ \\
\underline{430}\ \ \ \\
200\ \ \\
\underline{172}\ \ \\
280 \\
\underline{258} \\
22
\end{array}
$$

89.

Estimate	Exact	Check

$$\begin{array}{r} 10 \\ 30\overline{)300} \end{array}$$

$$\begin{array}{r} 10.629 \\ 27\overline{)287.000} \\ \underline{27} \\ 170 \\ \underline{162} \\ 80 \\ \underline{54} \\ 260 \\ \underline{243} \\ 17 \end{array}$$

$$\begin{array}{r} 27 \\ \times\ 1\ 0 \\ \hline 270 \end{array} \qquad \begin{array}{r} 270 \\ +\ 17 \\ \hline 287 \end{array}$$

Each volunteer collected $10.63.

91.   average, nearest hundredth

$$48.785 \approx 48.79 \text{ ft}$$

$$\begin{array}{r} {}^{1\ 3\ 2} \\ 42.34 \\ 38.97 \\ 51.95 \\ +\ 61.88 \\ \hline 195.14 \end{array} \qquad \begin{array}{r} 48.785 \\ 4\overline{)195.140} \\ \underline{16} \\ 35 \\ \underline{32} \\ 31 \\ \underline{28} \\ 34 \\ \underline{32} \\ 20 \\ \underline{20} \end{array}$$

93.   (a)   base $\rightarrow 7^{3 \leftarrow \text{exponent}}$

$7^3 = 7 \times 7 \times 7 = 343$

(b)   base $\rightarrow 2.3^{4 \leftarrow \text{exponent}}$

$2.3^4 = 2.3 \times 2.3 \times 2.3 \times 2.3 = 27.9841$

(c)   base $\rightarrow 8^{4 \leftarrow \text{exponent}}$

$8^4 = 8 \times 8 \times 8 \times 8 = 4,096$

95.   (a) $0.9^1 = 0.9$ Any number with an exponent of 1 is that number itself.

(b) $35^1 = 35$

(c) $1^1 = 1$

97.   (a) $1.7^0 = 1$ Any number (except 0) with an exponent of 0 equals 1.

(b) $1^0 = 1$

(c) $8^0 = 1$

(d) $149^0 = 1$

99.   (a) $1^2 = 1 \times 1 = 1$

(b) $125^2 = 125 \times 125 = 15,625$

(c) $5.6^2 = 5.6 \times 5.6 = 31.36$

(d) $21^2 = 21 \times 21 = 441$

some calculators: 21 $\boxed{x^2}$

other calculators: 21 $\boxed{x^2}$ $\boxed{=}$

101.   (a) $10 = 10^1$

(b) $1,000 = 10^3$

(c) $10,000 = 10^4$

(d) $100,000 = 10^5$

103.   (a) $700 \div 100 = 7$

(b) $40.56 \div 1,000 = 0.04056$

(c) $60.5 \div 100 = 0.605$

(d) $23,079 \div 10,000 = 2.3079$

(e) $44,582 \div 1,000 = 44.582$

105.
$$4^2 \times (12 - 7) - 8 + 3 =$$ Do operations within parentheses first.

$$4^2 \times 5 - 8 + 3 =$$ Evaluate exponentiation.

$$16 \times 5 - 8 + 3 =$$ Multiply.

$$80 - 8 + 3 =$$ Add and subtract from left to right.

$$72 + 3 =$$

$$75$$

107.
$$4 + 5 - 2 \times 3 =$$ Multiply.

$$4 + 5 - 6 =$$ Add and subtract from left to right.

$$9 - 6 =$$

$$3$$

109.
$$12 \div 4 \times 6 =$$ Divide.

$$3 \times 6 =$$ Multiply.

$$18$$

111.
$$5 + 21 \div 3 \cdot 7 =$$ Divide.

$$5 + 7 \cdot 7 =$$ Multiply.

$$5 + 49 =$$ Add.

$$54$$

113.
$$8 + 6 \div 2 \times 3 - 1 =$$ Divide.

$$8 + 3 \times 3 - 1 =$$ Multiply.

$$8 + 9 - 1 =$$ Add and subtract from left to right.

$$16$$

115.
$$21 + 7 \cdot 2 - 5 \cdot 4 =$$ Multiply left to right.

$$21 + 14 - 20 =$$ Add and subtract from left to right.

$$15$$

117.
$$18 - 5 \cdot 2 + 7 =$$ Multiply.

$$18 - 10 + 7 =$$ Add and subtract from left to right.

$$15$$

119.
$$5 - 2 \cdot 2 + 12 =$$ Multiply.

$$5 - 4 + 12 =$$ Add and subtract from left to right.

$$13$$

121.
$$3.1 \times 4 \times \sqrt{16} - 6^2 =$$ Evaluate exponentiation and square roots from left to right.

$$3.1 \times 4 \times 4 - 6^2 =$$

$$3.1 \times 4 \times 4 - 36 =$$ Multiply from left to right.

$$12.4 \times 4 - 36 =$$

$$49.6 - 36 =$$ Subtract.

$$13.6$$

123. $5.2^3 - \sqrt{81} \times (2+1) =$ Do operations within parentheses first.

$5.2^3 - \sqrt{81} \times 3 =$ Evaluate exponentiation and square roots from left to right.

$140.608 - \sqrt{81} \times 3 =$

$140.608 - 9 \times 3 =$ Multiply.

$140.608 - 27 =$ Subtract.

113.608

125. $584 \div 12 = 48.67$ or 49 boxes   **127.** $42,670 - 26,361 = 16,309$ people

129. $48 \cdot 100 \cdot 1.40 = \ \$6,720$

$40 \cdot 110 \cdot 1.40 = \ \underline{\$6,160}$

Total Rent $= \$12,880$

131. $(43 + 68 + 72 + 59 + 21) \div 5 = \$52.60$

Average cost per pair of shoes

133. $(12.19 + 10.87 + 15.21 + 6.50 + 8.95) \div 5 = \$10.74$

Average daily lunch cost

135. $2,160 \div 15 = 144$ so 15×144 would do.

$2,160 \div 16 = 135$ 16×135

$2,160 \div 18 = 120$ 18×120

$2,160 \div 20 = 108$ 20×108

$2,160 \div 24 = 90$ 24×90

$2,160 \div 27 = 80$ 27×80

$2,160 \div 30 = 72$ 30×72

$2,160 \div 36 = 60$ 36×60

$2,160 \div 40 = 54$ 40×54

$2,160 \div 45 = 48$ 45×48

Any of the sizes given would do, but the best
size is 45×48.

137.   (a) 0.03^2 $= 0.0009$

(b) 0.07^2 $= 0.0049$

(c) 0.005^2 $= 0.000025$

(d) 0.009^2 $= 0.000081$

(e) 0.02^2 $= 0.000008$

(f) 0.004^3 $= 0.000000064$

Chapter 1 Trial Test

1.   5,   030,   102
Millions Thousands Units
Five million, thirty thousand, one hundred two.

3.   Seven and twenty-seven thousandths.
7.027

5. $2,\textcircled{7}\underline{4}3$ 7 is in the hundreds place, 4 is the digit to the right, 4 is less than 5, so round down.
The rounded value is 2,700.

7.   smaller: 5.09   5.1
                ↑   ↑
              $\boxed{5.09}$ <   5.1

9.   nearest tenth $48.\textcircled{3}\underline{2}84$
                               48.3

11. $\overset{2\ 2}{37}$
         158
         764
         $+\ \ 48$
         $\overline{1,007}$

13. $\overset{2\ 1\quad 4}{13{,}207}$
         $\times\quad 702$
         $\overline{\overset{1\ 1}{26414}}$
         $\underline{92449}$
         $\overline{\$9{,}271{,}314}$

15. $3^2 + 5^3 =$ Evaluate exponentiation from left to right.
         $9 + 5^3 =$
         $9 + 125 =$ Add.
         134

17. $3 \times 6^2 - 4 \div 2 =$ Evaluate exponentiation.
         $3 \times 36 - 4 \div 2 =$ Multiply and divide from left to right.
         $108 - 4 \div 2 =$ Divide.
         $108 - 2 =$ Subtract.
         106

19. $86 \div 10^4 =$ Evaluate the exponent.
         $86 \div 10{,}000 =$ Divide from left to right.
         0.0086

21. Estimate: Exact:
         480   475
         $-\ 170$ $-\ 165$
         $\overline{\$310}$ $\overline{\$310}$
         There is $310 left from his paycheck.

23. Estimate: Exact:
         $\$10$ $\$14$
         $10\overline{)100}$ $9\overline{)126}$
                       $\underline{9}$
                       36
                       $\underline{36}$
                       0
         The cost per pizza is $14.

25. The commutative property means that values being added may be added in any order.
         $2 + 3 = 5$ $3 + 2 = 5$
         The associative property means that values being added may be grouped in any manner.
         $5 + (6 + 7) =$ $(5 + 6) + 7 =$
         $5 + 13 =$ $11 + 7 =$
         18   18

27. $42.73 \times 1,000 = 42{,}730 = 42{,}730$

29.   nearest tenth

$$
\begin{array}{r}
11.58 \approx 11.6 \\
7.2\,\overline{)\,83.410} \\
\underline{72} \\
114 \\
\underline{72} \\
421 \\
\underline{360} \\
610 \\
\underline{576} \\
34
\end{array}
$$

31.

$$
\begin{array}{r}
\overset{2}{8}2 \\
95 \\
76 \\
84 \\
72 \\
\underline{+\;91} \\
500
\end{array}
\qquad
\begin{array}{r}
83.3 \approx 83 \;\text{nearest whole number} \\
6\,\overline{)\,500.0} \\
\underline{48} \\
20 \\
\underline{18} \\
20 \\
\underline{18} \\
2
\end{array}
$$

33.   Estimate, nearest tenth

$$
\begin{array}{rr}
0.87 & 0.9 \\
-\,0.328 & -\,0.3 \\
\hline
 & 0.6
\end{array}
$$

35.   Estimate, round each number to one non-zero digit.

$$
37.2\,\overline{)\,2{,}987.5} \qquad
\begin{array}{r}
70 \\
40\,\overline{)\,3{,}000}
\end{array}
$$

37. $\$1.75 \times 10{,}000 = 1{,}7500 = \$17{,}500$
The heating oil costs $17,500.

chapter 2   Integers

Assignment Exercises

1.   −1 G   **3.**   −2 F   **5.**   −3 E   **7.**   −7 A   **9.**   5 L

11.   6 M   **13.**   5, 21, 987 Answers may vary.   **15.**   0; zero is not a natural number.

17.   1   **19.** $72 > -80$ **21.** $7 > -5$ **23.** $-9 < 5$ **25.** $|5| = 5$

27. $|-3| = 3$ **29.** $|+7| = 7$ **31.** $|-11| = 11$ **33.**   The opposite of -12 is $+12$.

35.   The opposite of 15 is -15.   **37.**   The opposite of -2 is $+2$.

39.   The opposite of -42 is $+42$.   **41.**   The opposite of $+87$ is -87.

43.–47.

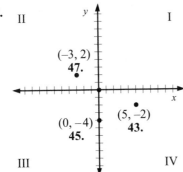

49.   The origin has coordinates $(0,0)$.

51. $A\ (3, 0)$
       $B\ (2, 2)$
       $C\ (2, -5)$
       $D\ (-4, -1)$
       $E\ (-3, 1)$

53. $5 + 12 = 17$
Same sign, add, common sign.

55. $(-15) + 8 = -7$
Different signs, subtract, sign of larger absolute value.

57. $-5 + (-8) = -13$
Same sign, add, common sign.

59. $8 + (-8) = 0$
These are opposites, so subtract absolute values.
Zero has no sign.

61. $0 + (-8) = -8$
Zero added to a number does not change that number.

63.
$$-25+0+12+7 =$$
$$-25+12+7 =$$
$$-13+7 =$$
$$-6$$

65. $+4-5+9 = -1+9 = 8;$ the team gained a net of $+8$ yards.

67.
$$\$500-\$42-\$18-\$21+\$150 =$$
$$458-18-21+150 =$$
$$440-21+150 =$$
$$419+150 =$$
$$\$569$$

69. The additive identity, 0, if added to any number will result in the same number. The sum of numbers that are additive inverses is zero.

71.
$$-9-4 =$$ Change subtraction sign to addition.
$$-9+(-4) =$$ Change sign of subtrahend.
$$-13$$ Add.

73.
$$11-(-3) =$$ Change subtraction sign to addition.
$$11+(+3) =$$ Change sign of subtrahend.
$$14$$ Add.

75.
$$\underbrace{-6+3}-5-7 =$$ Change subtraction sign to addition.
     Change sign of subtrahend.
$$\underbrace{-3-5}-7 =$$ Add.
     Repeat.
$$\underbrace{-3+(-5)}-7 =$$
$$-8-7 =$$
$$-8+(-7) =$$
$$-15$$

77. $-5-0 = -5$ Subtracting zero from an integer results in the same number with the same sign.

79.
$$0-(-2) =$$ Subtracting an integer from zero results in the opposite of the number.
$$0+(+2) =$$
$$2$$

81.
$$18-(-18) =$$ Change subtraction sign to addition.
$$18+(+18) =$$ Change sign of subtrahend.
$$36$$ Add.

83.
$$+43-(-27) =$$ Difference in $43°$ above 0 $(+43)$ and $27°$ below 0 (-27)
$$43+(+27) =$$ Change signs to addition.
$$70°$$ Add.

85. $97.8°-103.2° = -5.4°$

87. $14°-(-22°) = 14°+22° = 36°C$

89. $7 \times -2 = -14$ Different signs give negative product.

91. $6(-2) = -12$ Different signs give negative product.

93. $-8(0) = 0$ Multiplying an integer by zero results in zero, which has no sign.

95. $2(3)(-7)(0) = 0$ Multiplying by zero results in zero.

97. $4(3)(-2)(7) = -168$ Since number of negative factors is odd, product will be negative.

99. $(7)^3 = (7)(7)(7) = 343$ A positive number raised to a power is positive.

101. $-4^2 = -4 \cdot 4 = -16$ The exponent does not apply to the negative sign.

103. $5^2 = 5 \cdot 5 = 25$ A positive number raised to a power is positive.

105. $-2°(5) = -10°$ Product of drop in temperature $(-2°)$ and hours observed (5).

107. Higher, 20 pts.
$-4(5) = -20$ Drop of 4 points (-4) over a period of 5 weeks.

109. $12 \div 3 = 4$
Same signs give positive quotient.

111. $\dfrac{-5}{-5} = +1$
Same signs give a positive quotient.

113. $\dfrac{-20}{-5} = +4$
Same signs give positive quotient.

115. $\dfrac{-24}{6} = -4$
Different signs give negative quotient.

117. $\dfrac{-51}{-3} = +17$
Same signs give a positive quotient.

119. $\dfrac{-7}{0} =$ undefined or impossible
Division of an integer by zero is undefined or impossible.

121. $\dfrac{51}{-17} = -3$
Different signs give a negative quotient.

123. $\dfrac{90°}{-6} = -15°$

125. $7(3+5) =$ Parentheses.
$7(8) =$ Multiply
56
some calculator steps:

7 $\boxed{\times}$ $\boxed{(}$ 3 $\boxed{+}$ 5 $\boxed{)}$ $\boxed{=}$

other calculator steps:

7 3 $\boxed{+}$ 5

127. $\dfrac{15-7}{8} =$ Parentheses or grouping.

$\dfrac{8}{8} =$ Division.

1

129. $12 - 8(-3) =$ Multiply.

$12 + 24 =$ Add.

36

some calculator steps:

12 [−] 8 [×] 3 [+/−] [=]

other calculator steps:

12 [−] 8 [( ] [−] 3 [ )] [=]

131. $4 + (-3)^4 - 2(5 + 1) =$ Parentheses.

$4 + (-3)^4 - 2(6) =$ Exponentiation.

$4 + 81 - 2(6) =$ Multiply.

$4 + 81 - 12 =$ Add.

$85 - 12 =$ Subtract.

73

some calculator steps:

4 [+] 3 [+/−] [x^y] 4 [−] 2 [×] [( ] 5 [+] 1 [ )] [=]

other calculator steps:

4 [+] [( ] [(−)] 3 [ )] [^] 4 [−] 2 [( ] 5 [+] 1 [ )] [ENTER]

133. $-3 + 2^3 - 7 =$

$-3 + 8 - 7 =$ Exponentiation.

$5 - 7 =$ Addition and subtraction.

$5 + (-7) =$

-2

some calculator steps:

3 [+/−] [+] 2 [x^y] 3 [−] 7 [=]

other calculator steps:

[(−)] 3 [+] 2 [^] 3 [−] 7 [ENTER]

135. $296 - 382(-4)^5 =$ Exponentiation.

$296 - 382(-1024) =$ Multiplication.

$296 + 391,168 =$ Addition.

$391,464$

some calculator steps:

296 [−] 382 [×] 4 [+/−] [x^y] 5 [=]

other calculator steps:

296 [−] 382 [( ] [−] 4 [ )] [^] 5 [ENTER]

137.

8:00 AM:	$-3°C$	
9:00 AM: increase 2°	$-3° + 2° = -1°C$	
10:00 AM: increase 1°	$-1° + 1° = 0°C$	
11:00 AM: increase 0°	$0° + 0° = 0°C$	
12:00 PM: increase 1°	$0° + 1° = 1°C$	
1:00 PM: no change	$1°C$	
2:00 PM: increase 3°	$1° + 3° = 4°C$	
3:00 PM: decrease 4°	$4° - 4° = 0°C$	
4:00 PM: decrease 7°	$0° - 7° = -7°C$	
5:00 PM: decrease 8°	$-7° - 8° = -15°C$	
6:00 PM: decrease 12°	$15° - 12° = -27°C$	

Chapter 2 Trial Test

1. $-8 < 0$ **3.** $-5 > -10$ **5.** The opposite of 8 is -8.

7. $-3 + 7 =$ Adding unlike signs: subtract,
$\quad\quad 4$ answer has sign of number with larger absolute value.

9.
$2(6)(-4) =$
$12(-4) =$ Multiplying integers with unlike signs:
$\quad -48$ multiply absolute values, negative answer.

11. $8 + 4 + (-2) + (-7) =$ **13.** $2(-1)(-4) =$ **15.** $(-8)(3)(0)(-1) = 0$
$\quad 12 + (-2) + (-7) =$ $\quad -2(-4) =$ Multiplying by zero results in zero.
$\quad\quad 10 + (-7) =$ $\quad\quad 8$
$\quad\quad\quad 3$

17. $0 - 7 =$ **19.** $\dfrac{-7}{0}$ Undefined or impossible.   **21.** $5 + (-7) - (-3) + 2 - 6 =$
$\quad 0 + (-7) =$ $\quad -2 - (-3) + 2 - 6 =$
$\quad\quad -7$ $\quad -2 + 3 + 2 - 6 =$
$\quad\quad\quad 1 + 2 - 6 =$
$\quad\quad\quad\quad 3 - 6 =$
$\quad\quad\quad 3 + (-6) =$
$\quad\quad\quad\quad -3$

23. $\dfrac{4}{-2} = -2$ Dividing unlike signs gives negative answer.   **25.** $2(3 - 9) \div 2^2 + 7 =$
$\quad 2(-6) \div 4 + 7 =$
$\quad -12 \div 4 + 7 =$
$\quad -3 + 7 =$
$\quad\quad 4$

27. $5(6) - 2 + 10 \div 2 =$

$30 - 2 + 5 =$

$28 + 5 =$

33

some calculator steps:

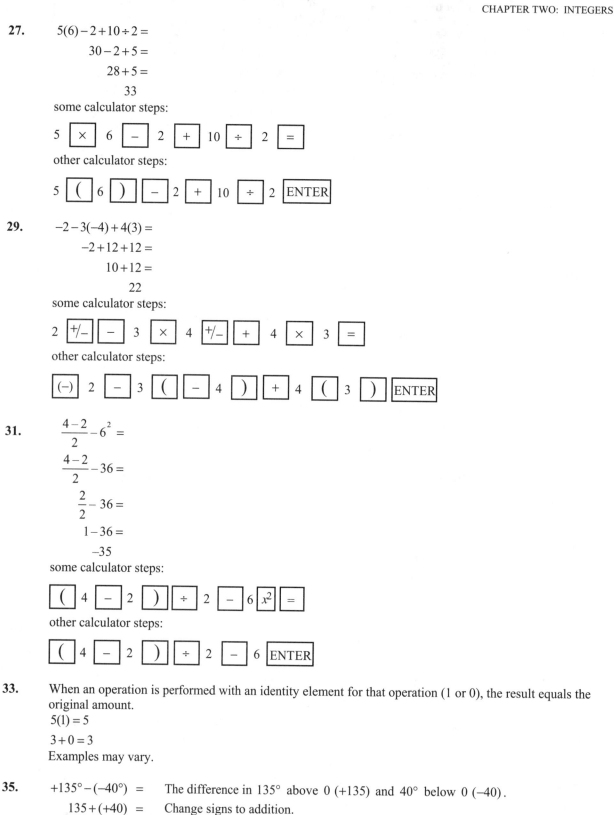

5 [×] 6 [−] 2 [+] 10 [÷] 2 [=]

other calculator steps:

5 [( ] 6 [ )] [−] 2 [+] 10 [÷] 2 [ENTER]

29. $-2 - 3(-4) + 4(3) =$

$-2 + 12 + 12 =$

$10 + 12 =$

22

some calculator steps:

2 [+/−] [−] 3 [×] 4 [+/−] [+] 4 [×] 3 [=]

other calculator steps:

[(−)] 2 [−] 3 [( ] [−] 4 [ )] [+] 4 [( ] 3 [ )] [ENTER]

31. $\dfrac{4-2}{2} - 6^2 =$

$\dfrac{4-2}{2} - 36 =$

$\dfrac{2}{2} - 36 =$

$1 - 36 =$

-35

some calculator steps:

[( ] 4 [−] 2 [ )] [÷] 2 [−] 6 [x^2] [=]

other calculator steps:

[( ] 4 [−] 2 [ )] [÷] 2 [−] 6 [ENTER]

33.   When an operation is performed with an identity element for that operation (1 or 0), the result equals the original amount.

$5(1) = 5$

$3 + 0 = 3$

Examples may vary.

35. $+135° - (-40°) =$ The difference in 135° above 0 (+135) and 40° below 0 (−40).

$135 + (+40) =$ Change signs to addition.

$175°F$ Add.

chapter 3 Fractions

Assignment Exercises

1. $\dfrac{3}{8}$ **3.** $\dfrac{3}{9}$ or $\dfrac{1}{3}$ **5.** $\dfrac{13}{24}$

7. $\dfrac{9}{4}$

(a) The numerator of the fraction is 9. (b) The denominator of the fraction is 4.
(c) One unit has been divided into 4 parts. (d) 9 of these parts are used.
(e) The fraction can be read as 9 divided by 4. (f) The divisor of the division is 4.
(g) The dividend of the division is 9. (h) This fraction is improper.
(i) This fraction has a value more than 1. (j) This fraction represents 9 out of 4 parts.

9. $\dfrac{5}{2}$ (f) Improper fraction **11.** $6\dfrac{1}{7}$ (d) Mixed number

13. $\dfrac{7}{11}$ (e) Proper fraction **15.** $33\dfrac{1}{3}$ (d) Mixed number

17. $20 = 10 \times 2,\ 30 = 10 \times 3,\ 40 = 10 \times 4,\ 50 = 10 \times 5,\ 60 = 10 \times 6$; answers may vary.

19. $42 = 21 \times 2,\ 63 = 21 \times 3,\ 84 = 21 \times 4,\ 105 = 21 \times 5,\ 126 = 21 \times 6$; answers may vary.

21. $14 = 7 \times 2,\ 21 = 7 \times 3,\ 28 = 7 \times 4,\ 35 = 7 \times 5,\ 42 = 7 \times 6$; answers may vary.

23. $16 = 8 \times 2,\ 24 = 8 \times 3,\ 32 = 8 \times 4,\ 40 = 8 \times 5,\ 48 = 8 \times 6$; answers may vary.

25. Yes; sum of digits is divisible by 3.

27. No; divisible by 2 but not by 3.

29. Yes; last digit is 0.

31. No; sum of digits is not divisible by 9.

33. 1, 48   1, 2, 3, 4, 6, 8, 12, 16, 24, 48   **35.** 1, 51   1, 3, 17, 51
    2, 24   3, 17
    3, 16
    4, 12
    6, 8

37. 1, 74   1, 2, 37, 74
    2, 37

39.　18, composite $1 \cdot 18$
$2 \cdot 9$
$3 \cdot 6$

41.　21, composite $1 \cdot 21$
$3 \cdot 7$

43.　$2 \cdot 3 \cdot 7$

45.　$2 \cdot 7 \cdot 7$ or $2 \cdot 7^2$

47.　$18 = 2 \cdot 3^2$
$40 = 2^3 \cdot 5$
$LCM = 2^3 \cdot 3^2 \cdot 5$
$= 360$

49.　$12 = 2^2 \cdot 3$
$18 = 2 \cdot 3^2$
$30 = 2 \cdot 3 \cdot 5$
$LCM = 2^2 \cdot 3^2 \cdot 5$
$= 180$

51.　$10 = 2 \cdot 5$
$12 = 2^2 \cdot 3$
$GCF = 2$

53.　$12 = 2^2 \cdot 3$
$18 = 2 \cdot 3^2$
$30 = 2 \cdot 3 \cdot 5$
$GCF = 2 \cdot 3$
$= 6$

55.　$\dfrac{5}{8} = \dfrac{?}{24}$
$8 \overline{)24}^{\,3}, \quad 3 \times 5 = 15$
$\dfrac{5}{8} = \dfrac{15}{24}$

57.　$\dfrac{5}{12} = \dfrac{?}{60}$
$12 \overline{)60}^{\,5}, \quad 5 \times 5 = 25$
$\dfrac{5}{12} = \dfrac{25}{60}$

59.　$\dfrac{2}{3} = \dfrac{?}{15}$
$3 \overline{)15}^{\,5}, \quad 5 \times 2 = 10$
$\dfrac{2}{3} = \dfrac{10}{15}$

61.　$\dfrac{3}{4} = \dfrac{?}{32}$
$4 \overline{)32}^{\,8}, \quad 8 \times 3 = 24$
$\dfrac{3}{4} = \dfrac{24}{32}$

63.　$\dfrac{1}{5} = \dfrac{?}{55}$
$5 \overline{)55}^{\,11}, \quad 11 \times 1 = 11$
$\dfrac{1}{5} = \dfrac{11}{55}$

65.　$\dfrac{4}{5} = \dfrac{?}{20}$
$5 \overline{)20}^{\,4}; \quad 4 \times 4 = 16$
$\dfrac{4}{5} = \dfrac{16}{20}$

67.　$\dfrac{6}{12} = \dfrac{6 \div 6}{12 \div 6} = \dfrac{1}{2}$

69.　$\dfrac{4}{32} = \dfrac{4 \div 4}{32 \div 4} = \dfrac{1}{8}$

71.　$\dfrac{2}{8} = \dfrac{2 \div 2}{8 \div 2} = \dfrac{1}{4}$

73.　$\dfrac{34}{64} = \dfrac{34 \div 2}{64 \div 2} = \dfrac{17}{32}$

75.　$\dfrac{12}{32} = \dfrac{12 \div 4}{32 \div 4} = \dfrac{3}{8}$

77.　$\dfrac{6}{8} = \dfrac{6 \div 2}{8 \div 2} = \dfrac{3}{4}$

79.　$0.7 = \dfrac{7}{10}$

81.　$0.95 = \dfrac{95 \div 5}{100 \div 5} = \dfrac{19}{20}$

83.　$0.872 = \dfrac{872 \div 8}{1,000 \div 8} = \dfrac{109}{125}$

85.　$0.02 = \dfrac{2 \div 2}{100 \div 2} = \dfrac{1}{50}$

87. $5\overline{)1.0}$ $\quad \dfrac{1}{5} = 0.2$
$\quad\quad \underline{1.0}$
with 0.2 above

89. $8\overline{)5.000}$ $\quad \dfrac{5}{8} = 0.625$
$\quad\quad \underline{48}$
$\quad\quad \ \ 20$
$\quad\quad \ \ \underline{16}$
$\quad\quad \ \ 40$
$\quad\quad \ \ \underline{40}$
with 0.625 above

91. $11\overline{)9.0000}$ $\quad \dfrac{9}{11} = 0.818 \text{ (rounded)}$
$\quad\quad \underline{88}$
$\quad\quad \ \ 20$
$\quad\quad \ \ \underline{11}$
$\quad\quad \ \ 90$
$\quad\quad \ \ \underline{88}$
$\quad\quad \ \ \ 20$
$\quad\quad \ \ \ \underline{11}$
$\quad\quad \ \ \ \ 9$
with 0.8181 above

93. $\dfrac{18}{5} = 5\overline{)18} = 3\dfrac{3}{5}$
$\quad\quad\quad \underline{15}$
$\quad\quad\quad \ 3$
with 3 above

95. $\dfrac{39}{8} = 8\overline{)39} = 4\dfrac{7}{8}$
$\quad\quad\quad \underline{32}$
$\quad\quad\quad \ 7$
with 4 above

97. $\dfrac{43}{8} = 8\overline{)43} = 5\dfrac{3}{8}$
$\quad\quad\quad \underline{40}$
$\quad\quad\quad \ 3$
with 5 above

99. $\dfrac{175}{2} = 2\overline{)175} = 87\dfrac{1}{2}$
$\quad\quad\quad\ \underline{16}$
$\quad\quad\quad\ 15$
$\quad\quad\quad\ \underline{14}$
$\quad\quad\quad\ \ 1$
with 87 above

101. $\dfrac{18}{12} = 12\overline{)18} = 1\dfrac{6}{12} = 1\dfrac{1}{2}$
$\quad\quad\quad\quad \underline{12}$
$\quad\quad\quad\quad \ 6$
with 1 above

103. $8 = \dfrac{8}{1}$

105. $7\dfrac{1}{8} = \dfrac{(8 \times 7)+1}{8} = \dfrac{57}{8}$

107. $9\dfrac{3}{16} = \dfrac{(16 \times 9)+3}{16} = \dfrac{147}{16}$

109. $4\dfrac{3}{5} = \dfrac{(5 \times 4)+3}{5} = \dfrac{23}{5}$

111. $12 = \dfrac{12}{1}$

113. $5\dfrac{1}{3} = \dfrac{(3 \times 5)+1}{3} = \dfrac{16}{3}$

115. $2 = \dfrac{?}{10}$

$2 = \dfrac{2}{1} = \dfrac{2 \times 10}{1 \times 10} = \dfrac{20}{10}$

117. $11 = \dfrac{?}{3}$

$11 = \dfrac{11}{1} = \dfrac{11 \times 3}{1 \times 3} = \dfrac{33}{3}$

119. $\dfrac{1}{4}, \dfrac{1}{3}, \dfrac{1}{5} \quad \dfrac{4}{2 \times 2} \quad \dfrac{3}{3} \quad \dfrac{5}{5}$
$\quad\quad\quad\quad\quad\quad\quad\quad\ 2^2$

$\text{LCD} = 2^2 \times 3 \times 5 = 4 \times 3 \times 5 = 60$

121. $\dfrac{3}{4}, \dfrac{1}{16} \quad \dfrac{4}{2 \times 2} \quad \dfrac{16}{2 \times 8}$
$\quad\quad\quad\quad\quad\ \ 2^2 \quad\quad\ 2 \times 2 \times 4$
$\quad\quad\quad\quad\quad\quad\quad\quad\ 2 \times 2 \times 2 \times 2$
$\quad\quad\quad\quad\quad\quad\quad\quad\quad\quad 2^4$

$\text{LCD} = 2^4 = 16$

123. $\dfrac{5}{12}, \dfrac{3}{10}, \dfrac{13}{15} \quad \dfrac{12}{2 \times 6} \quad \dfrac{10}{2 \times 5} \quad \dfrac{15}{3 \times 5}$
$\quad\quad\quad\quad\quad\quad\quad\ 2 \times 2 \times 3$
$\quad\quad\quad\quad\quad\quad\quad\quad 2^2 \times 3$

$\text{LCD} = 2^2 \times 3 \times 5 = 4 \times 3 \times 5 = 60$

125. $\dfrac{5}{8} \quad \dfrac{9}{16}$

$\dfrac{10}{16} > \dfrac{9}{16} \quad\quad \dfrac{5}{8} = \dfrac{5 \times 2}{8 \times 2} = \dfrac{10}{16}$

$\dfrac{5}{8} > \dfrac{9}{16}$

$\dfrac{5}{8}$ is greater than $\dfrac{9}{16}$

127. $\dfrac{3}{8} \overset{?}{<} \dfrac{1}{2}$

$\dfrac{3}{8} < \dfrac{4}{8}$ $\dfrac{1}{2} = \dfrac{1 \times 4}{2 \times 4} = \dfrac{4}{8}$

$\dfrac{3}{8} < \dfrac{1}{2}$

No, $\dfrac{3}{8}$ in. thick plaster board is not thicker than a $\dfrac{1}{2}$ in. thick piece.

129. $\dfrac{19}{32} \overset{?}{<} \dfrac{7}{8}$ **131.** $\dfrac{5}{8}, \dfrac{3}{8}$ **133.** $\dfrac{3}{8} < \dfrac{4}{8}$

$\dfrac{19}{32} < \dfrac{28}{32}$ $\dfrac{7}{8} = \dfrac{7 \times 4}{8 \times 4} = \dfrac{28}{32}$ $\dfrac{3}{8} < \dfrac{5}{8}$ $\dfrac{3}{8}$ is smaller

$\dfrac{19}{32} < \dfrac{7}{8}$ $\dfrac{3}{8}$ is smaller

A $\dfrac{19}{32}$ in. wrench is smaller than a $\dfrac{7}{8}$ in. bolt head.

135. $\dfrac{1}{4} \quad \dfrac{3}{16}$ **137.** $\dfrac{7}{8} \quad \dfrac{27}{32}$

$\dfrac{4}{16} > \dfrac{3}{16}$ $\dfrac{1}{4} = \dfrac{1 \times 4}{4 \times 4} = \dfrac{4}{16}$ $\dfrac{28}{32} > \dfrac{27}{32}$ $\dfrac{7}{8} = \dfrac{7 \times 4}{8 \times 4} = \dfrac{28}{32}$

$\dfrac{1}{4} > \dfrac{3}{16}$ $\dfrac{7}{8} > \dfrac{27}{32}$

$\dfrac{3}{16}$ is smaller $\dfrac{27}{32}$ is smaller

139. $\dfrac{1}{2} \quad \dfrac{9}{19}$

$\dfrac{19}{38} > \dfrac{18}{38}$ $\dfrac{1}{2} = \dfrac{1 \times 19}{2 \times 19} = \dfrac{19}{38}, \dfrac{9}{19} = \dfrac{9 \times 2}{19 \times 2} = \dfrac{18}{38}$

$\dfrac{1}{2} > \dfrac{9}{19}$

$\dfrac{9}{19}$ is smaller

141. $0.26 = \dfrac{26}{100}$ **143.** $0.272 = \dfrac{272}{1,000} = \dfrac{272 \times 11}{1,000 \times 11} = \dfrac{2,992}{11,000}$

$\dfrac{3}{4} = \dfrac{3 \times 25}{4 \times 25} = \dfrac{75}{100}$ $\dfrac{3}{11} = \dfrac{3 \times 1,000}{11 \times 1,000} = \dfrac{3,000}{11,000}$

$\dfrac{75}{100} > \dfrac{26}{100}$; $\dfrac{3}{4} > 0.26$; so, $\dfrac{3}{4}$ is larger. $\dfrac{2,992}{11,000} < \dfrac{3,000}{11,000}$; so, $\dfrac{3}{11}$ is larger.

145.
$$\frac{3}{16} = \frac{12}{64}$$
$$+\frac{9}{64} = \frac{9}{64}$$
$$\frac{21}{64}$$

147.
$$\frac{3}{5} = \frac{18}{30}$$
$$+\frac{5}{6} = \frac{25}{30}$$
$$\frac{43}{30} = 1\frac{13}{30}$$

149.
$$2\frac{7}{16} = 2\frac{14}{32}$$
$$+6\frac{5}{32} = 6\frac{5}{32}$$
$$8\frac{19}{32}$$

151.
$$3\frac{7}{8} = 3\frac{28}{32}$$
$$5\frac{3}{16} = 5\frac{6}{32}$$
$$+1\frac{7}{32} = 1\frac{7}{32}$$
$$9\frac{41}{32} = 9+1\frac{9}{32} = 10\frac{9}{32}$$

153.
$$7\frac{5}{8} = 7\frac{10}{16}$$
$$+10\frac{7}{16} = 10\frac{7}{16}$$
$$17\frac{17}{16} = 17+1\frac{1}{16} = 18\frac{1}{16}$$

The pipe was $18\frac{1}{16}$ in. before it was cut.

155.
$$7\frac{5}{16} = 7\frac{10}{32}$$
$$+5\frac{9}{32} = 5\frac{9}{32}$$
$$12\frac{19}{32}$$

The original piece of stock was $12\frac{19}{32}$ in.

157.
$$3\frac{1}{8} = 3\frac{4}{32}$$
$$5\frac{3}{32} = 5\frac{3}{32}$$
$$+7\frac{9}{16} = 7\frac{18}{32}$$
$$15\frac{25}{32}$$

The welded rod is $15\frac{25}{32}$ in.

159.
$$3\frac{1}{2} = 3\frac{2}{4}$$
$$+1\frac{1}{4} = 1\frac{1}{4}$$
$$4\frac{3}{4} \text{ in.}$$

161.
$$\frac{1}{2} = \frac{8}{16}$$
$$\frac{3}{16} = \frac{3}{16}$$
$$+\frac{3}{16} = \frac{3}{16}$$
$$\frac{14}{16} = \frac{7}{8} \text{ in.}$$

163.
$$\frac{5}{9}$$
$$-\frac{2}{9}$$
$$\frac{3}{9} = \frac{1}{3}$$

165.
$$3\frac{5}{8} = 3\frac{5}{8}$$
$$-2 = 2\frac{0}{8}$$
$$1\frac{5}{8}$$

167.
$$8\frac{7}{8} = 8\frac{28}{32} = 7\frac{32}{32} + \frac{28}{32} = 7\frac{60}{32}$$
$$-2\frac{29}{32} = 2\frac{29}{32} = 2\frac{29}{32} \qquad = 2\frac{29}{32}$$
$$5\frac{31}{32}$$

169.
$$12\frac{11}{16}$$
$$-5$$
$$7\frac{11}{16}$$

171.
$$122\frac{1}{2} = 121\frac{6}{4}$$
$$-87\frac{3}{4} = -87\frac{3}{4}$$
$$34\frac{3}{4}$$

173.

$$\frac{7}{8} = \frac{14}{16}$$

$$\frac{3}{16} = \frac{3}{16}$$

$$\frac{1}{16} = \frac{1}{16}$$

$$+\frac{7}{16} = \frac{7}{16}$$

$$\frac{25}{16} = 1\frac{9}{16}$$

$$2 = 1\frac{16}{16}$$

$$-1\frac{9}{16} = 1\frac{9}{16}$$

$$\frac{7}{16}$$

The metal is $\frac{7}{16}$ in. thick if it is flush with the bolt.

175.

$$2\frac{5}{16} = 2\frac{20}{64} = 1\frac{84}{64}$$

$$-\frac{55}{64} = \frac{55}{64} = \frac{55}{64}$$

$$1\frac{29}{64}$$

The difference in the diameters is $1\frac{29}{64}$ in.

177. $\dfrac{1}{3} \times \dfrac{7}{8} = \dfrac{7}{24}$

179. $\dfrac{7}{9} \times \dfrac{3}{8} = \dfrac{7}{\cancel{9}} \times \dfrac{\cancel{3}^{1}}{8} = \dfrac{7}{24}$ (denominator 3)

181. $\dfrac{15}{16} \times \dfrac{4}{5} \times \dfrac{2}{3} = \dfrac{\cancel{15}^{\,3}}{\cancel{16}_{\,2}} \times \dfrac{\cancel{4}^{1}}{\cancel{5}_{1}} \times \dfrac{\cancel{2}^{1}}{\cancel{3}_{1}} = \dfrac{1}{2}$

183. $\dfrac{7}{16} \times 18 = \dfrac{7}{16} \times \dfrac{18}{1} = \dfrac{7}{\cancel{16}_{8}} \times \dfrac{\cancel{18}^{9}}{1} = \dfrac{63}{8} = 7\dfrac{7}{8}$

185. $1\dfrac{1}{2} \times \dfrac{4}{5} = \dfrac{3}{2} \times \dfrac{4}{5} = \dfrac{3}{\cancel{2}_{1}} \times \dfrac{\cancel{4}^{2}}{5} = \dfrac{6}{5} = 1\dfrac{1}{5}$

187. $1\dfrac{3}{4} \times 1\dfrac{1}{7} = \dfrac{\cancel{7}^{1}}{\cancel{4}_{1}} \times \dfrac{\cancel{8}^{2}}{\cancel{7}_{1}} = \dfrac{1 \times 2}{1 \times 1} = \dfrac{2}{1} = 2$

189. $(12 \times 18) + \left(12 \times \dfrac{3}{8}\right) = (12 \times 18) + \left(\dfrac{\cancel{12}^{\,3}}{1} \times \dfrac{3}{\cancel{8}_{\,2}}\right)$

$$= 96 + \dfrac{9}{2}$$

$$= 96 + 4\dfrac{1}{2} = 100\dfrac{1}{2}$$

The wall will be $100\dfrac{1}{2}$ in. high.

191. $3\dfrac{2}{3} \times \dfrac{3}{4} = \dfrac{11}{\cancel{3}_{1}} \times \dfrac{\cancel{3}^{1}}{4} = \dfrac{11}{4} = 2\dfrac{3}{4}$

The dessert used $2\dfrac{3}{4}$ cups of flour.

193. $18\dfrac{3}{4} \times 8$

$$\dfrac{75}{\cancel{4}_{1}} \times \dfrac{\cancel{8}^{2}}{1} = \dfrac{75 \times 2}{1 \times 1} = \dfrac{150}{1} = 150 \text{ cm}$$

195. $\left(\dfrac{3}{4}\right)^{2} = \dfrac{3}{4} \cdot \dfrac{3}{4} = \dfrac{9}{16}$

197. $\left(\dfrac{4}{9}\right)^2 = \dfrac{4}{9} \cdot \dfrac{4}{9} = \dfrac{16}{81}$

199. $\left(\dfrac{1}{2}\right)^3 = \dfrac{1}{2} \cdot \dfrac{1}{2} \cdot \dfrac{1}{2} = \dfrac{1}{8}$

201. $\left(\dfrac{9}{10}\right)^2 = \dfrac{9}{10} \cdot \dfrac{9}{10} = \dfrac{81}{100}$

203. $\dfrac{4}{1}$

Reciprocal $= \dfrac{1}{4}$

205. $0.7 = \dfrac{7}{10}$

Reciprocal $= \dfrac{10}{7}$

207. $\dfrac{7}{8} \div \dfrac{3}{4} = \dfrac{7}{8} \times \dfrac{4}{3} = \dfrac{7}{\cancel{8}_2} \times \dfrac{\cancel{4}^1}{3} = \dfrac{7}{6} = 1\dfrac{1}{6}$

209. $\dfrac{7}{8} \div \dfrac{3}{32} = \dfrac{7}{8} \times \dfrac{32}{3} = \dfrac{7}{\cancel{8}_1} \times \dfrac{\cancel{32}^4}{3} = \dfrac{28}{3} = 9\dfrac{1}{3}$

211. $18 \div \dfrac{3}{4} = \dfrac{18}{1} \div \dfrac{3}{4} = \dfrac{\cancel{18}^6}{1} \times \dfrac{4}{\cancel{3}_1} = \dfrac{24}{1} = 24$

213. $5\dfrac{1}{10} \div 2\dfrac{11}{20} = \dfrac{51}{10} \div \dfrac{51}{20} = \dfrac{51}{10} \times \dfrac{20}{51} = \dfrac{\cancel{51}^1}{\cancel{10}_1} \times \dfrac{\cancel{20}^2}{\cancel{51}_1} = \dfrac{2}{1} = 2$

215. $7\dfrac{1}{5} \div 12 = \dfrac{36}{5} \div \dfrac{12}{1} = \dfrac{36}{5} \times \dfrac{1}{12} = \dfrac{\cancel{36}^3}{5} \times \dfrac{1}{\cancel{12}_1} = \dfrac{3}{5}$

217. $\dfrac{3}{16} \times 3 = \dfrac{3}{16} \times \dfrac{3}{1} = \dfrac{9}{16}$ Waste

$12 - \dfrac{9}{16} = 11\dfrac{16}{16} - \dfrac{9}{16} = 11\dfrac{7}{16}$

$11\dfrac{7}{16} \div 4 = \dfrac{183}{16} \div \dfrac{4}{1} = \dfrac{183}{16} \times \dfrac{1}{4} = \dfrac{183}{64} = 2\dfrac{55}{64}$

The maximum length that each pipe can be is $2\dfrac{55}{64}$ in.

219. $1\dfrac{1}{8} \div 6 = \dfrac{9}{8} \div \dfrac{6}{1} = \dfrac{9}{8} \times \dfrac{1}{6} = \dfrac{\cancel{9}^3}{8} \times \dfrac{1}{\cancel{6}_2} = \dfrac{3}{16}$ Each piece is $\dfrac{3}{16}$ yd long.

221. $22\dfrac{1}{2} \div \dfrac{5}{8} = \dfrac{45}{2} \div \dfrac{5}{8} = \dfrac{\cancel{45}^9}{\cancel{2}_1} \cdot \dfrac{\cancel{8}^4}{\cancel{5}_1} = \dfrac{9 \cdot 4}{1 \cdot 1} = 36$ lengths

223. $\dfrac{\frac{1}{3}}{6} = \dfrac{1}{3} \div 6 = \dfrac{1}{3} \div \dfrac{6}{1} = \dfrac{1}{3} \times \dfrac{1}{6} = \dfrac{1}{18}$

225. $\dfrac{8}{1\frac{1}{2}} = 8 \div 1\frac{1}{2} = \dfrac{8}{1} \div \dfrac{3}{2} = \dfrac{8}{1} \times \dfrac{2}{3} = \dfrac{16}{3} = 5\frac{1}{3}$

227. $\dfrac{2\frac{1}{5}}{8\frac{4}{5}} = 2\frac{1}{5} \div 8\frac{4}{5} = \dfrac{11}{5} \div \dfrac{44}{5} = \dfrac{11}{5} \times \dfrac{5}{44} = \dfrac{\overset{1}{\cancel{11}}}{\cancel{5}} \times \dfrac{\cancel{5}}{\underset{4}{\cancel{44}}} = \dfrac{1}{4}$

229. $\dfrac{12\frac{1}{2}}{100} = 12\frac{1}{2} \div 100 = \dfrac{25}{2} \div \dfrac{100}{1} = \dfrac{25}{2} \times \dfrac{1}{100} = \dfrac{\overset{1}{\cancel{25}}}{2} \times \dfrac{1}{\underset{4}{\cancel{100}}} = \dfrac{1}{8}$

231. $-\dfrac{3}{8} = \dfrac{-3}{8}$
$\phantom{-\dfrac{3}{8}} = \dfrac{3}{-8}$
$\phantom{-\dfrac{3}{8}} = -\dfrac{-3}{-8}$

233. $\dfrac{-7}{-8} = -\dfrac{-7}{8}$
$\phantom{\dfrac{-7}{-8}} = -\dfrac{7}{-8}$
$\phantom{\dfrac{-7}{-8}} = \dfrac{7}{8}$

235. $\dfrac{2}{-5} = \dfrac{-2}{-5}$
$\phantom{\dfrac{2}{-5}} = -\dfrac{2}{5}$
$\phantom{\dfrac{2}{-5}} = \dfrac{-2}{5}$

237. $\dfrac{5}{9} - \dfrac{-3}{7} = \dfrac{5}{9} + \dfrac{3}{7} = \dfrac{35}{63} + \dfrac{27}{63} = \dfrac{62}{63}$

239. $\dfrac{-4}{5} \div \dfrac{-7}{15} = \dfrac{-4}{\cancel{5}} \times \dfrac{\overset{3}{\cancel{15}}}{-7} = \dfrac{-12}{-7} = \dfrac{12}{7} = 1\frac{5}{7}$

241. $0.27 \times (0.13) = \begin{array}{r} 0.27 \\ \times\ \ 0.13 \\ \hline 081 \\ 0270 \\ \hline 0.0351 \end{array} = 0.0351$

243. $-12.4 \div 0.2 = 0.2\,\overline{)\,{-12.4}} = -62$
$\begin{array}{r} -62. \\ \hline -12.4 \\ 12 \\ \hline 04 \\ 4 \\ \hline 0 \end{array}$

245. $-\dfrac{7}{8} + \left(-\dfrac{5}{12}\right) = \dfrac{-7}{8} + \left(\dfrac{-5}{12}\right) = \dfrac{-21}{24} + \left(\dfrac{-10}{24}\right) = \dfrac{-31}{24} = -1\frac{7}{24}$

7 $\boxed{a\!\!\diagup\!\!^{b}_{c}}$ 8 $\boxed{+/-}$ $\boxed{+}$ $\boxed{(}$ 5 $\boxed{a\!\!\diagup\!\!^{b}_{c}}$ 12 $\boxed{+/-}$ $\boxed{)}$ $\boxed{=}$ $-1\dfrac{7}{24}$

247. $-2\dfrac{5}{8} \times 4\dfrac{1}{2} = \dfrac{-21}{8} \times \dfrac{9}{2} = \dfrac{-189}{16} = -11\dfrac{13}{16}$

2 $\boxed{a\!\!\diagup\!\!^{b}_{c}}$ 5 $\boxed{a\!\!\diagup\!\!^{b}_{c}}$ 8 $\boxed{+/-}$ $\boxed{\times}$ 4 $\boxed{a\!\!\diagup\!\!^{b}_{c}}$ 1 $\boxed{a\!\!\diagup\!\!^{b}_{c}}$ 2 $\boxed{=}$ $-11\dfrac{13}{16}$

249. $-\dfrac{1}{2} + \dfrac{3-5}{3} = -\dfrac{1}{2} + \dfrac{-2}{3} = \dfrac{-3}{6} + \dfrac{-4}{6} = -\dfrac{7}{6}$ or $-1\dfrac{1}{6}$

251. $0.2 - 3.1(-7.6) = 0.2 + 23.56 = 23.76$

253. $(-0.2)^2 + 5.7 = 0.04 + 5.7 = 5.74$

255. (a) Chapter 1 has an odd number of pages, so page 16 will be blank. Chapter 2 will begin on page 17.
(b) 74 pages; Chapter 1, 16 pages, including 1 blank page
Chapter 2, 18 pages, including 1 blank page
Chapter 3, 24 pages, including no blank pages
Chapter 4, 16 pages, including 1 blank page
(c) There will be three blank pages in the total document; 1 each in chapters 1, 2, and 4.

Chapter 3 Trial Test

1. 3 out of 4 people in a survey, $\dfrac{3}{4}$

3. $\dfrac{9}{3} = 3\overset{3}{\overline{)9}} = 3$ To convert an improper fraction to a whole number, perform the division indicated.

5. $4\dfrac{6}{7} = \dfrac{(4 \times 7) + 6}{7} = \dfrac{34}{7}$ To convert a mixed number to an improper fraction, multiply the denominator of the fractional part by the whole number and add the numerator of the fractional part to form new numerator, while denominator remains same.

7.
$$\frac{96}{} $$
$$= 2 \cdot 48$$
$$= 2 \cdot 2 \cdot 24$$
$$= 2 \cdot 2 \cdot 2 \cdot 12$$
$$= 2 \cdot 2 \cdot 2 \cdot 2 \cdot 6$$
$$= 2 \cdot 2 \cdot 2 \cdot 2 \cdot 2 \cdot 3$$
$$2^5 \cdot 3$$

9. $\dfrac{5}{6} \times \dfrac{3}{10} = \dfrac{\cancel{5}^{1}}{\cancel{6}_{2}} \times \dfrac{\cancel{3}^{1}}{\cancel{10}_{2}} = \dfrac{1}{4}$

11. $2\dfrac{2}{9} \times 1\dfrac{3}{4} = \dfrac{(2 \times 9) + 2}{9} \times \dfrac{(1 \times 4) + 3}{4}$

$$= \dfrac{20}{9} \cdot \dfrac{7}{4} = \dfrac{\cancel{20}^{5}}{9} \cdot \dfrac{7}{\cancel{4}_{1}} = \dfrac{35}{9}$$

$$= 9\overset{3}{\overline{)35}} = 3\dfrac{8}{9}$$
$$\underline{27}$$
$$8$$

13. $7\dfrac{1}{2} \div \dfrac{5}{9} = \dfrac{(7 \times 2) + 1}{2} \div \dfrac{5}{9} = \dfrac{15}{2} \div \dfrac{5}{9}$

$$= \dfrac{15}{2} \cdot \dfrac{9}{5} = \dfrac{\cancel{15}^{3}}{2} \cdot \dfrac{9}{\cancel{5}_{1}} = \dfrac{27}{2}$$

$$= 2\overset{13}{\overline{)27}} = 13\dfrac{1}{2}$$
$$\underline{2}$$
$$7$$
$$\underline{6}$$
$$1$$

15.
$$\dfrac{7}{12} = \dfrac{7}{12}$$
$$+\dfrac{5}{6} = \dfrac{10}{12} \qquad \left(\dfrac{5}{6} = \dfrac{5 \cdot 2}{6 \cdot 2} = \dfrac{10}{12}\right)$$
$$\overline{}$$
$$\dfrac{17}{12} = 1\dfrac{5}{12} \qquad 12\overset{1}{\overline{)17}}$$
$$\underline{12}$$
$$5$$

17.
$$2\dfrac{3}{7} = 2\dfrac{6}{14} \qquad \left(\dfrac{3}{7} = \dfrac{3 \cdot 2}{7 \cdot 2} = \dfrac{6}{14}\right)$$
$$5 \quad = 5$$
$$+\dfrac{1}{2} = \dfrac{7}{14} \qquad \left(\dfrac{1}{2} = \dfrac{1 \cdot 7}{2 \cdot 7} = \dfrac{7}{14}\right)$$
$$\overline{}$$
$$7\dfrac{13}{14}$$

19.
$$\dfrac{7}{9} = \dfrac{7}{9}$$
$$-\dfrac{2}{3} = \dfrac{6}{9} \qquad \left(\dfrac{2}{3} = \dfrac{2 \cdot 3}{3 \cdot 3} = \dfrac{6}{9}\right)$$
$$\overline{}$$
$$\dfrac{1}{9}$$

21. $\dfrac{5\frac{2}{3}}{1\frac{1}{9}} = \dfrac{\frac{(5\cdot3)+2}{3}}{\frac{(1\times9)+1}{9}} = \dfrac{\frac{17}{3}}{\frac{10}{9}} = \dfrac{17}{3} \div \dfrac{10}{9} =$

$\dfrac{17}{\cancel{3}} \cdot \dfrac{\overset{3}{\cancel{9}}}{10} = \dfrac{51}{10} = 10\overline{\smash{)}51.} = 5\dfrac{1}{10}$

$\dfrac{50}{1}$

23. $-1.3 - (3.1 - 5.4) =$

$-1.3 - (-2.3) \quad = -1.3 + 2.3 = 1.0$

25. $\dfrac{7}{32}, \dfrac{5}{16}$ larger?

$\dfrac{7}{32} < \dfrac{10}{32} \qquad \left(\dfrac{5}{16} = \dfrac{5\cdot2}{16\cdot2} = \dfrac{10}{32}\right)$

$\dfrac{7}{32} < \boxed{\dfrac{5}{16}} \qquad \dfrac{5}{16}$ is larger.

27. $\dfrac{3}{5} \quad 5\overline{\smash{)}3.0}^{\;.6} \quad \dfrac{3}{5} = 0.6$

$\dfrac{3\,0}{0}$

29. $\dfrac{2}{7}$ received safety awards

31. $5\dfrac{1}{2} = 5\dfrac{3}{6} = 4\dfrac{6}{6} + \dfrac{3}{6} = 4\dfrac{9}{6}$

$-1\dfrac{2}{3} = 1\dfrac{4}{6} = 1\dfrac{4}{6} \quad = 1\dfrac{4}{6}$

$3\dfrac{5}{6}$

There was $3\dfrac{5}{6}$ cups of sugar left.

33. $2\dfrac{2}{3} \cdot 3 = \dfrac{(2\times3)+2}{3} \cdot \dfrac{3}{1} = \dfrac{8}{3} \cdot \dfrac{3}{1} = \dfrac{8}{\cancel{3}} \cdot \dfrac{\overset{1}{\cancel{3}}}{1} = \dfrac{8}{1} = 8$

To make three costumes, 8 yards of red satin material would be needed.

chapter 4   Percents

Assignment Exercises

1. $\dfrac{72}{100} = 72\%$ **3.** $\dfrac{23}{100} = 23\%$ **5.** $0.7 = 70\%$

7. $0.83 = 83\%$ **9.** $3\dfrac{1}{5} = 3.20 = 320\%$ **11.** $125 = 12,500\%$

13. $17.3 = 1,730\%$ **15.** $72\% = 0.72 = \dfrac{72}{100} = \dfrac{18}{25}$

17. $12\dfrac{1}{2}\% = 0.125 = \dfrac{12.5}{100} = \dfrac{125}{1,000} = \dfrac{1}{8}$

19. $\dfrac{2}{3}\% = 0.67\% = 0.0067$ or $\dfrac{\frac{2}{3}}{100} = \dfrac{2}{3} \cdot \dfrac{1}{100} = \dfrac{2}{300} = \dfrac{1}{150}$

21. $275\% = 2.75 = \dfrac{275}{100} = 2\dfrac{75}{100} = 2\dfrac{3}{4}$

23. $112\dfrac{1}{2}\% = 1.125 = \dfrac{1,125}{1,000} = 1\dfrac{1}{8}$

25. $227.2\% = 2.272$

27. $340\% = 3.4$ **29.** $83\% = 0.83$

31. $62\dfrac{1}{2}\% = 62.5\% = 0.625$

33. $\dfrac{1}{2} = \dfrac{a}{9}$ $\quad 2\overline{)9.0}$ $\;\dfrac{4.5}{}$; $4.5 \times 1 = 4.5$; $a = 4.5$

$\quad\quad\quad\quad\quad \dfrac{8}{10}$

$\quad\quad\quad\quad\quad\; \underline{10}$

35. $\dfrac{7}{16} = \dfrac{21}{y}$ $\quad 7\overline{)21}$ $\;\dfrac{3}{}$; $3 \times 16 = 48$; $y = 48$

$\quad\quad\quad\quad\quad \underline{21}$

37.
$\overset{\text{R}}{5\%} \;\; \overset{\text{B}}{\text{of } 180} \;\; \overset{\text{P}}{\text{is what number?}}$
percent $\quad$ total $\quad\quad$ part

39.
$\overset{\text{R}}{45 \text{ percent of}} \;\; \overset{\text{B}}{\text{how many dollars}} \;\; \overset{\text{P}}{\text{is } \$36 ?}$
percent $\quad\quad$ total $\quad\quad\quad\quad$ part

41.
$\overset{\text{P}}{\text{Six is what}} \;\; \overset{\text{R}}{\text{percent of}} \;\; \overset{\text{B}}{25} \text{ sacks of grass seed?}$
part $\quad\quad$ percent $\quad\quad$ total

43.
　　　　　R　　　B　　　　　　　　P
　　18% of 150 pieces of sod is how many?
　　percent　percent　　　　　　part

45. 5% "of" 480

　　R　　　　B

$$\frac{R}{100} = \frac{P}{B}$$

$$\frac{5}{100} = \frac{P}{480}$$

$$5 \times 480 = 100 \times P$$

$$2,400 = 100 \times P$$

$$\frac{2,400}{100} = P$$

$$24 = P$$

47. $\frac{1}{4}$% "of" 175

　　R　　　　B

$$\frac{R}{100} = \frac{P}{B}$$

$$\frac{\frac{1}{4}}{100} = \frac{P}{175}$$

$$\frac{1}{4} \times 175 = 100 \times P$$

$$43\frac{3}{4} = 100 \times P$$

$$\frac{43\frac{3}{4}}{100} = P$$

$$\frac{7}{16} = P$$

or

$$0.4375 = P$$

49. 39 "is" "of" 65
　　　　P　　　　　B

$$\frac{R}{100} = \frac{P}{B}$$

$$\frac{R}{100} = \frac{39}{65}$$

$$R \times 65 = 100 \times 39$$

$$R \times 65 = 3,900$$

$$R = \frac{3,900}{65}$$

$$R = 60\%$$

51. "of" 65 "is" 162.5
　　　　B　　　　P

$$\frac{R}{100} = \frac{P}{B}$$

$$\frac{R}{100} = \frac{162.5}{65}$$

$$R \times 65 = 100 \times 162.5$$

$$R = \frac{16,250}{65}$$

$$R = 250\%$$

53. 24% "is" 19.92
　　　R　　　　P

$$\frac{R}{100} = \frac{P}{B}$$

$$\frac{24}{100} = \frac{19.92}{B}$$

$$24 \times B = 100 \times 19.92$$

$$24 \times B = 1,992$$

$$B = \frac{1,992}{24}$$

$$B = 83$$

55. 260% "is" 395.2
　　　R　　　　P

$$\frac{R}{100} = \frac{P}{B}$$

$$\frac{260}{100} = \frac{395.2}{B}$$

$$260 \times B = 100 \times 395.2$$

$$260 \times B = 39,520$$

$$B = \frac{39,520}{260}$$

$$B = 152$$

57. 38.25 "is" "of" 250
　　　P　　　　　　B

$$\frac{R}{100} = \frac{P}{B}$$

$$\frac{R}{100} = \frac{38.25}{250}$$

$$250 \times R = 100 \times 38.25$$

$$250 \times R = 3,825$$

$$R = \frac{3,825}{250}$$

$$R = 15.3\%$$

59. "of" 26 "is" 130
        B   P

$$\frac{R}{100} = \frac{P}{B}$$

$$\frac{R}{100} = \frac{130}{26}$$

$$R \times 26 = 100 \times 130$$

$$R \times 26 = 13{,}000$$

$$R = \frac{13{,}000}{26}$$

$$R = 500\%$$

61. $10\frac{1}{3}\%$ "is" 8.68
        R   P

$$\frac{R}{100} = \frac{P}{B}$$

$$\frac{10\frac{1}{3}}{100} = \frac{8.68}{B}$$

$$10\frac{1}{3} \times B = 100 \times 8.68$$

$$10\frac{1}{3} \times B = 868$$

$$B = \frac{868}{10\frac{1}{3}}$$

$$B = 84$$

63. 84 part 224 total
        P   B

$$\frac{R}{100} = \frac{P}{B}$$

$$\frac{R}{100} = \frac{84}{224}$$

$$R = \frac{100 \times 84}{224}$$

$$R = 37.5\%$$

or

$$37\frac{1}{2}\%$$

The alloy is $37\frac{1}{2}\%$ zinc.

65. 27 part 2374 total
        P   B
(nearest hundredth percent)

$$\frac{R}{100} = \frac{P}{B}$$

$$\frac{R}{100} = \frac{27}{2374}$$

$$R = \frac{100 \times 27}{2374}$$

$$R = 1.14\%$$

There was 1.14% defective.

67. 28% 950 total
        P   B

$$\frac{R}{100} = \frac{P}{B}$$

$$\frac{28}{100} = \frac{P}{950}$$

$$P = \frac{28 \times 950}{100}$$

$$P = 266$$

Of the paycheck, $266 goes for food.

69. 1475 part 36,875 total
        P   B

$$\frac{R}{100} = \frac{P}{B}$$

$$\frac{R}{100} = \frac{1475}{36{,}875}$$

$$R = \frac{100 \times 1475}{36{,}875}$$

$$R = 4\%$$

Of those receiving traffic citations, 4% were prosecuted.

71. 67 part 33.5%
        P   R

$$\frac{R}{100} = \frac{P}{B}$$

$$\frac{33.5}{100} = \frac{67}{B}$$

$$B = \frac{100 \times 67}{33.5}$$

$$B = 200$$

The total number of student demonstrators was 200.

73. $3{,}296 \times 6.2\% = 3{,}296 \times 0.062 = \$204.35$ social security tax

75.

$$\begin{array}{r} 4{,}873 \\ -2{,}500 \\ \hline 2{,}373 \end{array} \quad \text{all}$$

$$\text{base for} \atop \text{commission}$$

$$\frac{8}{100} = \frac{P}{2{,}373}$$

$$P = \frac{8 \times 2{,}373}{100}$$

$$P = 189.84$$

$$\begin{array}{r} 189.84 \\ +250 \\ \hline 439.84 \end{array}$$

The distributor's salary is $439.84 for the given week.

77.

$$\begin{array}{r} 100\% \\ +\ 5\% \\ \hline 105\% \end{array} \quad \text{all} \atop \text{tax}$$

$$\frac{105}{100} = \frac{P}{348.25}$$

$$P = \frac{105 \times 348.25}{100}$$

$$P = 365.66$$

The total bill is $365.66.

79.

$$\frac{6.2}{100} = \frac{P}{27{,}542}$$

$$P = \frac{6.2 \times 27{,}542}{100}$$

$$P = 1{,}707.60$$

The employer's contributions were $1,707.60.

81.

$$\frac{R}{100} = \frac{4.96}{283.15}$$

$$R = \frac{100 \times 4.96}{283.15}$$

$$R = 1.75\%$$

The monthly interest rate is 1.75% on the account.

83.

$$\frac{5}{100} = \frac{P}{52{,}475} \qquad \frac{18}{12} \times 2{,}623.75 = 3{,}935.63$$

$$P = \frac{5 \times 52{,}475}{100} \quad \text{(18 months)}$$

$$P = 2{,}623.75$$

There was $3,935.63 interest earned.

85.

$$\frac{3.25}{100} = \frac{P}{27.45}$$

$$P = \frac{3.25 \times 27.45}{100}$$

$$P = 0.89$$

There is $0.89 sales tax on the purchase.

87.

$$\frac{R}{100} = \frac{170}{2{,}000}$$

$$R = \frac{100 \times 170}{2{,}000}$$

$$R = 8.5\%$$

The interest rate was 8.5%.

89.

$$\frac{9.75}{100} = \frac{P}{6{,}500} \qquad \frac{7}{12} \times 633.75 = 369.69$$

$$P = \frac{9.75 \times 6{,}500}{100} \quad \text{(7 months)}$$

$$P = 633.75$$

The interest was $369.69 on the business loan after 7 months.

91.

$$\frac{3}{100} = \frac{10.65}{B}$$

$$B = \frac{100 \times 10.65}{3}$$

$$B = 355$$

The sales were $355 for the weekend.

93. $100\% - 12.9\% = 87.1\%$

95. $100\% - 21.5\% = 78.5\%$

97. $100\% - 32\frac{2}{5}\% = 67\frac{3}{5}\%$

99. $100\% - 92\% = 8\%$

101.

$$\begin{array}{r} 800 \\ -750 \\ \hline 50 \end{array} \quad \begin{array}{l} \text{end} \\ \text{original, required, B} \\ \text{increase, P} \end{array}$$

$$\frac{R}{100} = \frac{P}{B}$$

$$\frac{R}{100} = \frac{50}{750}$$

$$R = \frac{100 \times 50}{750}$$

$$R = 6\frac{2}{3}\% \text{ or } 7\%$$

There was 7% ordered for waste.

103.

$$\begin{array}{r} 600 \\ -516 \\ \hline 84 \end{array} \quad \begin{array}{l} \text{original, B} \\ \text{end} \\ \text{decrease, P} \end{array}$$

$$\frac{R}{100} = \frac{P}{B}$$

$$\frac{R}{100} = \frac{84}{600}$$

$$R = \frac{100 \times 84}{600}$$

$$R = 14\%$$

The percent of decrease in the price of the lathe is 14%.

105.

$$\begin{array}{r} 100\% \\ - \quad 2\% \\ \hline 98\% \end{array} \quad \begin{array}{l} \text{all} \\ \text{loss} \end{array}$$

$$\frac{R}{100} = \frac{P}{B}$$

$$\frac{98}{100} = \frac{P}{145}$$

$$P = \frac{98 \times 145}{100}$$

$$P = 142.1$$

The dried casting will weigh 142.1 kg.

107.

$$\frac{R}{100} = \frac{P}{B}$$

$$\frac{0.8}{100} = \frac{P}{62.5}$$

$$P = \frac{0.8 \times 62.5}{100}$$

$$P = 0.5$$

$$\begin{array}{rr} 62.5 & 62.5 \\ + \ 0.5 & - \ 0.5 \\ \hline 63.0 & 62.0 \end{array}$$

The limit dimensions of the length of the part are 62 cm to 63 cm.

109.

$$\begin{array}{r} 100\% \\ - \ 25\% \\ \hline 75\% \end{array} \quad \begin{array}{l} \text{all} \\ \text{less} \end{array}$$

$$\frac{R}{100} = \frac{P}{B}$$

$$\frac{75}{100} = \frac{P}{2.25}$$

$$P = \frac{75 \times 2.25}{100}$$

$$P = 1.69$$

(assume rounding to the nearest cent)
The floppy disk now sells for $1.69.

111.

$$\frac{R}{100} = \frac{300}{2,400}$$

$$R = \frac{100 \times 300}{2,400}$$

$$R = 12.5\%$$

The percent of increase is 12.5%.

113.

$$\begin{array}{r} 100\% \\ + \ 15\% \\ \hline 115\% \end{array} \quad \begin{array}{l} \text{all} \\ \text{more} \end{array}$$

$$\frac{R}{100} = \frac{P}{B}$$

$$\frac{115}{100} = \frac{P}{50}$$

$$P = \frac{115 \times 50}{100}$$

$$P = 57.5$$

The stronger carton will hold 57.5 pounds.

115.

$$\begin{array}{r} 24 \\ -18 \\ \hline 6 \end{array} \quad \begin{array}{l} \text{end} \\ \text{original, B} \\ \text{increase, P} \end{array}$$

$$\frac{R}{100} = \frac{P}{B}$$

$$\frac{R}{100} = \frac{6}{18}$$

$$r = \frac{100 \times 6}{18}$$

$$R = 33\frac{1}{3}\%$$

The percent of increase was $33\frac{1}{3}\%$.

117.

$$\begin{array}{r} 168 \\ -160 \\ \hline 8 \end{array} \quad \begin{array}{l} \text{original, B} \\ \text{end} \\ \text{loss, P} \end{array}$$

(nearest tenth)

$$\frac{R}{100} = \frac{P}{B}$$

$$\frac{R}{100} = \frac{8}{168}$$

$$R = \frac{100 \times 8}{168}$$

$$R = 4.8\%$$

The percent of weight loss was about 4.8%.

119.

$$\begin{array}{r} 100\% \\ -17.4\% \\ \hline 82.6\% \end{array} \quad \begin{array}{l} \text{all} \\ \text{less} \end{array}$$

(nearest whole number)

$$\frac{R}{100} = \frac{P}{B}$$

$$\frac{82.6}{100} = \frac{P}{350}$$

$$P = \frac{82.6 \times 350}{100}$$

$$P = 289.1 \approx 289$$

The horsepower of the new car is about 289.

121.

$$\begin{array}{ll} 3{,}900 & \text{jobs in 2010} \\ -\,2{,}095 & \text{jobs in 2000} \\ \hline 1{,}805 & \text{increase} \end{array}$$

$$\frac{R}{100} = \frac{P}{B}$$

$$\frac{R}{100} = \frac{1{,}805}{2{,}095}$$

$$R = \frac{100 \cdot 1{,}805}{2{,}095} = 86.16\%$$

$$86\% \text{ increase}$$

123.

$$\begin{array}{r} 3{,}420 \\ 652 \\ 625 \\ +\,150 \\ \hline 4{,}847 \end{array}$$

$$\frac{R}{100} = \frac{4{,}847}{18{,}250}$$

$$R = \frac{100 \times 4{,}847}{18{,}250}$$

$$R = 26.6\%$$

Of the motorist's annual income, 26.6% is used for automotive transportation.

125.

$$\begin{array}{ll} 35 & \text{total} \\ -\,25 & \text{women} \\ \hline 10 & \text{men} \end{array}$$

$$\frac{R}{100} = \frac{10}{35}$$

$$R = \frac{100 \times 10}{35}$$

$$R = 28.6\%$$

The class had 28.6% men.

Chapter 4 Trial Test

1. $\dfrac{4}{5} = 0.8 = 80\%$

3. $0.3\% = 0.003$

5.
$$\overset{R}{\underset{\text{percent}}{40\%}} \quad \text{of} \quad \overset{B}{\underset{\text{total}}{10}} \text{ x-ray techniques is how many? } \overset{P}{\underset{\text{part}}{}}$$

7.
$$\overset{P}{\underset{\text{part}}{9}} \text{ is what } \overset{R}{\underset{\text{percent}}{\text{percent}}} \text{ of } \overset{B}{\underset{\text{total}}{27}} \text{ dogwood trees?}$$

9.
$$\overset{R}{\underset{\text{percent}}{12\%}} \quad \text{of} \quad \overset{B}{\underset{\text{total}}{50}} \text{ grass plugs is how many? } \overset{P}{\underset{\text{part}}{}}$$

11. $6\frac{1}{4}\%$ "of" 144
$$\quad\quad R \quad\quad\quad B$$

$$\frac{R}{100} = \frac{P}{B}$$

$$\frac{6\frac{1}{4}}{100} = \frac{P}{144}$$

$$6\frac{1}{4} \times 144 = 100 \times P$$

$$900 = 100 \times P$$

$$\frac{900}{100} = P$$

$$9 = P$$

13. 45.75 "is" 15%
$$\quad\quad P \quad\quad\quad R$$

$$\frac{R}{100} = \frac{P}{B}$$

$$\frac{15}{100} = \frac{45.75}{B}$$

$$15 \times B = 100 \times 45.75$$

$$15 \times B = 4{,}575$$

$$B = \frac{4{,}575}{15}$$

$$B = 305$$

15.

250% "is" 287.5
R $\qquad$ P

$$\frac{R}{100} = \frac{P}{B}$$

$$\frac{250}{100} = \frac{287.5}{B}$$

$$250 \times B = 100 \times 287.5$$

$$250 \times B = 28,750$$

$$B = \frac{28,750}{250}$$

$$B = 115$$

17.

245% "is" 164.4
R $\qquad$ P
nearest hundredth

$$\frac{R}{100} = \frac{P}{B}$$

$$\frac{245}{100} = \frac{164.4}{B}$$

$$245 \times B = 100 \times 164.4$$

$$245 \times B = 16,440$$

$$B = \frac{16,440}{245}$$

$$B = 67.10$$

19. $100\% - 88\% = 12\%$

21.

$15,000 total   14%
B $\qquad$ P

3 months

$\frac{3}{12} \times 2,100$

$\frac{1}{4} \times 2,100$

525

$$\frac{R}{100} = \frac{P}{B}$$

$$\frac{14}{100} = \frac{P}{15,000}$$

$$14 \times 15,000 = 100 \times P$$

$$210,000 = 100 \times P$$

$$\frac{210,000}{100} = P$$

$$2,100 = P$$

There is $525 interest earned on the investment.

23.

$$\frac{R}{100} = \frac{P}{B}$$

$$\frac{7}{100} = \frac{175}{B}$$

$$B = \frac{100 \times 175}{7}$$

$$B = 2,500$$

The sales person sold $2,500.

25.

$\begin{array}{r} 149 \\ -123 \\ \hline 26 \end{array}$ end
original, B
increase, P

(nearest hundredth)

$$\frac{R}{100} = \frac{P}{B}$$

$$\frac{R}{100} = \frac{26}{123}$$

$$R = \frac{100 \times 26}{123}$$

$$R = 21.14\%$$

The percent increase of women students was 21.14%.

27.

$\begin{array}{r} 372 \\ -323 \\ \hline 49 \end{array}$ original, B
end
decrease, P

(nearest hundredth)

$$\frac{R}{100} = \frac{P}{B}$$

$$\frac{R}{100} = \frac{49}{372}$$

$$R = \frac{100 \times 49}{372}$$

$$R = 13.17\%$$

The percent of decrease was 13.17%.

29.

$\begin{array}{r} 36.6 \\ -34.7 \\ \hline 1.9 \end{array}$ original, B
end
loss, P

(nearest whole number)

$$\frac{R}{100} = \frac{P}{B}$$

$$\frac{R}{100} = \frac{1.9}{36.6}$$

$$R = \frac{100 \times 1.9}{36.6}$$

$$R = 5\%$$

The percent of weight loss is about 5%.

31.

$$\frac{R}{100} = \frac{P}{B} \quad \text{(nearest cent)}$$

$$\frac{12}{100} = \frac{P}{873.92}$$

$$P = \frac{12 \times 873.92}{100}$$

$$P = 104.87$$

The discount was $104.87.

chapter 5 Direct Measurement

ASSIGNMENT EXERCISES

1. Package of spaghetti
   ounces or pounds

3. Container of motor oil
   quarts

5. Package of taco shells
   ounces

7. Shipment of iron
   tons

9. Size of an aluminum pot
   quarts

11. Sugar for a pie recipe
    cups

13. Fabric for a pair of kitchen curtains
    yards

15. $\dfrac{4c}{1qt}, \dfrac{1qt}{4c}$

17. $\dfrac{2,000\,lb}{1\,T}, \dfrac{1\,T}{2,000\,lb}$

19. 12 ft = ____ yd

    $\dfrac{12\,\cancel{ft}}{1}\left(\dfrac{1\,yd}{3\,\cancel{ft}}\right) = 4\,yd$

21. $1\dfrac{1}{5}$ mi = ____ ft

    $1\dfrac{1}{5}mi = \dfrac{6\,\cancel{mi}}{5}\left(\dfrac{5,280\,ft}{1\,\cancel{mi}}\right) = 6,336\,ft$

23. 5 lb = ____ oz

    $\dfrac{5\,\cancel{lb}}{1}\left(\dfrac{16\,oz}{1\,\cancel{lb}}\right) = 80\,oz$

25. 680 oz = ____ lb

    $\dfrac{680\,\cancel{oz}}{1}\left(\dfrac{1\,lb}{16\,\cancel{oz}}\right) = 42.5\,lb$

27. $19\,oz \times 16 = 304\,oz$

    $\dfrac{304\,\cancel{oz}}{1}\left(\dfrac{1\,lb}{16\,\cancel{oz}}\right) = 19\,lb$

    The case weighs 304 oz, or 19 lb.

29. $7\dfrac{1}{2}$ qt = ____ pt

    $7\dfrac{1}{2}qt = \dfrac{15\,\cancel{qt}}{2}\left(\dfrac{2\,pt}{1\,\cancel{qt}}\right) = 15\,pt$

31. 3 gal = ____ pt

    $\left(\dfrac{3\,\cancel{gal}}{1}\right)\left(\dfrac{4\,\cancel{qt}}{1\,\cancel{gal}}\right)\left(\dfrac{2\,pt}{1\,\cancel{qt}}\right) = 24\,pt$

33. $1\dfrac{1}{4}$ mi = ____ ft

    $1\dfrac{1}{4}mi = \dfrac{5\,\cancel{mi}}{4}\left(\dfrac{5,280\,ft}{1\,\cancel{mi}}\right) = 6,600\,ft$

    To fence the property line, 6,600 ft of wire is needed.

35. 6 ft 17 in.

17 in. = 1 ft 5 in.

7 ft 5 in.

37. 12 lb $17\frac{1}{2}$ oz

$17\frac{1}{2}$ oz = 1 lb $1\frac{1}{2}$ oz

13 lb $1\frac{1}{2}$ oz

39. 1 gal 2 qt 5 pt

5 pt = 2 qt 1 pt

1 gal 4 qt 1 pt

4 qt = 1 gal

2 gal 1 pt

41. 3 yd 2 ft 16 in.

16 in. = 1 ft 4 in.

3 yd 3 ft 4 in.

3 ft = 1 yd

4 yd 4 in.

43. $3\frac{1}{4}$ ft 10 in.

$3\frac{1}{4}$ ft = 1 yd $\frac{1}{4}$ ft

1 yd $\frac{1}{4}$ ft 10 in.

$\frac{1}{4}$ ft = 3 in.

1 yd 13 in.

13 in. = 1 ft 1 in.

1 yd 1 ft 1 in. or 4 ft 1 in.

45. 1 gal 3 qt 48 oz

48 oz = 6 c

1 gal 3 qt 6 c

6 c = 3 pt

1 gal 3 qt 3 pt

3 pt = 1 qt 1 pt

1 gal 4 qt 1 pt

4 qt = 1 gal

2 gal 1 pt

47. 8 ft − 49 in.

96 in. − 49 in. = 47 in.

47 in. = 3 ft 11 in.

49. 2 ft 9 in.

+ 8 ft 2 in.

10 ft 11 in. or 3 yd 1 ft 11 in.

51. 5 gal 3 qt

+ 2 gal 3 qt

7 gal 6 qt

8 gal 2 qt

53. 4 lb 9 oz = 3 lb 16 oz + 9 oz = 3 lb 25 oz

− 3 lb 11 oz   = 3 lb 11 oz

14 oz

55. 12 ft 6 in. = 11 ft 18 in.

− 10 ft 9 in. = 10 ft 9 in.

1 ft 9 in.

To make the rug fit the room, 1 ft 9 in. should be trimmed.

57. 2 ft − 7 in. = 1 ft 12 in. − 7 in. = 1 ft 5 in.

The length of the water hose was 1 ft 5 in. after it was cut.

59. 42 ft

×12 ft

84

42

504 ft^2

61. 9 in.

×7 in.

63 in^2

63. 20 yd 2 ft 6 in. ÷ 2

10 yd 1 ft 3 in.

2$\overline{)20\text{ yd 2 ft 6 in.}}$

20 yd 2 ft 6 in.

65. 65 ft ÷ 12

$5\frac{5}{12}$ ft or 5.42 ft

12$\overline{)65\text{ ft}}$

60

5

67. 18 lb ÷ 4

4 lb   8 oz

4$\overline{)18\text{ lb}}$

16 lb

2 lb → 32 oz

32 oz

Each box would weigh 4 lb 8 oz.

69. 14 ft ÷ 4 ft = $\frac{14\ \cancel{ft}}{4\ \cancel{ft}} = 3\frac{1}{2}$ or 3.5

71. $\quad 400 \text{ lb} \div 90 \text{ lb} = \dfrac{400 \cancel{\text{lb}}}{90 \cancel{\text{lb}}} = 4\dfrac{4}{9}$

73. $\quad 5\dfrac{\text{mi}}{\text{min}} = \underline{\qquad}\dfrac{\text{mi}}{\text{hr}}$

$\dfrac{5\,\text{mi}}{\cancel{\text{min}}}\left(\dfrac{60\,\cancel{\text{min}}}{1\,\text{hr}}\right) = 300\dfrac{\text{mi}}{\text{hr}}$

75. $\quad 88\dfrac{\text{ft}}{\text{sec}} = \underline{\qquad}\dfrac{\text{mi}}{\text{hr}}$

$\dfrac{88\,\cancel{\text{ft}}}{\cancel{\text{sec}}}\left(\dfrac{1\,\text{mi}}{5{,}280\,\cancel{\text{ft}}}\right)\left(\dfrac{60\,\cancel{\text{sec}}}{1\,\cancel{\text{min}}}\right)\left(\dfrac{60\,\cancel{\text{min}}}{1\,\text{hr}}\right) = 60\dfrac{\text{mi}}{\text{hr}}$

77. $\quad 75\dfrac{\text{gal}}{\text{hr}} = \underline{\qquad}\dfrac{\text{gal}}{\text{min}}$

$\dfrac{75\,\text{gal}}{\cancel{\text{hr}}}\left(\dfrac{1\,\cancel{\text{hr}}}{60\,\text{min}}\right) = 1\dfrac{1}{4}\dfrac{\text{gal}}{\text{min}}$

The pump can move $1\dfrac{1}{4}$ or 1.25 gallons per minute.

79. $\quad 3 \text{ pt} = \underline{\qquad} \text{ qt}$

$\dfrac{3\,\cancel{\text{pt}}}{1}\left(\dfrac{1\,\text{qt}}{2\,\cancel{\text{pt}}}\right) = \dfrac{3}{2}\text{ qt} = 1\dfrac{1}{2}\text{ qt}$

The recipe calls for $1\dfrac{1}{2}$ qt of milk.

81.   1,000 times

kilo -

83. $\dfrac{1}{1000}$ of

milli -

85. $\dfrac{1}{100}$ of

centi -

87.   dekameter (dkm)

deka - means 10 times.

89.   milligram (mg)

milli - means $\dfrac{1}{1,000}$ of.

91.   kiloliter (kL)

kilo - means 1,000 times.

93.   Height of the Washington Monument
(a)   200 m

95.   Weight of an egg
(a)   50 g

97.   Weight of a man's shoe
(c)   0.25 kg

99.   Bottle of medicine
(b)   50 mL

101. $67.1 \text{ m} = \underline{\qquad} \text{ dkm}$

From m to dkm, move one space to the left.
$67.1 \text{ m} = 6\underaccent{\cdot}{7{.}}1 = 6.71 \text{ dkm}$

103. $2.3 \text{ m} = \underline{\qquad} \text{ mm}$

From m to mm, move 3 spaces to the right.
$2.3 \text{ m} = 2{.}\underaccent{\cdot}{300} = 2{,}300 \text{ mm}$

105. $0.123 \text{ hm} = \underline{\qquad} \text{ mm}$

From hm to mm, move 5 spaces to the right.
$0.123 \text{ hm} = 0{.}\underaccent{\cdot}{12300} = 12{,}300 \text{ mm}$

107. $23 \text{ dkm} = \underline{\qquad} \text{ mm}$

From dkm to mm, move 4 spaces to the right.
$23 \text{ dkm} = 23{.}\underaccent{\cdot}{0000} = 230{,}000 \text{ mm}$

109. $41{,}327 \text{ dkm} = \underline{\qquad} \text{ km}$

From dkm to km, move 2 spaces to the left.
$41{,}327 \text{ dkm} = 413\underaccent{\cdot}{27{.}} = 413.27 \text{ km}$

111. $394.5 \text{ g} = \underline{\qquad} \text{ hg}$

From g to hg, move 2 spaces to the left.
$394.5 \text{ g} = 3\underaccent{\cdot}{94{.}}5 = 3.945 \text{ hg}$

113. $3{,}000{,}974 \text{ cg} = \underline{\qquad} \text{ kg}$

From cg to kg, move 5 spaces to the left.
$3{,}000{,}974 \text{ cg} = 30\underaccent{\cdot}{00974{.}} = 30.00974 \text{ kg}$

115. $12 \text{ g} + 5 \text{ m}$

Since g (grams) is a measure of weight, and m (meters) is a measure of length, these cannot be added.

117. $8 \text{ g} - 52 \text{ cg}$

$800 \text{ cg} - 52 \text{ cg} = 748 \text{ cg}$

or

$8 \text{ g} - 0.52 \text{ g} = 7.48 \text{ g}$

119. $6.83 \text{ cg} \times 9 = 61.47 \text{ cg}$

121. $7.5 \text{ kg} \div 0.5 \text{ kg} = \dfrac{7.5 \text{ kg}}{0.5 \text{ kg}} = 15$

123. $34 \text{ hL} \div 4 = 8\dfrac{1}{2} \text{ hL}$ or 8.5 hL

125. $2.7 \text{ m} \times 7 = 18.9 \text{ m}$

18.9 m of fabric must be purchased.

127. $5 \text{ mL} + 24 \text{ cL}$

$5 \text{ mL} + 240 \text{ mL} = 245 \text{ mL}$

or

$0.5 \text{ cL} + 24 \text{ cL} = 24.5 \text{ cL}$

The recipe calls for 245 mL or 24.5 cL of liquid.

129. $42 \text{ m} \div 7 = 6 \text{ m}$

Each piece is 6 m long.

131. $25 \text{ L} \div 25 \text{ cL} = \dfrac{25 \text{ L}}{25 \text{ cL}} = \dfrac{2500 \text{ cL}}{25 \text{ cL}} = 100$

There are 100 servings of punch.

133. $6.8 \text{ dkm} \div 1.7 \text{ m} = \dfrac{68 \text{ m}}{1.7 \text{ m}} = 40$

From the bolt, 40 shirts can be made.

135. $215 \text{ m} = \underline{\quad} \text{ yards}$

$\dfrac{215 \text{ m}}{1} \left(\dfrac{1.093 \text{ yd}}{1 \text{ m}} \right) = 235.124 \text{ yd}$

137. $15 \text{ L} = \underline{\quad} \text{ liquid quarts}$

$\dfrac{15 \text{ L}}{1} \left(\dfrac{1.0567 \text{ qt}}{1 \text{ L}} \right) = 15.8505 \text{ qt}$

139. $32 \text{ kg} = \underline{\quad} \text{ pounds}$

$\dfrac{32 \text{ kg}}{1} \left(\dfrac{2.2046 \text{ lb}}{1 \text{ kg}} \right) = 70.5472 \text{ lb}$

141. $9 \text{ in.} = \underline{\quad} \text{ centimeters}$

$\dfrac{9 \text{ in.}}{1} \left(\dfrac{2.54 \text{ cm}}{1 \text{ in.}} \right) = 22.86 \text{ cm}$

143. $14.8 \text{ dkL} = \underline{\quad} \text{ quarts}$

$14.8 \text{ dkL} = 148 \text{ L}$

$\dfrac{148 \text{ L}}{1} \left(\dfrac{1.0567 \text{ qt}}{1 \text{ L}} \right) = 156.3916 \text{ qt}$

145. $200 \text{ ft} = \underline{\quad} \text{ m}$

$\dfrac{200 \text{ ft}}{1} \left(\dfrac{0.3048 \text{ m}}{1 \text{ ft}} \right) = 60.96 \text{ m}$

147. $175 \text{ mi} = \underline{\quad} \text{ km}$

$\dfrac{175 \text{ mi}}{1} \left(\dfrac{1.6093 \text{ km}}{1 \text{ mi}} \right) = 281.6275 \text{ km}$

149. $142 \times 0.4536 = 64.4112$ Change lb to kg.

$5 \text{ ft } 9 \text{ in.} = 5 \times 12 + 9$ Change ft to in.

$= 60 + 9$

$= 69 \text{ in.}$

$69 \times 0.0254 = 1.7526$ Change in. to meters.

(*Cont.*)

149.   (*Cont.*) $BMI = \dfrac{w}{h^2}$

$$= \frac{64.4112}{(1.7526)^2}$$

$$= \frac{64.4112}{3.07160676}$$

$$= 20.96987181$$

$$BMI = 21$$

151. $\dfrac{72 \text{ hr}}{1}\left(\dfrac{1 \text{ day}}{24 \text{ hr}}\right) = 3 \text{ days}$ **153.** $\dfrac{158 \text{ min}}{1}\left(\dfrac{1 \text{ hr}}{60 \text{ min}}\right) = 2 \text{ hr } 38 \text{ min}$

155. $\dfrac{96 \text{ hr}}{1}\left(\dfrac{1 \text{ day}}{24 \text{ hr}}\right) = 4 \text{ days}$ **157.** $\dfrac{39 \text{ mo}}{1}\left(\dfrac{1 \text{ yr}}{12 \text{ mo}}\right) = 3 \text{ yr } 3 \text{ mo}$

159.   304,243   6 significant digits   **161.**   4.010   4 significant digits

163. $2\dfrac{1}{2}$ in. $Precision = \dfrac{1}{2}$

$\dfrac{1}{2} \times \dfrac{1}{2} = \dfrac{1}{4}$ Greatest possible error

165. $3\dfrac{5}{16}$ ft $Precision = \dfrac{1}{16}$

$\dfrac{1}{2} \times \dfrac{1}{16} = \dfrac{1}{32}$ Greatest possible error

167.   5.8 cm   Precision = 0.1
$0.5 \times 0.1 = 0.05$ Greatest possible error

169   15.3 cm   Precision = 0.1
$0.5 \times 0.1 = 0.05$ Greatest possible error

171.   The line segment is past 5 in. but before 6 in.; thus the measure will be a mixed number. $5\dfrac{1}{4}$ inch

173. $4\dfrac{7}{16}$ inch   **175.** $3\dfrac{15}{16}$ inch   **177.** $3\dfrac{9}{16}$ inch   **179.** $2\dfrac{3}{4}$ inch

181.   117 mm or 118 mm   **183.**   99 mm   **185.**   60 mm

187.   45 mm   **189.**   20 mm

191. $12\dfrac{7}{8}$ in.

$-7\dfrac{5}{8}$ in.

$\overline{}$
$5\dfrac{2}{8}$ in. $= 5\dfrac{1}{4}$ in.

193. 8 in. $= 7\dfrac{32}{32}$ in.

$-3\dfrac{5}{32}$ in. $= -3\dfrac{5}{32}$ in.

$\overline{}$
$4\dfrac{27}{32}$ in.

195.   20.5 cm
$\underline{-17.8 \text{ cm}}$
2.7 cm

197. $15\dfrac{3}{8}$ in.

$+25\dfrac{1}{8}$ in.

$\overline{}$
$40\dfrac{4}{8} = 40\dfrac{1}{2}$ in.

$40\dfrac{1}{2} \div 2 = \dfrac{81}{2} \cdot \dfrac{1}{2} = \dfrac{81}{4} = 20\dfrac{1}{4}$ in.

199.   8.9 cm
          $\underline{+\ 2.3\ \text{cm}}$
          11.2 cm
          $11.2 \div 2 = 5.6$ cm

201.   9.8 cm
          $\underline{+5\quad\text{cm}}$
          14.8 cm
          14.8 cm $\div 2 = 7.4$ cm

203. $78°C = \underline{\quad\quad} K$
          $K = °C + 273$
          $K = 78 + 273$
          $K = 351$

205. $12°F = \underline{\quad\quad} °R$
          $°R = °F + 460$
          $°R = 12 + 460$
          $°R = 472$

207. $95°C = \underline{\quad\quad} °F$
          $°F = \frac{9}{5}°C + 32$
          $°F = \frac{9}{5}(95) + 32$
          $°F = 203$

209. $40°C = \underline{\quad\quad} °F$
          $°F = \frac{9}{5}°C + 32$
          $°F = \frac{9}{5}(40) + 32$
          $°F = 72 + 32$
          $°F = 104$

211. $365°F = \underline{\quad\quad} °C$
          $°C = \frac{5}{9}(°F - 32)$
          $°C = \frac{5}{9}(365 - 32)$
          $°C = \frac{5}{9}(333)$
          $°C = 185$

213.   The U.S. Customary or English system of measurement has always been used in the United States. Unity ratios are needed to convert from one unit to another, and there are many varying units of measure. The metric system is an international system of measurement that uses three standard units and prefixes to indicate their powers of 10. Converting from one unit to another involves merely moving the decimal placement.

Chapter 5 Trial Test

1. $3\ \text{ft} = \underline{\quad\quad}$ in.
       $\frac{3\ \cancel{ft}}{1}\left(\frac{12\ \text{in.}}{1\ \cancel{ft}}\right) = 36$ in.

3. $32\ \text{qt} = \underline{\quad\quad}$ gal
       $\frac{32\ \cancel{qt}}{1}\left(\frac{1\ \text{gal}}{4\ \cancel{qt}}\right) = 8$ gal

5. $60\ \frac{\text{gal}}{\text{min}} = \frac{\quad\quad}{\text{sec}}\ \text{qt}$
       $\frac{60\ \cancel{gal}}{\cancel{min}}\left(\frac{4\ \text{qt}}{1\ \cancel{gal}}\right)\left(\frac{1\ \cancel{min}}{60\ \text{sec}}\right) = 4\ \frac{\text{qt}}{\text{sec}}$

7. $495\ \text{ft} = \underline{\quad\quad}$ yd
       $\frac{495\ \cancel{ft}}{1}\left(\frac{1\ \text{yd}}{3\ \cancel{ft}}\right) = 165$ yd

       The section of highway is 165 yd.

9. $\frac{55\ \text{mi}}{\text{hr}} = \frac{\quad\quad}{\text{sec}}\ \text{ft}$
       $\frac{55\ \cancel{mi}}{\cancel{hr}}\left(\frac{5280\ \text{ft}}{1\ \cancel{mi}}\right)\left(\frac{1\ \cancel{hr}}{60\ \cancel{min}}\right)\left(\frac{1\ \cancel{min}}{60\ \text{sec}}\right) = 80\frac{2}{3}\ \frac{\text{ft}}{\text{sec}}$

       The automobile is traveling $80\frac{2}{3}$ feet per second.

11. $1\frac{1}{4}$ inch

13. 1 gal 3 qt 6 c 20 oz

$(20\text{ oz}=2\text{ c }4\text{ oz})$

1 gal 3 qt 8 c 4 oz

$(8\text{ c}=4\text{ pt})$

1 gal 3 qt 4 pt 4 oz

$(4\text{ pt}=2\text{ qt})$

1 gal 5 qt 4 oz

$(5\text{ qt}=1\text{ gal }1\text{ qt})$

2 gal 1 qt 4 oz

15. 1 hr

17. $\frac{1}{10}$ of standard unit

deci -

19. 298 m = _____ km

From m to km, move 3 spaces to the left.

298 m = 298 = 0.298 km

21. $10\text{ L}-5.2\text{ dL}$

$100\text{ dL}-5.2\text{ dL}=94.8\text{ dL}$

or

$10\text{ L}-0.52\text{ L}=9.48\text{ L}$

There are 94.8 dL or 9.48 L of liquid remaining in the container.

23. 75 mi = _____ km

$\frac{75\text{ mi}}{1}\left(\frac{1.6093\text{ km}}{1\text{ mi}}\right)=120.6975\text{ km}$

25. 4 L = _____ pt

$\frac{4\text{ L}}{1}\left(\frac{1.0567\text{ qt}}{1\text{ L}}\right)\left(\frac{2\text{ pt}}{1\text{ qt}}\right)=8.4536\text{ pt}$

27. $2,450\frac{\text{ft}}{\text{sec}}=\dfrac{\text{m}}{\text{sec}}$

$\frac{2,450\text{ ft}}{\text{sec}}\left(\frac{0.3048\text{ m}}{1\text{ ft}}\right)=746.76\frac{\text{m}}{\text{sec}}$

The bullet travels $746.76\frac{\text{m}}{\text{sec}}$.

29. $48°\text{F} = \text{\_\_\_\_\_ }°\text{C}$

$C=\frac{5}{9}(F-32)$

$C=\frac{5}{9}(48-32)$

$C=\frac{5}{9}(16)$

$C=8.888888889$

$C=9°C$

31. 3.8 cm

+5.9 cm

9.7 cm

$9.7\div2=4.85\text{ cm}$

chapter 6

Perimeter, Area, and Volume

ASSIGNMENT EXERCISES

1.

$10\frac{1}{2}$ cm, 9 cm, 18 cm

Perimeter $\quad P = 2(b+s)$

$$= 2\left(18 + 10\frac{1}{2}\right)$$

$$= 2\left(28\frac{1}{2}\right)$$

$$= 57 \text{ cm}$$

3. 35 mm, 70 mm

$P = 2(l+w)$

$= 2(70+35)$

$= 2(105)$

$= 210 \text{ mm}$

5.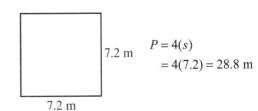

7.2 m, 7.2 m

$P = 4(s)$

$= 4(7.2) = 28.8 \text{ m}$

7. 7.5 in., 6.8 in., 6.1 in., 7.2 in., 14.3 in.

$P = b_1 + b_2 + s_1 + s_2$

$= 7.5 + 14.3 + 6.8 + 7.2$

$= 35.8 \text{ in.}$

9.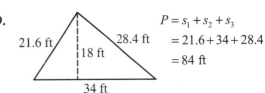

21.6 ft, 18 ft, 28.4 ft, 34 ft

$P = s_1 + s_2 + s_3$

$= 21.6 + 34 + 28.4$

$= 84 \text{ ft}$

11.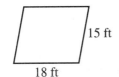

15 ft, 18 ft

$P = 2(b) + 2(s)$

$= 2(18) + 2(15)$

$= 36 + 30 = 66 \text{ ft}$

13. 60 in., 84 in.

$P = 2(l) + 2(w)$

$= 2(84) + 2(60)$

$= 168 + 120 = 288$

15.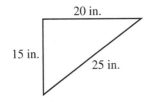

20 in., 15 in., 25 in.

$P = a + b + c$

$= 15 + 20 + 25$

$= 60 \text{ in.}$

17.

$h = 9$ cm, $b = 18$ cm

$A = bh$

$A = 18(9)$

$A = 162 \text{ cm}^2$

19. 35 mm, 70 mm

$A = lw$

$A = 70(35)$

$A = 2{,}450 \text{ mm}^2$

21. 7.2 m, 7.2 m

$A = s^2$

$A = (7.2)^2$

$A = 51.84 \text{ m}^2$

41

23.

7.5 in.

6.1 in.

14.3 in.

$A = \dfrac{1}{2}h(b_1 + b_2)$

$A = \dfrac{1}{2}(6.1)(7.5 + 14.3)$

$A = 3.05(21.8)$

$A = 66.49$ or 66.5 in^2

25.

21.6 ft   28.4 ft

18 ft

34 ft

$A = \dfrac{1}{2}\,bh$

$A = \dfrac{1}{2}(34)(18)$

$A = 306$ ft^2

or use Heron's formula

$s = \dfrac{1}{2}(a + b + c)$

$s = \dfrac{1}{2}(21.6 + 28.4 + 34)$

$s = \dfrac{1}{2}(84)$

$s = 42$

$A = \sqrt{s(s-a)(s-b)(s-c)}$

$A = \sqrt{42(42 - 21.6)(42 - 28.4)(42 - 34)}$

$A = \sqrt{42(20.4)(13.6)(8)}$

$A = \sqrt{93,219.84}$

$A = 305.3192428$

$A = 305.3$ ft^2

27. $A = lw$

$A = 275(120)$

$A = 33,000$ ft^2

29. $A = lw$

$A = 18\left(16\dfrac{1}{2}\right)$

$A = 297$ ft^2

$A = \dfrac{297 \text{ ft}^2}{1}\left(\dfrac{1 \text{ yd}^2}{9 \text{ ft}^2}\right) = 33$ yd^2

31. $A = lw$

$A = 20(16)$

$A = 320$ ft^2

$\dfrac{320 \text{ ft}^2}{1}\left(\dfrac{1 \text{ gal}}{150 \text{ ft}^2}\right)\left(\dfrac{\$4.75}{1 \text{ gal}}\right) = \$14.25$

33.
$$A_{wall} = lw$$
$$= 25(11)$$
$$= 275 \text{ ft}^2$$
$$A_{window} = bh$$
$$= 5(2)$$
$$= 10 \text{ ft}^2$$
$$A_{4\ window} = 4(10) = 40 \text{ ft}^2$$
$$A_{to\ stain} = 275 - 40 = 235 \text{ ft}^2$$

35.
$$A_{room} = lw$$
$$= 12(8)$$
$$= 96 \text{ ft}^2$$
$$A_{roll} = lw$$
$$= 20(2)$$
$$= 40 \text{ ft}^2$$

$$\text{since } 24 \text{ in.} = \frac{24 \text{ in.}}{1}\left(\frac{1 \text{ ft}}{12 \text{ in.}}\right) = 2 \text{ ft}$$

$$\text{rolls} = 96 \text{ ft}^2 \div 40 \text{ ft}^2 = \frac{96 \text{ ft}^2}{40 \text{ ft}^2} = 2\frac{2}{5} \text{ rolls}$$

Need 3 rolls.

37.
$$A = \pi r^2$$
$$= \pi (4)^2$$
$$= 50.27 \text{ m}^2$$

39.
$$A = \pi r^2$$
$$A = \pi (6.35)^2$$
$$A = 126.68 \text{ m}^2$$
$$r = \frac{d}{2}$$
$$r = \frac{12.7}{2}$$
$$r = 6.35 \text{ m}$$

41.
$$A = lw$$
$$= 4(3)$$
$$= 12 \text{ cm}^2$$

43.
$$A_{small} = \pi r^2$$
$$= \pi (1.25)^2$$
$$= 4.91 \text{ m}^2$$
$$r = \frac{1}{2}d = \frac{1}{2}(2.5) = 1.25 \text{ m}$$
$$A_{large} = \pi r^2$$
$$= \pi (1.85)^2$$
$$= 10.75 \text{ m}^2$$
$$d = 2.5 + 1.2 = 3.7 \text{ m}$$
$$r = \frac{1}{2}d = \frac{1}{2}(3.7) = 1.85 \text{ m}$$
$$A_{difference} = 10.75 - 4.91 = 5.84 \text{ m}^2$$
$$= 5.8 \text{ m}^2$$

45. $\text{total area} = 1 + 1\frac{1}{2} + 2 = 4\frac{1}{2}\ \text{in}^2\ \text{ or }\ 4.5\ \text{in}^2$

$A = \pi r^2$

$4.5 = \pi r^2$

$r^2 = 4.5 \div \pi$

$r^2 = 1.4324$

$r = \sqrt{1.4324}$

$r = 1.2\ \text{in. (rounded)}$

$d = 2r = 2(1.2) = 2.4\ \text{in.}$

47. $C = \pi d$

$\quad = \pi(5)$

$\quad = 15.71\ \text{in.}$

$\dfrac{15.71\ \text{in.}}{1}\left(\dfrac{1\ \text{ft}}{12\ \text{in.}}\right) = 1.31\ \text{ft}$

$\text{Cutting speed} = C \times \text{rpm}$

$\quad\quad\quad\quad = 1.31(25)$

$\quad\quad\quad\quad = 32.75$

$\quad\quad\quad\quad = 33\ \text{ft/min}$

49. $C = \pi d$

$47 = \pi d$

$d = 47 \div \pi$

$d = 14.96 = 15.0\ \text{in.}$

51. $A_{\text{circle}} = \pi r^2$

$\quad\quad = \pi(48)^2$

$\quad\quad = 7{,}238.229474\ \text{in}^2$

$\dfrac{7{,}238.229474\ \text{in}^2}{1}\left(\dfrac{1\ \text{ft}^2}{144\ \text{in}^2}\right)\left(\dfrac{1\ \text{yd}^2}{9\ \text{ft}^2}\right) = 5.59\ \text{yd}^2$

$\dfrac{5.59}{4} = 1.396 = 1.4\ \text{yd}^2$

53. $C = 2\pi r$

$C = 2\pi(9.4)$

$C = 59.1\ \text{in.}$

55.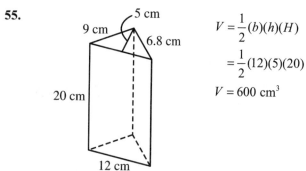

$V = \dfrac{1}{2}(b)(h)(H)$

$\quad = \dfrac{1}{2}(12)(5)(20)$

$V = 600\ \text{cm}^3$

57.

$V = \pi(r)^2(h)$

$\quad = \pi(10)^2(25)$

$\quad = \pi(100)(25)$

$V = 7.854\ \text{cm}^3$

$r = \dfrac{d}{2} = \dfrac{20\ \text{cm}}{2}$

$\quad = 10\ \text{cm}$

59. $V = lwh$

$V_{\text{top soil}} = (85)(65)(0.5)$

$\quad\quad\quad = 2{,}762.5\ \text{ft}^3$

$\dfrac{2{,}762.5\ \text{ft}^3}{1}\left(\dfrac{1\ \text{yd}^3}{27\ \text{ft}^3}\right) = 102\ \text{yd}^3$

61.

$$V_{\text{pipe}} = \pi(r^2)(l)$$

$$= \pi\left(\frac{1.5}{2}\right)^2 (5 \cdot 5,280) \qquad 18 \text{ in.} = 1.5 \text{ ft}$$

$$= \pi(0.5625)(26,400)$$

$$V_{\text{pipe}} = 46,652.65091 \text{ ft}^3$$

$$\frac{46,652.65091 \text{ ft}^3}{1}\left(\frac{7.48 \text{ gal}}{1 \text{ ft}^3}\right) = 348,961.8288$$

$$= 348,962 \text{ gal}$$

63.

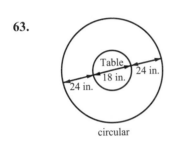

circular

$$d = 24 + 18 + 24$$

$$= 66 \text{ in.}$$

The fabric must be circular with a 66 in. diameter.

$$A = \pi r^2 \qquad r = \frac{d}{2} = \frac{66 \text{ in.}}{2} = 33 \text{ in.}$$

$$A = \pi(33)^2$$

$$A = 3,421.1944 \text{ in}^2$$

$$\frac{3,421.1944 \text{ in}^2}{1}\left(\frac{1 \text{ ft}^2}{144 \text{ in}^2}\right) = 23.75829444$$

so 24 ft^2 are needed.

Chapter 6 Trial Test

1.

$$24 \text{ ft } 6 \text{ in.} = 24.5 \text{ ft}$$

$$P = 2(l + w)$$

$$= 2(24.5 + 21)$$

$$= 2(45.5)$$

$$P = 91 \text{ ft}$$

$$A = lw$$

$$= 24.5(21)$$

$$A = 514.5 \text{ ft}^2$$

3.

$$P = 2(b + s)$$

$$= 2(3.8 + 2.3)$$

$$= 2(6.1)$$

$$P = 12.2 \text{ in.}$$

$$A = bh$$

$$= 3.8(1.6)$$

$$A = 6.08 \text{ in}^2$$

5.

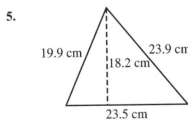

$$P = a + b + c$$

$$P = 19.9 + 23.9 + 23.5$$

$$P = 67.3 \text{ cm}$$

$$A = \frac{1}{2}(b)(h)$$

$$A = \frac{1}{2}(23.5)(18.2)$$

$$A = 213.85 \text{ cm}^2$$

7.

8 cm   12 cm

17 cm

$$P = a + b + c$$

$$P = 8 + 12 + 17$$

$$P = 37 \text{ cm}$$

$$s = \frac{1}{2}(a + b + c)$$

$$s = \frac{1}{2}(8 + 12 + 17)$$

$$s = 18.5 \text{ cm}$$

(cont.)

7.   *(cont.)*

$$A = \sqrt{s(s-a)(s-b)(s-c)}$$
$$A = \sqrt{18.5(18.5-8)(18.5-12)(18.5-17)}$$
$$A = \sqrt{18.5(10.5)(6.5)(1.5)}$$
$$A = 43.5 \text{ cm}^2$$

9.

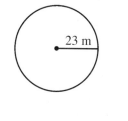

$$C = 2\pi r$$
$$C = 2\pi(23)$$
$$C = 46\pi$$
$$C = 144.5 \text{ m}$$
$$A = \pi r^2$$
$$A = \pi(23)^2$$
$$A = \pi(529)$$
$$A = 1{,}661.9 \text{ m}^2$$

11. $V = lwh$
$$V = (8.3)(8.3)(8.3)$$
$$V = 571.787$$
$$V = 571.8 \text{ cm}^3$$

13. $V = \pi r^2 h$
$$V = \pi(10)^2(14)$$
$$V = \pi(100)14$$
$$V = 4{,}398 \text{ cm}^3$$

15. $A = lw$
$$= 13(12)$$
$$= 156 \text{ ft}^2$$

$$\frac{156 \text{ ft}^2}{1}\left(\frac{1 \text{ yd}^2}{9 \text{ ft}^2}\right) = 17\frac{1}{3} \text{ yd}^2$$

$$\frac{\$3.00}{\text{yd}^2}\left(\frac{17\frac{1}{3} \text{ yd}^2}{1}\right) = \$52.00$$

17. $A = lw$
$$11 \times 12 = 132 \text{ ft}^2$$
$$\underline{10 \times 15 = 150 \text{ ft}^2}$$
$$282 \text{ ft}^2$$

19. $C = 2\pi r$
$$C = 2\pi(6)$$
$$C = 37.70 \text{ in.}$$

21.

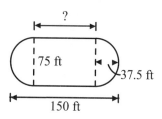

Diameter of semicircles is 75 ft

Radius $r = \dfrac{1}{2}d = \dfrac{1}{2}(75) = 37.5$ ft

Length of interior rectangle
$$150 - (37.5) - (37.5) = 75 \text{ ft}$$
Thus, interior is a square of side length 75 ft.

$$P = C + 75 + 75$$
$$= 2\pi r + 150$$
$$= 2\pi(37.5) + 150$$
$$= 235.619449 + 150$$
$$= 385.62 \text{ ft (rounded)}$$

23.

$$A_{\text{outside}} = \pi r^2$$
$$= \pi (0.4375)^2$$
$$= 0.60 \text{ in}^2$$

$$\frac{7}{8} = 0.875$$

$$r = \frac{1}{2}d = \frac{1}{2}(0.875) = 0.4375 \text{ in.}$$

$$A_{\text{inside}} = \pi r^2$$
$$= \pi (0.3125)^2$$
$$= 0.31 \text{ in}^2$$

$$\frac{5}{8} = 0.625$$

$$r = \frac{1}{2}d = \frac{1}{2}(0.625) = 0.3125 \text{ in.}$$

$$A_{\text{ring}} = A_{\text{outside}} - A_{\text{inside}}$$
$$= 0.60 - 0.31$$
$$= 0.29 \text{ in}^2$$

25.

$$A_{\text{outside}} = \pi r^2$$
$$= \pi \left(\frac{1}{4}\right)^2$$
$$= 0.196 \text{ in}^2$$

$$r = \frac{1}{2}d = \frac{1}{2}\left(\frac{1}{2}\right) = \frac{1}{4} \text{ in.}$$

$$A_{\text{inside}} = \pi r^2$$
$$= \pi \left(\frac{1}{8}\right)^2$$
$$= 0.049 \text{ in}^2$$

$$r = \frac{1}{2}d = \frac{1}{2}\left(\frac{1}{4}\right) = \frac{1}{8} \text{ in.}$$

$$A_{\text{ring}} = A_{\text{outside}} - A_{\text{inside}}$$
$$= 0.196 - 0.049$$
$$= 0.147$$
$$= 0.15 \text{ in}^2$$

chapter 7 Interpreting and Analyzing Data

ASSIGNMENT EXERCISES

1. Women used more sick days than men in 1999, 2001, and 2002.

3. Men used more sick days than women in 2000, 2003, and 2004.

5. $$\frac{R}{100} = \frac{8,500}{66,000}$$
$$66,000 \times R = 8,500 \times 100$$
$$R = \frac{850,000}{66,000}$$
$$R = 12.9\%$$

7. $$\begin{array}{r} 8,500 \\ + 3,000 \\ \hline 11,500 \end{array}$$
$$\frac{R}{100} = \frac{11,500}{66,000}$$
$$66,000 \times R = 11,500 \times 100$$
$$R = \frac{1,150,000}{66,000}$$
$$R = 17.4\%$$

9. 7-10-2004 at 4:00 PM

11. 50 computers

13. $$\begin{array}{r} 50 \\ 40 \\ + 20 \\ \hline 110 \end{array}$$
The system has 110 computers.

15. $$\frac{20}{40} = \frac{1}{2}$$

The ratio of 24 G (–) 32 G computers to 12 G (–) 16 G computers is $\frac{1}{2}$.

17.

Class Interval	Midpoint	Tally	Class Frequency
56–65	60.5	ЖТ ЖТ	10

19.

Class Interval	Midpoint	Tally	Class Frequency
36–45	40.5	ЖТ ЖТ II	12

21.

Class Interval	Midpoint	Tally	Class Frequency
16–25	20.5	ЖТ II	7

23.

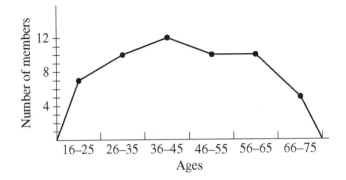

25. The age group 36–45 has the greatest number of members with 12 members.

27.
$$\begin{array}{r} 10 \\ +\ 5 \\ \hline 15 \end{array}$$

There are 15 members over age 55.

29. $\dfrac{5}{10} = \dfrac{1}{2}$

The ratio of the number of members age 66 to 75 to members age 46 to 55 is $\dfrac{1}{2}$.

31. $\dfrac{R}{100} = \dfrac{10}{54}$

$54 \times R = 10 \times 100$

$R = \dfrac{1,000}{54}$

$R = 18.5\%$

33.

miles per gallon	Midpoint	Tally	MPG Frequency
20–24	22	⊮ II	7
25–29	27	⊮ I	6
30–34	32	IIII	4

Answers may vary.

35.

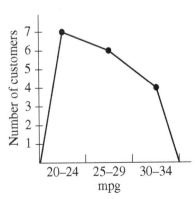

37.

$$
\begin{array}{r}
12.6 \\
5\,\overline{)63.0} \\
\underline{5} \\
13 \\
\underline{10} \\
30 \\
\underline{30}
\end{array}
$$

The automobile salesperson sold an average of 12.6 cars per month.

39.

$$
\begin{array}{r}
13.76 \approx 13.8 \\
21\,\overline{)289.00} \\
\underline{21} \\
79 \\
\underline{63} \\
160 \\
\underline{147} \\
130 \\
\underline{126} \\
4
\end{array}
$$

The delivery truck used an average of 13.8 miles per gallon.

41. $7.90

$\left.\begin{array}{l}\$6.20 \\ \$5.85\end{array}\right\}\ \dfrac{6.20+5.85}{2}=\dfrac{12.05}{2}$

$5.85

$5.45 $= \$6.03$ median

43.   The mode is $1.85, as it is the most frequent.

45.

$$
\begin{array}{c}
\text{Points} \\
\text{Hours} \quad \text{per Hour} \\
\begin{array}{rcccr}
3 & \times & 4 & = & 12 \\
3 & \times & 3 & = & 9 \\
+3 & \times & 4 & = & +12 \\
\hline
9 & & & & 33
\end{array}
\end{array}
$$

$$
\begin{array}{r}
3.666 \approx 3.67 \\
9\,\overline{)33.000} \\
\underline{27} \\
60 \\
\underline{54} \\
60 \\
\underline{54} \\
60 \\
\underline{54} \\
6
\end{array}
$$

The student's QPA is 3.67.

47.

$$
\begin{array}{ccc}
\begin{array}{r} 75 \\ \times\ \ 6 \\ \hline 450 \end{array}
&
\begin{array}{r} 79 \\ 73 \\ 71 \\ 78 \\ +\ 86 \\ \hline 387 \end{array}
&
\begin{array}{r} 450 \\ -387 \\ \hline 63 \end{array}
\end{array}
$$

An 83 is needed on the last test for a 90 A average.

49.

$$
\begin{array}{l}
98 \\
92 \\
90 \\
88 \\
83 \\
\underline{39} \\
490
\end{array}
$$

$\text{Mean} = 6\,\overline{\smash{\big)}\,490}\; = 81.67$

$\text{Median} = 89$

Mode: None

$\text{Range} = 98 - 39 = 59$

51. $\text{Mean} = 81.67$

x	$\overline{x}$		$x - \overline{x}$	$(x - \overline{x})^2$
98	$-\,81.67$	$=$	16.33	266.67
92	$-\,81.67$	$=$	10.33	106.71
90	$-\,81.67$	$=$	8.33	69.39
88	$-\,81.67$	$=$	6.33	40.07
83	$-\,81.67$	$=$	1.33	1.77
39	$-\,81.67$	$=$	-42.67	1820.73
490			0	2305.34

$$s = \sqrt{\frac{2305.34}{6-1}} = 21.47$$

53. $3 \times 4 \times 2 = 24$ outfits

55. $\dfrac{10}{13}$ probability of choosing a fashion magazine on the first draw

$\dfrac{10-1}{13-1} = \dfrac{9}{12} = \dfrac{3}{4}$ probability of choosing a fashion magazine on the second draw if first was successful

57.

HHHH	THHH
HHHT	THHT
HHTH	THTH
HHTT	THTT
HTHH	TTHH
HTHT	TTHT
HTTH	TTTH
HTTT	TTTT

16 combinations

$2 \cdot 2 \cdot 2 \cdot 2 = 16$

59. $\dfrac{1}{5}$

61.

$$
\begin{array}{r}
12 \\
24 \\
+12 \\
\hline
48
\end{array}
$$

$\dfrac{12}{48} = \dfrac{1}{4}$ probability

Chapter 7 Trial Test

1. bar

3. line

5.
$$
\begin{array}{r}
14 \\
-12 \\
\hline
2°C
\end{array}
$$

7.
$$
\begin{array}{r}
50 \\
+15 \\
\hline
\$65
\end{array}
$$

9. $\dfrac{R}{100} = \dfrac{50}{200}$

$200 \times R = 50 \times 100$

$R = \dfrac{5,000}{200}$

$R = 25\%$

11. $\dfrac{15}{200} = \dfrac{3}{40}$

13. Women make more than men in the English and Electronic departments.

15. $\dfrac{R}{100} = \dfrac{50}{48}$

$48 \times R = 50 \times 100$

$R = \dfrac{5,000}{48}$

$R = 104.1666667\%$

$R = 104.2\%$

17. $\dfrac{44}{42} = \dfrac{22}{21}$

19.
$$\begin{array}{r} 3 \\ 2 \\ +1 \\ \hline 6 \end{array}$$

21. $\dfrac{2}{4} = \dfrac{1}{2}$

23.

Class Interval	Midpoint	Tally	Class Frequency
4–6	5	ЖHT IIII	9

25.   14

27.   Exact number of employees cannot be determined from the data given.

29.   range: $93 - 68 = 25$

$$\begin{array}{r} 93 \\ \left.\begin{array}{r}81 \\ 81\end{array}\right\} \longleftarrow \text{mode} \\ 78 \longleftarrow \text{median} \\ 75 \\ 69 \\ +\ 68 \\ \hline 545 \end{array}$$

$$77.85 \approx 77.9 \text{ mean}$$
$$\begin{array}{r} 7\,\overline{\smash{\big)}\,545.00} \\ \underline{49} \\ 55 \\ \underline{49} \\ 60 \\ \underline{56} \\ 40 \\ \underline{35} \\ 5 \end{array}$$

31.   Mean $= \dfrac{81 + 78 + 69 + 75 + 81 + 93 + 68}{7} = \dfrac{545}{7} = 77.85714286$

33. $2 \times 3 = 6$

x	$\overline{x}$	$x - \overline{x}$	$(x - \overline{x})^2$
81	77.85714286	3.142857143	9.87755102
78	77.85714286	0.14285714	0.0204081624
69	77.85714286	-8.85714286	78.44897964
75	77.85714286	-2.8571423	8.163265322
81	77.85714286	3.14285714	9.877551002
93	77.85714286	15.14285714	229.3061224
68	77.85714286	-9.85714286	97.16326536

$\sum (x - \overline{x})^2 = 432.8571429$

Standard deviation $= \sqrt{\dfrac{\sum (x - \overline{x})^2}{n - 1}}$

$= \sqrt{\dfrac{432.8571429}{6}}$

$= 8.493695141$

$s = 8.49$ (rounded)

35.
$$\begin{array}{r} 2 \\ +3 \\ \hline 5 \end{array}$$
$\dfrac{3}{5}$ probability

chapter 8   Linear Equations

ASSIGNMENT EXERCISES

1. $5 + (+7)$
$5 + 7 = 12$

3. $-7 + (-12)$
$-7 - 12 = -19$

5. $23 + 84$
$23 + 84 = 107$

7. $-6 + 5 = -1$

9. $-9 + 15 = 6$

11. $14 + (-19)$
$14 - 19 = -5$

13. $5 - 8 = -3$

15. $-7 - 18 = -25$

17. $-5 - (-3)$
$-5 + 3 = -2$

19. $11 - (-12)$
$11 + 12 = 23$

21. $5 - 2 + 3 - 7$
$3 + 3 - 7$
$6 - 7 = -1$

23. $6 + 2 - 8 - 3 + 4$
$8 - 8 - 3 + 4$
$0 - 3 + 4 = 1$

25. $5(3) = 15$

27. $(-5)(-8) = 40$

29. $-11(-3) = 33$

31. $\dfrac{28}{7} = 4$

33. $\dfrac{-84}{7} = -12$

35. $\dfrac{54}{-6} = -9$

37. $5 + 7(3 - 9)$
$5 + 7(-6)$
$5 - 42 = -37$

39. $(-6)^2 + 3(-5)$
$36 + (-15)$
$36 - 15 = 21$

41. $-3^2 - 5^2 + 12 \cdot 3$
$-9 - 25 + 36$
$-34 + 36 = +2$

43. $5 - 7(4 - 13)^2 + 8$
$5 - 7(-9)^2 + 8$
$5 - 7(81) + 8$
$5 - 567 + 8 = -554$

45. $5 + 7 = 18 - 6$
$12 = 12$

47. $8 - 9 + 3^2 = -2^2 + 12$
$-1 + 9 = -4 + 12$
$8 = 8$

49. $x = 5 + 9$
$x = 14$

51. $y = \dfrac{48}{-6} = -8$

53. $\boxed{15x} - \boxed{\dfrac{3a}{7}} + \boxed{\dfrac{x-7}{5}}$

55. Five more than a number is two, or a number increased by 5 equals 2. Answers will vary.

57. A number divided by 8 is 7.
Answers will vary.

59. Three times the sum of a number and seven equals -3. Answers will vary.

61. $2x + 7 = 11$

63. $2(x + 8) = 40$

65. $3a + 2a = 5a$

67. $3(2y - 4) + y$
$6y - 12 + y$
$7y - 12$

69. $-3(a + 2) - 5$
$-3a - 6 - 5$
$-3a - 11$

71. $11 - 2(x - 5)$
$11 - 2x + 10$
$21 - 2x \text{ or } -2x + 21$

73. $\begin{aligned} x - 5 &= 8 \\ +5 \quad &+5 \\ x \quad &= 13 \end{aligned}$

75. $\begin{aligned} x - 21 &= 17 \\ +21 \quad &+21 \\ x \quad &= 38 \end{aligned}$

77. $\begin{aligned} x - 8 &= -10 \\ +8 \quad &+8 \\ x \quad &= -2 \end{aligned}$

79. $\begin{aligned} x - 5 &= 14 \\ +5 \quad &+5 \\ x \quad &= 19 \end{aligned}$

81. $3x = 21$

$\dfrac{\cancel{3}x}{\cancel{3}} = \dfrac{\overset{7}{\cancel{21}}}{\cancel{3}}$

$x = 7$

Check:
$3x = 21$
$3(7) = 21$
$21 = 21$

83. $-15 = 2b$

$\dfrac{-15}{2} = \dfrac{\cancel{2}b}{\cancel{2}}$

$\dfrac{-15}{2} = b$

$b = \dfrac{-15}{2} \text{ or } -7\dfrac{1}{2} \text{ or } -7.5$

Check:
$-15 = 2b$
$-15 = 2(-7.5)$
$-15 = -15$

85. $-7y = -49$

$\dfrac{\cancel{-7}y}{\cancel{-7}} = \dfrac{\overset{7}{\cancel{-49}}}{\cancel{-7}}$

$y = 7$

Check:
$-7y = -49$
$-7(7) = -49$
$-49 = -49$

87. $8 = -x$
$8 = -1x$

$\dfrac{8}{-1} = \dfrac{-1x}{-1}$

$-8 = x$

$x = -8$

Check:
$8 = -x$
$8 = -(-8)$
$8 = 8$

89.
$$3 = \frac{1}{5}x$$

$$\left(\frac{5}{1}\right)3 = \left(\frac{\cancel{5}}{\cancel{1}}\right)\frac{\cancel{1}}{\cancel{5}}x$$

$$15 = x$$

$$x = 15$$

Check:

$$3 = \frac{1}{5}x$$

$$3 = \frac{1}{5}(15)$$

$$3 = 3$$

91.
$$\frac{-3}{8}x = -24$$

$$\left(\frac{-8}{\cancel{3}}\right)\frac{\cancel{-3}}{\cancel{8}}x = \left(\frac{-8}{\cancel{3}}\right)\frac{\overset{8}{-\cancel{24}}}{1}$$

$$x = 64$$

Check:

$$-\frac{3}{8}x = -24$$

$$-\frac{3}{8}(64) = -24$$

$$-24 = -24$$

93.
$$42 = \frac{-6}{7}x$$

$$\left(\frac{-7}{\cancel{6}}\right)\left(\frac{\overset{7}{\cancel{42}}}{1}\right) = \left(\frac{-7}{\cancel{6}}\right)\left(\frac{\cancel{-6}}{\cancel{7}}x\right)$$

$$-49 = x$$

$$x = -49$$

check:

$$42 = -\frac{6}{7}x$$

$$42 = \frac{-6}{7}(-49)$$

$$42 = 42$$

95.
$$\frac{1}{7}x = 12$$

$$\left(\frac{7}{1}\right)\frac{\cancel{1}}{\cancel{7}}x = \left(\frac{7}{1}\right)\frac{12}{1}$$

$$x = 84$$

Check:

$$\frac{1}{7}x = 12$$

$$\frac{1}{7}(84) = 12$$

$$12 = 12$$

97.
$$4x + x = 25$$
$$5x = 25$$
$$\frac{5x}{5} = \frac{25}{5}$$
$$x = 5$$

99.
$$2b - 7b = 10$$
$$-5b = 10$$
$$\frac{-5b}{-5} = \frac{10}{-5}$$
$$b = -2$$

101.
$$21 = x + 2x$$
$$21 = 3x$$
$$\frac{21}{3} = \frac{3x}{3}$$
$$7 = x$$
$$x = 7$$

103.
$$20 - 4 = 2x - 6x$$
$$16 = -4x$$
$$\frac{16}{-4} = \frac{-4x}{-4}$$
$$-4 = x$$
$$x = -4$$

105.
$$x + 7 = 10$$
$$x + 7 - 7 = 10 - 7$$
$$x + 0 = 3$$
$$x = 3$$

107.
$$x - 3 = -4$$
$$x - 3 + 3 = -4 + 3$$
$$x + 0 = -1$$
$$x = -1$$

109.
$$1 = a - 4$$
$$1 + 4 = a - 4 + 4$$
$$5 = a + 0$$
$$5 = a$$
$$a = 5$$

111.
$$3x + 4 = 19$$
$$3x + 4 - 4 = 19 - 4$$
$$3x = 15$$
$$\frac{3x}{3} = \frac{15}{3}$$
$$x = 5$$

113.
$$15 - 3x = -6$$
$$15 - 15 - 3x = -6 - 15$$
$$-3x = -21$$
$$\frac{-3x}{-3} = \frac{-21}{-3}$$
$$x = 7$$

115.
$$-7 = 6x - 31$$
$$-7 + 31 = 6x - 31 + 31$$
$$24 = 6x$$
$$\frac{24}{6} = \frac{6x}{6}$$
$$4 = x$$
$$x = 4$$

117.
$$-12 = -8 - 2x$$
$$-12 + 8 = -8 + 8 - 2x$$
$$-4 = -2x$$
$$\frac{-4}{-2} = \frac{-2x}{-2}$$
$$2 = x$$
$$x = 2$$

119.
$$5x - 12 = 9x$$
$$5x - 5x - 12 = 9x - 5x$$
$$-12 = 4x$$
$$\frac{-12}{4} = \frac{4x}{4}$$
$$-3 = x$$
$$x = -3$$

121.
$$3x + 9 = 10 + 3x + 1$$
$$3x + 9 - 9 = 10 - 9 + 3x + 1$$
$$3x = 1 + 3x + 1$$
$$3x - 3x = 1 + 1$$
$$0 = 2 \text{ False}$$
No real solutions

123.
$$4y + 8 = 3y - 4$$
$$4y - 3y = -4 - 8$$
$$y = -12$$

125.
$$7 - 4y = y + 22$$
$$-4y - y = 22 - 7$$
$$-5y = 15$$
$$\frac{-5y}{-5} = \frac{15}{-5}$$
$$y = -3$$

127.
$$4x - 3 = 2x + 6$$
$$4x - 2x = 6 + 3$$
$$2x = 9$$
$$\frac{2x}{2} = \frac{9}{2}$$
$$x = \frac{9}{2} \text{ or } 4\frac{1}{2} \text{ or } 4.5$$

129.
$$8 - 2y = 15 - 3y$$
$$-2y + 3y = 15 - 8$$
$$y = 7$$

131.
$$5x - 12 = 2x + 15$$
$$5x - 2x = 15 + 12$$
$$3x = 27$$
$$\frac{3x}{3} = \frac{27}{3}$$
$$x = 9$$

133.
$$7x - 5 + 2x = 3 - 4x + 12$$
$$9x - 5 = 15 - 4x$$
$$9x + 4x = 15 + 5$$
$$13x = 20$$
$$\frac{13x}{13} = \frac{20}{13}$$
$$x = \frac{20}{13} \text{ or } 1\frac{7}{13} \text{ or } \approx 1.54$$

135.
$$3x - 5x + 2 = 6x - 5 + 12x$$
$$-2x + 2 = 18x - 5$$
$$-2x - 18x = -5 - 2$$
$$-20x = -7$$
$$\frac{-20x}{-20} = \frac{-7}{-20}$$
$$x = \frac{7}{20} \text{ or } 0.35$$

137.
$$0 = \frac{8}{9}c + \frac{1}{4}$$
$$0 - \frac{1}{4} = \frac{8}{9}c$$
$$-\frac{1}{4} = \frac{8}{9}c$$
$$\left(\frac{9}{8}\right)\left(-\frac{1}{4}\right) = \left(\frac{9}{8}\right)\frac{8}{9}c$$
$$c = -\frac{9}{32} \text{ or } \approx -0.28$$

139.
$$6.7y - y = 8.4 \quad \text{(round to tenths)}$$
$$5.7y = 8.4$$
$$\frac{5.7y}{5.7} = \frac{8.4}{5.7}$$
$$y = 1.5$$

$$\begin{array}{r} 6.7 \\ -1. \\ \hline 5.7 \end{array}$$

$$\begin{array}{r} 1.47 \\ 5.7{\overline{\smash{\big)}\,8.400}} \\ \underline{57} \\ 270 \\ \underline{228} \\ 420 \\ \underline{399} \\ 21 \end{array}$$

141.
$$0.86 = R + 0.4R$$
$$0.86 = 1.4R$$
$$\frac{0.86}{1.4} = \frac{1.4R}{1.4}$$
$$0.61 = R$$
$$R = 0.61$$

$$\begin{array}{r} 1. \\ +0.4 \\ \hline 1.4 \end{array}$$
(round to hundredths)

$$\begin{array}{r} 0.614 \\ 1.4{\overline{\smash{\big)}\,0.860}} \\ \underline{84} \\ 20 \\ \underline{14} \\ 60 \\ \underline{56} \\ 4 \end{array}$$

143.
$$18 = 6(2 - y)$$
$$18 = 12 - 6y$$
$$18 - 12 = -6y$$
$$6 = -6y$$
$$\frac{6}{-6} = \frac{-6y}{-6}$$
$$-1 = y$$
$$y = -1$$

145.
$$3x = 3(9 + 2x)$$
$$3x = 27 + 6x$$
$$3x - 6x = 27$$
$$-3x = 27$$
$$\frac{-3x}{-3} = \frac{27}{-3}$$
$$x = -9$$

147.
$$7x - 3(x - 8) = 28$$
$$7x - 3x + 24 = 28$$
$$4x = 28 - 24$$
$$4x = 4$$
$$\frac{4x}{4} = \frac{4}{4}$$
$$x = 1$$

149.
$$5x = 7 + (x+5)$$
$$5x = 7 + 1(x+5)$$
$$5x = 7 + 1x + 5$$
$$5x - 1x = 7 + 5$$
$$4x = 12$$
$$\frac{4x}{4} = \frac{12}{4}$$
$$x = 3$$

151.
$$4(3 - x) = 2x$$
$$12 - 4x = 2x$$
$$12 = 2x + 4x$$
$$12 = 6x$$
$$\frac{12}{6} = \frac{6x}{6}$$
$$2 = x$$
$$x = 2$$

153.
$$-2(4 - 2x) = -16 + 2x$$
$$-8 + 4x = -16 + 2x$$
$$4x - 2x = -16 + 8$$
$$2x = -8$$
$$\frac{2x}{2} = \frac{-8}{2}$$
$$x = -4$$

155.
$$5(3 - 2x) = -5$$
$$15 - 10x = -5$$
$$-10x = -5 - 15$$
$$-10x = -20$$
$$\frac{-10x}{-10} = \frac{-20}{-10}$$
$$x = 2$$

157.
$$8 = 6 - 2(3x - 1)$$
$$8 = 6 - 6x + 2$$
$$8 = 8 - 6x$$
$$8 - 8 = -6x$$
$$0 = -6x$$
$$\frac{0}{-6} = \frac{-6x}{-6}$$
$$0 = x$$
$$x = 0$$

159.
$$3(x - 1) = 18 - 2(x + 3)$$
$$3x - 3 = 18 - 2x - 6$$
$$3x - 3 = 12 - 2x$$
$$3x + 2x = 12 + 3$$
$$5x = 15$$
$$\frac{5x}{5} = \frac{15}{5}$$
$$x = 3$$

161.
$$-(2x + 1) = -7$$
$$-1(2x + 1) = -7$$
$$-2x - 1 = -7$$
$$-2x = -7 + 1$$
$$-2x = -6$$
$$\frac{-2x}{-2} = \frac{-6}{-2}$$
$$x = 3$$

163.
$$7 = 3 + 4(x + 2)$$
$$7 = 3 + 4x + 8$$
$$7 = 11 + 4x$$
$$7 - 11 = 4x$$
$$-4 = 4x$$
$$\frac{-4}{4} = \frac{4x}{4}$$
$$-1 = x$$
$$x = -1$$

165.
$$3(4x + 3) = 3 - 4(x - 1)$$
$$12x + 9 = 3 - 4x + 4$$
$$12x + 9 = 7 - 4x$$
$$12x + 4x = 7 - 9$$
$$16x = -2$$
$$\frac{16x}{16} = \frac{-2}{16}$$
$$x = -\frac{1}{8} \text{ or } -0.125$$

167.
$$x - 6 = 8$$
$$x = 8 + 6$$
$$x = 14$$

169.
$$5(x + 6) = x + 42$$
$$5x + 30 = x + 42$$
$$5x - x = 42 - 30$$
$$4x = 12$$
$$\frac{4x}{4} = \frac{12}{4}$$
$$x = 3$$

171.
$$x + (x - 3) = 51$$
$$x + x - 3 = 51$$
$$2x - 3 = 51$$
$$2x = 51 + 3$$
$$2x = 54$$
$$\frac{2x}{2} = \frac{54}{2}$$
$$x = 27$$
$$x - 3 = 27 - 3 = 24$$

One technician works 27 hours and the other works 24 hours.

173. $c = \pi d$

$6 = \pi d$

$\dfrac{6}{\pi} = d$

$1.9 = d$

No, a tube with a diameter of 1.9 in. will not fit into a hole 1.5 in. in diameter.

175. $P = 2(l + w); \; l = 2w$

$720 = 2(2w + w)$

$720 = 4w + 2w$

$720 = 6w$

$\dfrac{720}{6} = \dfrac{6w}{6}$

$120 \text{ ft} = w; \; l = 2w = 2(120) = 240 \text{ ft}$

177. $3x - 8 = 4$ Values selected for x may vary.

x	$3x - 8$	4	Observations
0	$3(0) - 8 = -8$	4	$4 - (-8) = 12$; difference of 12
2	$3(2) - 8 = -2$	4	$4 - (-2) = 6$; difference of 6
4	$3(4) - 8 = 4$	4	$4 - 4 = 0$; difference of 0, so $x = 4$ is the solution.

The solution is $x = 4$.

179. $6x = 7x + 3$ Values selected for x may vary.

x	$6x$	$7x + 3$	Observations
0	$6(0) = 0$	$7(0) + 3 = 3$	$3 - 0 = 3$; difference of 3
1	$6(1) = 6$	$7(1) + 3 = 10$	$10 - 1 = 9$; difference of 9
-1	$6(-1) = -6$	$7(-1) + 3 = -4$	$-4 - (-6) = 2$; difference of 2
-2	$6(-2) = -12$	$7(-2) + 3 = -11$	$-11 - (-12) = 1$; difference of 1
-3	$6(-3) = -18$	$7(-3) + 3 = -18$	$-18 - (-18) = 0$; solution

The solution is $x = -6$.

181. $5(x + 1) = 3x - 7$ Values selected for x may vary.

x	$5(x + 1)$	$3x - 7$	Observations
2	$5(2 + 1) = 15$	$3(2) - 7 = -1$	$-1 - (15) = -16$; difference of -16
-2	$5(-2 + 1) = -5$	$3(-2) - 7 = -13$	$-13 - (-5) = -8$; difference of -8
-3	$5(-3 + 1) = -10$	$3(-3) - 7 = -16$	$-16 - (-10) = -6$; difference of -6
-5	$5(-5 + 1) = -20$	$3(-5) - 7 = -22$	$-22 - (-20) = -2$; difference of -2
-6	$5(-6 + 1) = -25$	$3(-6) - 7 = -25$	$-25 - (-25) = 0$; solution

The solution is $x = -6$.

183. $\dfrac{12}{r+1} = 4$ Values selected for r may vary.

Additional Robots	Time Required to Complete the Task		Observations
r	$\dfrac{12 \text{ hr}}{r+1}$	4	First robot and additional robots complete the task in 4 hr.
0	$\dfrac{12 \text{ hr}}{0+1} = 12$	4	$4 - 12 = -8$; difference of -8 hr
1	$\dfrac{12 \text{ hr}}{1+1} = \dfrac{12}{2} = 6$	4	$4 - 6 = -2$; difference of -2 hr
2	$\dfrac{12 \text{ hr}}{2+1} = \dfrac{12}{3} = 4$	4	$4 - 4 = 0$; solution

Two additional robots are needed.

185. $f(x) = 2x - 1$

-2	-5
-1	-3
0	-1
1	1
2	3

187. $f(x) = -x + 1$

-3	4
0	1
3	-2
5	-4

189. $f(x) = -3x + 2$

The range is the set of real numbers.

191. $g(x) = 3x$

The range is the set of positive numbers that are multiples of 3.

193. $f(x) = x + 5$

-4	1
0	5
2	7

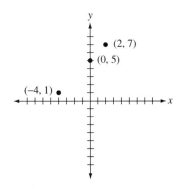

195. $f(x) = x$

-1	-1
2	2
3	3

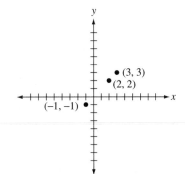

197.

$f(x) = 3x$

x	
-2	-6
0	0
3	9

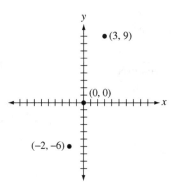

199.

$f(x) = 3x - 2$

x	$f(x)$
-1	-5
0	-2
2	4

$3(-1) - 2 = -3 - 2 = -5$

$3(0) - 2 = 0 - 2 = \ -2$

$3(2) - 2 = 6 - 2 = \ \ \ 4$

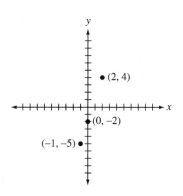

Chapter 8 Trial Test

1.
$$x + 5 = 19$$
$$\underline{-5 \ \ -5}$$
$$x = 14$$

3.
$$5x = 30$$
$$\frac{5x}{5} = \frac{30}{5}$$
$$x = 6$$

5.
$$\frac{x}{2} = 5$$
$$\left(\frac{2}{1}\right)\left(\frac{x}{2}\right) = \left(\frac{2}{1}\right)\left(\frac{5}{1}\right)$$
$$x = 10$$

7.
$$x = 5 - 8$$
$$x = 5 + -8$$
$$x = -3$$

9.
$$y - 2y = 15$$
$$-y = 15$$
$$\frac{-y}{-1} = \frac{15}{-1}$$
$$y = -15$$

11.
$$5 - 2x = 3x - 10$$
$$-2x - 3x = -10 - 5$$
$$-5x = -15$$
$$\frac{-5x}{-5} = \frac{-15}{-5}$$
$$x = 3$$

13.
$$3(x + 4) = 18$$
$$3x + 12 = 18$$
$$3x = 18 - 12$$
$$3x = 6$$
$$\frac{3x}{3} = \frac{6}{3}$$
$$x = 2$$

15.
$$7 - (x - 3) = 4x$$
$$7 - 1(x - 3) = 4x$$
$$7 - x + 3 = 4x$$
$$-x + 10 = 4x$$
$$10 = 4x + x$$
$$10 = 5x$$
$$\frac{10}{5} = \frac{5x}{5}$$
$$2 = x$$
$$x = 2$$

17.

$$4.5x - 3.4 = 2.1x - 0.4$$
$$4.5x - 2.1x = -0.4 + 3.4$$
$$2.4x = 3.0$$
$$\frac{2.4x}{2.4} = \frac{3.0}{2.4}$$
$$x = 1.25$$

$$\begin{array}{cc} 4.5 & 3.4 \\ -\ 2.1 & -\ 0.4 \\ \hline 2.4 & 3.0 \end{array}$$

$$2.4\overline{)3.000}$$
$$\begin{array}{r} 1.25 \\ \underline{24} \\ 60 \\ \underline{48} \\ 120 \\ \underline{120} \end{array}$$

19.

$$2(x+3) = 10$$
$$2x + 6 = 10$$
$$2x = 10 - 6$$
$$2x = 4$$
$$\frac{2x}{2} = \frac{4}{2}$$
$$x = 2$$

21.

Ross Prarie WMA $= x$
Potts WMA $= x + 4,980$
$$x + (x + 4,980) = 11,034$$
$$2x + 4,980 = 11,034$$
$$2x = 11,034 - 4,980$$
$$\frac{2x}{2} = \frac{6,054}{2}$$
$$x = 3,027$$

Ross Prarie has $3,027$ acres.
Potts has $3,027 + 4,980$ or $8,007$ acres.

23.

$$f(x) = -6x - 5$$

x	$f(x)$
-2	7
5	-35

$$f(x) = -6x - 5$$
$$f(-2) = -6(-2) - 5$$
$$f(-2) = 7$$
$$f(5) = -6(5) - 5$$
$$f(5) = -30 - 5$$
$$f(5) = -35$$

Equations with Fractions and Decimals

chapter **9**

ASSIGNMENT EXERCISES

1.
$$m + \frac{1}{4} = \frac{3}{4}$$
$$m + \frac{1}{4} - \frac{1}{4} = \frac{3}{4} - \frac{1}{4}$$
$$m = \frac{2}{4} = \frac{1}{2}$$

3.
$$p = \frac{1}{2} + \frac{1}{3}$$
$$(3)(2)p = (3)(\cancel{2})\frac{1}{\cancel{2}} + (\cancel{3})(2)\frac{1}{\cancel{3}}$$
$$6p = 3 + 2$$
$$6p = 5$$
$$\frac{6p}{6} = \frac{5}{6}$$
$$p = \frac{5}{6}$$

5.
$$\frac{2}{5} - x = \frac{1}{2}x + \frac{4}{5}$$
$$(\cancel{5})(2)\frac{2}{\cancel{5}} - (5)(2)x = (5)(\cancel{2})\frac{1}{\cancel{2}}x + (\cancel{5})(2)\frac{4}{\cancel{5}}$$
$$4 - 10x = 5x + 8$$
$$-10x - 5x = 8 - 4$$
$$-15x = 4$$
$$\frac{-15x}{-15} = \frac{4}{-15}$$
$$x = -\frac{4}{15}$$

7.
$$\frac{3}{7}m - \frac{1}{2} = \frac{2}{3}$$
$$(\cancel{7})(2)(3)\frac{3}{\cancel{7}}m - (7)(\cancel{2})(3)\frac{1}{\cancel{2}} = (7)(2)(\cancel{3})\frac{2}{\cancel{3}}$$
$$18m - 21 = 28$$
$$18m = 49$$
$$\frac{18m}{18} = \frac{49}{18}$$
$$m = \frac{49}{18} \text{ or } 2\frac{13}{18}$$

9.
$$\frac{2}{15}p - p = 4$$
$$(\cancel{15})\frac{2}{\cancel{15}}p - (15)p = (15)4$$
$$2p - 15p = 60$$
$$-13p = 60$$
$$\frac{-13p}{-13} = \frac{60}{-13}$$
$$-\frac{60}{13}p = \text{or} - 4\frac{8}{13}$$

11.
$$m = 2 + \frac{1}{4}m$$
$$(4)m = (4)2 + (\cancel{4})\frac{1}{\cancel{4}}m$$
$$4m = 8 + m$$
$$4m - m = 8$$
$$3m = 8$$
$$\frac{3m}{3} = \frac{8}{3}$$
$$m = \frac{8}{3} \text{ or } 2\frac{2}{3}$$

13.

$$\frac{1}{12}x = \frac{1}{4} + \frac{1}{8}$$

$$\frac{\cancel{12}}{1} \cdot \frac{1}{\cancel{12}}x = \left(\frac{2}{8} + \frac{1}{8}\right)\frac{12}{1}$$

$$x = \frac{3}{8} \cdot \frac{12}{1} = \frac{36}{8}$$

$$= \frac{9}{2} \text{ or } 4\frac{1}{2} \text{ or } 4.5$$

15.

$$2x + 4 = \frac{1}{2}$$

$$(2)2x + (2)4 = (\cancel{2})\frac{1}{\cancel{2}}$$

$$4x + 8 = 1$$

$$4x = 1 - 8$$

$$4x = -7$$

$$\frac{4x}{4} = \frac{-7}{4}$$

$$x = -\frac{7}{4} \text{ or } -1\frac{3}{4} \text{ or } -1.75$$

17.

$$\frac{3}{10}x = \frac{1}{8}x + \frac{2}{5}$$

$$(\cancel{10})(8)\frac{3}{\cancel{10}}x = (10)(\cancel{8})\frac{1}{\cancel{8}}x + (10)(8)\overset{2}{\cancel{\frac{2}{5}}}$$

$$24x = 10x + 32$$

$$24x - 10x = 32$$

$$14x = 32$$

$$\frac{14x}{14} = \frac{32}{14}$$

$$x = \frac{16}{7} \text{ or } 2\frac{2}{7}$$

19.

$$\frac{1}{x} = \frac{2}{5} + \frac{3}{10}$$

$$(10)(\cancel{x})\frac{1}{\cancel{x}} = (\cancel{10})(x)\overset{2}{\cancel{\frac{2}{5}}} + (\cancel{10})(x)\frac{3}{\cancel{10}}$$

$$10 = 4x + 3x$$

$$10 = 7x$$

$$\frac{10}{7} = \frac{7x}{7}$$

$$\frac{10}{7} = x$$

$$x = \frac{10}{7} \text{ or } 1\frac{3}{7}$$

21.

$$\frac{2}{p} = \frac{1}{2} + \frac{1}{4} - \frac{5}{12}$$

$$(12)(\cancel{p})\frac{2}{\cancel{p}} = (\cancel{12})(p)\overset{6}{\cancel{\frac{1}{2}}} + (\cancel{12})(p)\overset{3}{\cancel{\frac{1}{4}}} - (\cancel{12})(p)\frac{5}{\cancel{12}}$$

$$24 = 6p + 3p - 5p$$

$$24 = 4p$$

$$\frac{24}{4} = \frac{4p}{4}$$

$$p = 6$$

23.

$$\frac{5}{12}x - \frac{3}{4} = \frac{1}{9} - \frac{2}{3}x$$

$$(\cancel{36})\overset{3}{\cancel{\frac{5}{12}}}x - (\cancel{36})\overset{9}{\cancel{\frac{3}{4}}} = (\cancel{36})\overset{4}{\cancel{\frac{1}{9}}} - (\cancel{36})\overset{12}{\cancel{\frac{2}{3}}}x$$

$$15x - 27 = 4 - 24x$$

$$15x + 24x = 4 + 27$$

$$39x = 31$$

$$\frac{39x}{39} = \frac{31}{39}$$

$$x = \frac{31}{39}$$

25.

$$\frac{1}{3}x + \frac{1}{7}x = 1$$

$$(3)(7)\frac{1}{3}x + (3)(7)\frac{1}{7}x = (3)(7)1$$

$$7x + 3x = 21$$

$$10x = 21$$

$$\frac{10x}{10} = \frac{21}{10}$$

$$x = \frac{21}{10} \text{ or } 2\frac{1}{10} \text{ hr}$$

$$\text{or } 2.1 \text{ hrs}$$

$$\text{or } 2 \text{ hr } 6 \text{ min}$$

27.

$$\frac{5}{x} = \frac{2}{10} \quad \text{or} \quad \frac{5}{2} = \frac{x}{10}$$

$$2x = 50$$

$$\frac{2x}{2} = \frac{50}{2} \qquad \frac{50}{2} = \frac{2x}{2}$$

$$x = 25 \text{ fixtures} \quad 25 = x$$

29.

$$\frac{1}{R} = \frac{1}{2} + \frac{1}{6} + \frac{1}{12}$$

$$(12R)\frac{1}{R} = (12R)\left(\frac{1}{2}\right) + (12R)\left(\frac{1}{6}\right) + (12R)\left(\frac{1}{12}\right)$$

$$12 = 6R + 2R + R$$

$$\frac{12}{9} = \frac{9R}{9}$$

$$\frac{12}{9} = R$$

$$R = \frac{4}{3}$$

$$R = 1\frac{1}{3} \text{ ohms or } 1.33 \text{ ohms}$$

31.

$$3.4 = 1.5 + T$$

$$(10)\,3.4 = (10)\,1.5 + (10)\,T$$

$$34 = 15 + 10T$$

$$34 - 15 = 10T$$

$$19 = 10T$$

$$\frac{19}{10} = \frac{10T}{10}$$

$$\frac{19}{10} = T$$

$$T = \frac{19}{10} \text{ or } 1\frac{9}{10} \text{ or } 1.9$$

33.

$$2.3x - 4.1 = 0.5$$

$$(10)\,2.3x - (10)\,4.1 = (10)\,0.5$$

$$23x - 41 = 5$$

$$23x = 5 + 41$$

$$23x = 46$$

$$\frac{23x}{23} = \frac{46}{23}$$

$$x = 2$$

35.

$$6.8 = 0.2y - 8.64$$

$$(100)6.8 = (100)0.2y - (100)8.64$$

$$680 = 20y - 864$$

$$680 + 864 = 20y$$

$$1544 = 20y$$

$$\frac{1544}{20} = \frac{20y}{20}$$

$$y = \frac{386}{5} \text{ or } 77\frac{1}{5} \text{ or } 77.2$$

37.

$$0.3x - 2.15 = 0.8x + 3.75$$

$$(100)0.3x - (100)2.15 = (100)0.8x + (100)3.75$$

$$30x - 215 = 80x + 375$$

$$30x - 80x = 375 + 215$$

$$-50x = 590$$

$$\frac{-50x}{-50} = \frac{590}{-50}$$

$$x = \frac{590}{-50}$$

$$x = -11.8$$

39.

$$2.7 - x = 5 + 2x$$

$$(10)2.7 - (10)x = (10)5 + (10)2x$$

$$27 - 10x = 50 + 20x$$

$$-10x - 20x = 50 - 27$$

$$-30x = 23$$

$$\frac{-30x}{-30} = \frac{23}{-30}$$

$$x = -\frac{23}{30}$$

$$x = -0.7666666667$$

$$x = -0.8$$

41. $6.7y - y = 8.4$ (round to tenths)

$$5.7y = 8.4$$

$$\frac{5.7y}{5.7} = \frac{8.4}{5.7}$$

$$y = 1.473684211$$

$$y = 1.5$$

43. $\dfrac{4x}{0.7} = \dfrac{3}{1.2}$

$$4.8x = 2.1$$

$$\frac{4.8x}{4.8} = \frac{2.1}{4.8}$$

$$x = 0.4375$$

$$x = 0.44 \quad \text{(round to hundredths)}$$

45. $0.04y = 0.02 - y$

$$0.04y + y = 0.02$$

$$1.04y = 0.02$$

$$\frac{1.04y}{1.04} = \frac{0.02}{1.04}$$

$$y = 0.0192307692$$

$$y = 0.02 \quad \text{(round to hundredths)}$$

47. $\dfrac{2.1}{x} = \dfrac{4.3}{7}$ (round to tenths)

$$4.3x = 2.1(7)$$

$$4.3x = 14.7$$

$$\frac{4.3x}{4.3} = \frac{14.7}{4.3}$$

$$x = 3.418604651$$

$$x = 3.4$$

49. $\Omega = \dfrac{V}{A}$

$$\Omega = \frac{8.5}{0.5}$$

$$\Omega = 17$$

51. $V = \dfrac{W}{A}$

$$V = \frac{385}{3.5}$$

$$V = 110$$

53. $F = P \times A$

$$F = 30(12.5)$$

$$F = 375 \ \text{lb}$$

55. $\dfrac{3x}{8} = \dfrac{3}{4}$

$$12x = 24$$

$$\frac{12x}{12} = \frac{24}{12}$$

$$x = 2$$

57. $\dfrac{7}{x} = 6$

$$\frac{7}{x} = \frac{6}{1}$$

$$7 = 6x$$

$$\frac{7}{6} = \frac{6x}{6}$$

$$x = \frac{7}{6} \ \text{or} \ 1\frac{1}{6}$$

59. $\dfrac{4x+3}{15} = \dfrac{1}{3}$

$$12x + 9 = 15$$

$$12x = 15 - 9$$

$$12x = 6$$

$$\frac{12x}{12} = \frac{6}{12}$$

$$x = \frac{1}{2}$$

61.
$$\frac{5}{4x-3} = \frac{3}{8}$$
$$40 = 12x - 9$$
$$40 + 9 = 12x$$
$$49 = 12x$$
$$\frac{49}{12} = \frac{12x}{12}$$
$$\frac{49}{12} = x$$
$$x = \frac{49}{12} \text{ or } 4\frac{1}{12}$$

63.
$$\frac{4x}{7} = \frac{2x+3}{3}$$
$$12x = 14x + 21$$
$$12x - 14x = 21$$
$$-2x = 21$$
$$\frac{-2x}{-2} = \frac{21}{-2}$$
$$x = -\frac{21}{2} \text{ or } -10\frac{1}{2}$$

65.
$$\frac{5x}{3} = \frac{2x+1}{4}$$
$$20x = 6x + 3$$
$$20x - 6x = 3$$
$$14x = 3$$
$$\frac{14x}{14} = \frac{3}{14}$$
$$x = \frac{3}{14}$$

67.
$$\frac{7}{x} = \frac{5}{4x+3}$$
$$28x + 21 = 5x$$
$$21 = 5x - 28x$$
$$21 = -23x$$
$$\frac{21}{-23} = \frac{-23x}{-23}$$
$$x = -\frac{21}{23}$$

69.
$$\frac{15}{x} = \frac{4}{6}$$
$$90 = 4x$$
$$\frac{90}{4x} = \frac{4x}{4}$$
$$x = \frac{45}{2} \text{ or } 22\frac{1}{2}$$
23 machines

71.
$$\frac{50}{40} = \frac{x}{2}$$
$$100 = 40x$$
$$\frac{100}{40} = \frac{40x}{40}$$
$$x = 2\frac{1}{2} \text{ hours}$$

73.
$$\frac{25}{x} = \frac{35}{6300}$$
$$35x = 157,500$$
$$x = 4,500 \text{ women}$$

75.
$$\frac{45}{30} = \frac{x}{1000}$$
$$45,000 = 30x$$
$$\frac{45,000}{30} = \frac{30x}{30}$$
$$x = 1,500 \text{ rpm}$$

77.
$$\frac{3}{5} = \frac{x}{5}$$
$$15 = 5x$$
$$\frac{15}{5} = \frac{5x}{5}$$
$$x = 3 \text{ days}$$

79.
$$\frac{\frac{5}{8}}{2} = \frac{1\frac{5}{16}}{x}$$
$$\frac{\frac{5}{8}}{2} = \frac{\frac{21}{16}}{x}$$
$$\frac{5}{8}x = \overset{1}{\cancel{2}}\left(\frac{21}{\underset{8}{\cancel{16}}}\right)$$
$$\frac{5}{8}x = \frac{21}{8}$$
$$\left(\frac{\overset{1}{\cancel{8}}}{\underset{1}{\cancel{5}}}\right)\frac{\overset{1}{\cancel{5}}}{\underset{1}{\cancel{8}}}x = \left(\frac{\overset{1}{\cancel{8}}}{5}\right)\frac{21}{\underset{1}{\cancel{8}}}$$
$$x = \frac{21}{5}$$
$$x = 4\frac{1}{5} \text{ or } 4.2 \text{ ft}$$

81.
$$\frac{81.2}{x} = \frac{845}{1,350}$$
$$109,620 = 845x$$
$$\frac{109,620}{845} = \frac{845x}{845}$$
$$x = 129.7278107$$
$$x = 129.7 \text{ gal}$$

83.
$$\frac{300}{425} = \frac{3.5}{x}$$
$$300x = 1,487.5$$
$$\frac{300x}{300} = \frac{1,487.5}{300}$$
$$x = 4.958333333$$
$$x = 5.0 \text{ hr}$$

85.
$$\frac{825}{x} = \frac{1.983}{3.247}$$
$$1.983x = 2,678.775$$
$$\frac{1.983x}{1.983} = \frac{2,678.775}{1.983}$$
$$x = 1,350.869894$$
$$x = 1,351 \text{ ft}$$

87.
$$\frac{4}{2} = \frac{x}{30}$$
$$2x = 120$$
$$\frac{2x}{2} = \frac{120}{2}$$
$$x = 60 \text{ rpm}$$

89.
$$\frac{2}{x} = \frac{4}{6}$$
$$4x = 12$$
$$\frac{4x}{4} = \frac{12}{4}$$
$$x = 3 \text{ machines}$$

91.
$$\frac{AC}{RS} = \frac{AB}{RT} = \frac{BC}{TS}$$

93.
$$\frac{6}{AB} = \frac{12}{20} \leftarrow 12 + 8 = 20$$
$$12AB = 120$$
$$\frac{12AB}{12} = \frac{120}{12}$$
$$AB = 10$$

95. $\dfrac{130}{65} = \dfrac{x}{50}$

$65x = 6,500$

$\dfrac{65x}{65} = \dfrac{6,500}{65}$

$x = 100 \text{ teeth}$

97. 2 water to 5 antifreeze = 7 parts

$\dfrac{2}{7} = \dfrac{x}{10}$

$7x = 20$

$\dfrac{7x}{7} = \dfrac{20}{7}$

$x = \dfrac{20}{7}$ or $2\dfrac{6}{7}$ gal or 2.9 gal of water

$\dfrac{5}{7} = \dfrac{x}{10}$

$7x = 50$

$\dfrac{7x}{7} = \dfrac{50}{7}$

$x = \dfrac{50}{7}$ or $7\dfrac{1}{7}$ gal

or 7.1 gal of antifreeze

Chapter 9 Trial Test

1. $\dfrac{3}{8}y = 6$

$\left(\dfrac{\cancel{8}}{\cancel{3}}\right)\dfrac{\cancel{3}}{\cancel{8}}y = \left(\dfrac{8}{\cancel{3}}\right)\left(\dfrac{\cancel{6}^{2}}{1}\right)$

$y = 16$

3. $\dfrac{3a}{7} = 9$

$\left(\dfrac{7}{3}\right)\dfrac{3a}{7} = \left(\dfrac{7}{\cancel{3}}\right)\left(\dfrac{\cancel{9}^{3}}{1}\right)$

$a = 21$

5. $\dfrac{3+Q}{1} = \dfrac{4}{5}$

$5(3+Q) = 4$

$15 + 5Q = 4$

$5Q = 4 - 15$

$5Q = -11$

$\dfrac{5Q}{5} = \dfrac{-11}{5}$

$Q = -\dfrac{11}{5}$ or $-2\dfrac{1}{5}$ or -2.2

7. $\dfrac{8}{y+2} = -7$

$\dfrac{8}{y+2} = \dfrac{-7}{1}$

$8 = -7(y+2)$

$8 = -7y - 14$

$8 + 14 = -7y$

$22 = -7y$

$\dfrac{22}{-7} = \dfrac{-7y}{-7}$

$y = -\dfrac{22}{7}$ or $-3\dfrac{1}{7}$

9. $\dfrac{2}{7}x = \dfrac{1}{2}x + 4$

$(\cancel{7})(2)\dfrac{2}{\cancel{7}}x = (7)(\cancel{2})\dfrac{1}{\cancel{2}}x + (7)(2)4$

$4x = 7x + 56$

$4x - 7x = 56$

$-3x = 56$

$\dfrac{-3x}{-3} = \dfrac{56}{-3}$

$x = -\dfrac{56}{3}$ or $-18\dfrac{2}{3}$

11.

$$5x + \frac{3}{5} = 2$$

$$(5)5x + (\cancel{5})\frac{3}{\cancel{5}} = (5)2$$

$$25x + 3 = 10$$

$$25x = 10 - 3$$

$$25x = 7$$

$$\frac{25x}{25} = \frac{7}{25}$$

$$x = \frac{7}{25} \text{ or } 0.28$$

13.

$$\frac{3}{5}x + \frac{1}{10}x = \frac{1}{3}$$

$$(\overset{6}{\cancel{30}})\frac{3}{\cancel{5}}x + (\overset{3}{\cancel{30}})\frac{1}{\cancel{10}}x = (\overset{10}{\cancel{30}})\frac{1}{\cancel{3}}$$

$$18x + 3x = 10$$

$$21x = 10$$

$$\frac{21x}{21} = \frac{10}{21}$$

$$x = \frac{10}{21}$$

15.

$$1.3x = 8.02$$

$$(100)1.3x = (100)8.02$$

$$130x = 802$$

$$\frac{130x}{130} = \frac{802}{130}$$

$$x = \frac{401}{65} \text{ or } 6\frac{11}{65} \text{ or } \approx 6.17$$

17.

$$\frac{1.2}{x} = 4.05$$

$$\frac{1.2}{x} = \frac{4.05}{1}$$

$$4.05x = 1.2$$

$$\frac{4.05x}{4.05} = \frac{1.2}{4.05}$$

$$x = 0.2962962963$$

$$x = 0.30 \text{ or } \frac{8}{27}$$

19.

$$0.18x = 300 - x$$

$$0.18x + x = 300$$

$$1.18x = 300$$

$$\frac{1.18x}{1.18} = \frac{300}{1.18}$$

$$x = 254.2372881$$

$$x = 254.24 \text{ or } \frac{15,000}{59}$$

21.

$$3x + 1.4 = 8.9$$

$$3x = 8.9 - 1.4$$

$$3x = 7.5$$

$$\frac{3x}{3} = \frac{7.5}{3}$$

$$x = 2.5 \text{ or } 2\frac{1}{2} \text{ or } \frac{5}{2}$$

23.

$$0.23 + 7.1x = -0.8 \qquad \qquad 0.8$$

$$7.1x = -0.8 - 0.23 \qquad + 0.23$$

$$7.1x = -1.03 \qquad \qquad \overline{1.03}$$

$$\frac{7.1x}{7.1} = \frac{-1.03}{7.1}$$

$$x = -0.15$$

25. inverse proportion

$$\frac{9}{4} = \frac{x}{75}$$

$$4x = 675$$

$$\frac{4x}{4} = \frac{675}{4}$$

$$x = \frac{675}{4} \text{ or } 168\frac{3}{4} \text{ or } 168.75 \text{ rpm}$$

27.

$$P = \frac{F}{A}$$

$$P = \frac{32.75}{24.65}$$

$$P = 1.328600406$$

$$P = 1.33 \text{ psi}$$

29.   direct proportion

$$\frac{62.5}{x} = \frac{400}{350}$$

$$400x = 21{,}875$$

$$\frac{400x}{400} = \frac{21{,}875}{400}$$

$$x = 54.6875$$

$$x = 54.7 \text{ L}$$

31.

$$R = \frac{V}{A}$$

$$R = \frac{40}{3.5}$$

$$R = 11.42857143$$

$$R = 11.429 \text{ ohms}$$

33.   direct proportion

$$\frac{75}{x} = \frac{3\frac{1}{2}}{5} \qquad \left(3\frac{1}{2} = \frac{7}{2}\right)$$

$$3\frac{1}{2}x = 75(5)$$

$$\frac{7}{2}x = 375$$

$$(2)\frac{7}{2}x = (2)375$$

$$7x = 750$$

$$\frac{7x}{7} = \frac{750}{7}$$

$$x = 107.1428571$$

$$x = 107 \text{ lb}$$

35.

$$\frac{9}{15} = \frac{12}{15 + x} \qquad \text{let } DB = x$$

$$9(15 + x) = 12(15)$$

$$9x + 135 = 180$$

$$9x = 180 - 135$$

$$9x = 45$$

$$\frac{9x}{9} = \frac{45}{9}$$

$$x = 5$$

ASSIGNMENT EXERCISES

1. $x^5 \cdot x^5 = x^{10}$
   The exponent of the product is the *sum* of the exponents.

3. $3x^4 \cdot 7x^5 = 21x^9$

5. $\dfrac{x^8}{x^5} = x^3$
   The exponent of the quotient is the *difference* between the exponents.

7. $\dfrac{21x^4}{3x} = 7x^3$

9. $\dfrac{x^3 y^{-1}}{x^2 y^2} = x^{3-2} y^{-1-2} = xy^{-3} = \dfrac{x}{y^3}$

11. $(x^3)^4 = x^{3(4)} = x^{12}$
    To raise a power to a power, multiply exponents.

13. $(x^{-3})^{-5} = x^{15}$
    To raise a power to a power, multiply exponents.

15. $(-3x^2)^3 = (-3)^3 (x^2)^3 = (-3)(-3)(-3)x^{2(3)} = -27x^6$

17. $\dfrac{xy^3}{xy^5} = x^{1-1} y^{3-5} = x^0 y^{-2} = \dfrac{1}{y^2}$

19. $2x^3 y^2 - 15xy^3 + 21y^4$
    Degree: 5
    Degree of $2x^3 y^2$ is $3 + 2 = 5$

21. $5x + 3x^3 - 8 + x^2$

Descending order:	$3x^3 + x^2 + 5x - 8$
Degree:	3
Leading term:	$3x^3$
Leading coefficient:	3

23. $5x^2 - 12x + 2x^4 - 32$

Descending order: $2x^4 + 5x^2 - 12x - 32$

Degree: 4

Leading term: $2x^4$

Leading coefficient: 2

25. $8x - 2x^4 - (3x^3 + 5x - x^3) = -2x^4 - 2x^3 + 3x$

To simplify remove grouping symbols, then combine like terms

27. $4x^2 - (3y^2 + 7x^2 - 8y^2) = 4x^2 - 3y^2 - 7x^2 + 8y^2 = -3x^2 + 5y^2$ **29.** $-7x^8(-3x^{-2}) = 21x^6$

Multiply the coefficients and add the exponents.

31. $2x(x^2 + 3x - 5) =$ **33.** $-2x(x^3 - 7x^2 + 15) =$

$2x^3 + 6x^2 - 10x$ $-2x^4 + 14x^3 - 30x$

35. $\dfrac{12x^7}{-18x^4} = -\dfrac{2}{3}x^3$ or $-\dfrac{2x^3}{3}$ **37.** $\dfrac{42x^3 y}{-15x^3 y^3} = -\dfrac{14}{5y^2}$

Reduce coefficients and subtract the exponents.

39. $\dfrac{6x^3 - 12x^2 + 21x}{3x} = \dfrac{6x^3}{3x} - \dfrac{12x^2}{3x} + \dfrac{21x}{3x}$ **41.** $\dfrac{4x^5}{8x^2} - 3x^2(2x^4) =$

$= 2x^2 - 4x + 7$ $\dfrac{1x^3}{2} - 6x^6 = \dfrac{x^3}{2} - 6x^6$

43. $10^5 \cdot 10^7 = 10^{12} = 1,000,000,000,000$ **45.** $10^7 \cdot 10^{-10} = 10^{-3} = \dfrac{1}{1000} = 0.001$

47. $8.73 \div 10^{-3} = 8.73 \times 10^3$ **49.** $3.75 \times 10^5 =$ **51.** $3.87 \times 10^{-5} =$

$= 8.\underaccent{\frown}{730}$ $375,000$ 0.0000387

$= 8,730.$

or

$8.73 \div 10^{-3} = 8.73 \div \dfrac{1}{1,000}$

$= 8.73 \times \dfrac{1,000}{1}$

$= 8,730$

53. $52,000 \rightarrow 5_{\wedge}2000$ **55.** $670 \rightarrow 6_{\wedge}70$ **57.** $0.00017 \rightarrow 0.0001_{\wedge}7$

5.2×10^4 6.7×10^2 1.7×10^{-4}

59. $5,600 \rightarrow 5_{\wedge}600$ **61.** $52,000 \rightarrow 5_{\wedge}2000$

5.6×10^3 5.2×10^4

63. $5,830,000 \rightarrow 5_{\wedge}830\ 000$ **65.** $41,980,000 \rightarrow 4_{\wedge}1980\ 000$

5.83×10^6 4.198×10^7

67. $0.033 \rightarrow 0.03_{\wedge}3$ **69.** $0.000\ 000\ 008 \rightarrow 0.000\ 000\ 008_{\wedge}$

3.3×10^{-2} 8×10^{-9}

71. $0.000\ 0719 \rightarrow 0.000\ 07_\wedge 19$

7.19×10^{-5}

73. $0.000\ 675 \rightarrow 0.0006_\wedge 75$

6.75×10^{-4}

75. $0.004 \rightarrow 0.004_\wedge$

4×10^{-3}

77. $0.000\ 0008 \rightarrow 0.000\ 0008_\wedge$

8×10^{-7}

79. $1,600 \rightarrow 1_\wedge 600$

1.6×10^{3}

81. $97,000,000 \rightarrow 9_\wedge 7000\ 000$

9.7×10^{7}

83. $0.000\ 52 \rightarrow 0.000\ 5_\wedge 2$

5.2×10^{-4}

85. $10.53 \rightarrow 1_\wedge 0.53$

1.053×10^{1}

87. $5,082 \rightarrow 5_\wedge 082$

5.082×10^{3}

89. $7,800 \rightarrow 7_\wedge 800$

7.8×10^{3}

91. $25,000 \rightarrow 2_\wedge 5000$

2.5×10^{4}

93. $4,000 \rightarrow 4_\wedge 000$

4×10^{3}

95. $0.0047 \rightarrow 0.004_\wedge 7$

4.7×10^{-3}

97. $(7.8 \times 10^{53})(5.6 \times 10^{72}) = 43.68 \times 10^{125}$

$$= 4.368 \times 10^{1} \times 10^{125}$$

$$= 4.368 \times 10^{126}$$

99. $\dfrac{1.25 \times 10^{3}}{3.7 \times 10^{-8}} = 0.3378378378 \times 10^{11}$

$$= 3.4 \times 10^{-1} \times 10^{11} \text{ (rounded)}$$

$$= 3.4 \times 10^{10}$$

101. $250,000,000 \rightarrow 2_\wedge 50,000,000$

2.5×10^{8}

103. $6,000,000,000,000\ (0.2) =$

$(6 \times 10^{12})(0.2) = 1.2 \times 10^{12}$ mm $=$

1.2×10^{6} km or $1,200,000$ km

Chapter 10 Trial Test

1. $x^{4}(x) = x^{4}(x^{1}) = x^{4+1} = x^{5}$

3. $\left(\dfrac{4}{7}\right)^{2} = \dfrac{4^{2}}{7^{2}} = \dfrac{16}{49}$

5. $\left(\dfrac{x^{2}}{y}\right)^{2} = \dfrac{(x^{2})^{2}}{y^{2}} = \dfrac{x^{4}}{y^{2}}$

7. $4a(3a^{2} - 2a + 5) = 12a^{3} - 8a^{2} + 20a$

9. $(10^{3})^{2} = 10^{6}$

11. $5x^{2} - 3x - (2x + 4x^{2}) =$

$5x^{2} - 3x - 2x - 4x^{2} =$

$x^{2} - 5x$

13. $42 \times 10^3 = 42\underline{.000} = 42,000.$

15. $5.9 \times 10^{-2} =$
          0.059

17. $240 = 2_{\wedge}40$
          $= 2.4 \times 10^2$

19. $0.021 =$
          2.1×10^{-2}

21. $783 \times 10^{-5} = 7_{\wedge}83 \times 10^{-5}$
          $= 7.83 \times 10^2 \times 10^{-5}$
          $= 7.83 \times 10^{-3}$

23. $\dfrac{5.25 \times 10^4}{1.5 \times 10^2} = \dfrac{5.25}{1.5} \cdot \dfrac{10^4}{10^2} = 3.5 \times 10^2$

25. $\dfrac{3 \times 10^3}{2 \times 10^{-3}} = 1.5 \times 10^6 \text{ ohms}$

chapter 11 Roots and Radicals

ASSIGNMENT EXERCISES

1. $\sqrt{49}$ radical notation

$49^{1/2}$ exponential notation

3. $\sqrt[4]{16}$ radical notation

$16^{1/4}$ exponential notation

5. $\sqrt{121}$ radical notation

$121^{1/2}$ exponential notation

7. $\sqrt{36}$ $\sqrt{38}$ $\sqrt{49}$

$\downarrow$ $\downarrow$

6 and 7

$\sqrt{38}$ is between 6 and 7.

9. $\sqrt{121}$ $\sqrt{135}$ $\sqrt{144}$

$\downarrow$ $\downarrow$

11 and 12

$\sqrt{135}$ is between 11 and 12.

11. $\sqrt[3]{27}$ $\sqrt[3]{60}$ $\sqrt[3]{64}$

$\downarrow$ $\downarrow$

3 and 4

$\sqrt[3]{60}$ is between 3 and 4.

13. $\sqrt{15}$

15. $\sqrt{5}$

17. $\left(x^7\right)^{1/2}, \sqrt{x^7} = x^{7/2}$

19. $\left(x^{1/3}\right)^2, \left(\sqrt[3]{x}\right)^2 = x^{2/3}$

21. $\sqrt{x} = x^{1/2}$

23. $\sqrt[5]{x^4} = x^{4/5}$

25. $\left(\sqrt[3]{xy}\right)^4 = \left((xy)^{1/3}\right)^4 = (xy)^{4/3}$ or $x^{4/3}y^{4/3}$

27. $\sqrt{7} = 7^{1/2}$

29. $y^{3/5} = \sqrt[5]{y^3}$

31. $\sqrt{y^{12}} = \left(y^{12}\right)^{1/2} = y^6$

33. $-\sqrt{b^{18}} = -\left(b^{18}\right)^{\frac{1}{2}} = -b^9$

35. $\sqrt[3]{x} = x^{1/3}$

37. $\sqrt[5]{y^4} = (4y)^{1/5}$ or $4^{1/5}y^{1/5}$ or $2^{2/5}y^{1/5}$

39. $\sqrt[3]{8b^{12}} = \left(8b^{12}\right)^{1/3} = 8^{1/3}b^{12/3} = \left(2^3\right)^{1/3}b^4 = 2b^4$

41. $\left(a^{1/2}\right)\left(a^{3/2}\right) = a^{1/2+3/2} = a^{4/2} = a^2$

43. $y^{3/4} \cdot y^{1/4} = y^{3/4+1/4} = y^{4/4} = y^1 = y$

45. $\left(3x^{1/4}y^2\right)^3 = (3)^3\left(x^{1/4}\right)^3\left(y^2\right)^3 = 27x^{1/4\cdot3}y^{2\cdot3} = 27x^{3/4}y^6$

47. $\left(4ax^{1/2}\right)^3 = 4^3\left(a^1\right)^3\left(x^{1/2}\right)^3 = 64a^{1\cdot3}x^{1/2\cdot3} = 64a^3x^{3/2}$

49. $\dfrac{x^{3/4}}{x^{1/4}} = x^{3/4-1/4} = x^{2/4} = x^{1/2}$ **51.** $\dfrac{a^{5/6}}{a^{-1/3}} = a^{5/6-(-1/3)} = a^{5/6+2/6} = a^{7/6}$

53. $\dfrac{x^{5/8}}{x^{3/4}} = x^{5/8-3/4} = x^{5/8-6/8} = x^{-1/8} = \dfrac{1}{x^{1/8}}$ **55.** $\dfrac{a^3}{a^{1/3}} = a^{3-1/3} = a^{9/3-1/3} = a^{8/3}$

57. $\dfrac{12a^4}{6a^{1/2}} = 2a^{4-1/2} = 2a^{8/2-1/2} = 2a^{7/2}$;

$\dfrac{12(2)^4}{6(2^{1/2})} = \dfrac{192}{8.485281374} = 22.627$

$2(2^{7/2}) = 22.627$

59. $\dfrac{15a^{3/5}}{10a^5} = \dfrac{3}{2}a^{3/5-5} = \dfrac{3}{2}a^{3/5-25/5} = \dfrac{3}{2}a^{-22/5} = \dfrac{3}{2a^{22/5}}$;

$\dfrac{15(2^{3/5})}{10(2^5)} = \dfrac{22.7357485}{320} = 0.071$

$\dfrac{3}{2(2^{22/5})} = \dfrac{3}{42.22425314} = 0.071$

61. $a^{2.3}\left(a^4\right) = a^{6.3}$; $2^{2.3}(2^4) = 78.793$
$\phantom{a^{2.3}\left(a^4\right) = a^{6.3};\quad} 2^{6.3} = 78.793$

63. $\left(\sqrt{5}\right)^2 = \left(5^{1/2}\right)^2 = 5$ **65.** $\sqrt{x^2} = \left(x^2\right)^{1/2} = x$

67. $\sqrt{9p^3} = \sqrt{9}\sqrt{p^3} = \sqrt{9}\sqrt{p^2}\sqrt{p} = 3p\sqrt{p}$

69. $\sqrt{18a^2b} = \sqrt{18}\sqrt{a^2}\sqrt{b} = \sqrt{9\cdot2}\sqrt{a^2}\sqrt{b} = \left(3\sqrt{2}\right)(a)\left(\sqrt{b}\right) = 3a\sqrt{2b}$

71. $\sqrt{32x^5y^2} = \sqrt{32}\sqrt{x^5}\sqrt{y^2} = \sqrt{16\cdot2}\sqrt{x^4\cdot x}\sqrt{y^2} = \left(4\sqrt{2}\right)\left(x^2\sqrt{x}\right)(y) = 4x^2y\sqrt{2x}$

73. $\sqrt{75x^{10}y^9} = \sqrt{75}\sqrt{x^{10}}\sqrt{y^9} = \sqrt{25\cdot3}\sqrt{x^{10}}\sqrt{y^8\cdot y} = \left(5\sqrt{3}\right)\left(x^5\right)\left(y^4\sqrt{y}\right) = 5x^5y^4\sqrt{3y}$

75. $5\sqrt{3} - 7\sqrt{3} = -2\sqrt{3}$

77. $3\sqrt{7} - 2\sqrt{28} =$ **79.** $2\sqrt{6} + 3\sqrt{54} =$ **81.** $4\sqrt{3} - 8\sqrt{48} =$
$\ \ 3\sqrt{7} - 2\sqrt{4\cdot7} =$ $\ \ 2\sqrt{6} + 3\sqrt{9\cdot6} =$ $\ \ 4\sqrt{3} - 8\sqrt{16\cdot3} =$
$\ \ 3\sqrt{7} - 2\left(2\sqrt{7}\right) =$ $\ \ 2\sqrt{6} + 3\left(3\sqrt{6}\right) =$ $\ \ 4\sqrt{3} - 8\left(4\sqrt{3}\right) =$
$\ \ \ \ 3\sqrt{7} - 4\sqrt{7} =$ $\ \ \ \ 2\sqrt{6} + 9\sqrt{6} =$ $\ \ \ \ 4\sqrt{3} - 32\sqrt{3} =$
$\ \ \ \ \ \ \ \ -1\sqrt{7} =$ $\ \ \ \ \ \ \ \ 11\sqrt{6}$ $\ \ \ \ \ \ \ \ -28\sqrt{3}$
$\ \ \ \ \ \ \ \ -1\sqrt{7}$

83.
$$5\sqrt{8} - 3\sqrt{50} =$$
$$5\sqrt{4\cdot2} - 3\sqrt{25\cdot2} =$$
$$5\left(2\sqrt{2}\right) - 3\left(5\sqrt{2}\right) =$$
$$10\sqrt{2} - 15\sqrt{2} =$$
$$-5\sqrt{2}$$

85.
$$3\sqrt{2} - 5\sqrt{32} =$$
$$3\sqrt{2} - 5\sqrt{16\cdot2} =$$
$$3\sqrt{2} - 5\left(4\sqrt{2}\right) =$$
$$3\sqrt{2} - 20\sqrt{2} =$$
$$-17\sqrt{2}$$

87.
$$2\sqrt{8}\cdot3\sqrt{6} = 6\sqrt{48}$$
$$= 6\sqrt{16\cdot3}$$
$$= 6\left(4\sqrt{3}\right)$$
$$= 24\sqrt{3}$$

89.
$$5\sqrt{3}\cdot8\sqrt{7} = 40\sqrt{21}$$

91.
$$-8\sqrt{5}\cdot4\sqrt{30} = -32\sqrt{150}$$
$$= -32\sqrt{25\cdot6}$$
$$= -32\left(5\sqrt{6}\right)$$
$$= -160\sqrt{6}$$

93.
$$\sqrt{3}\left(\sqrt{12} - 5\right) =$$
$$\sqrt{36} - 5\sqrt{3} =$$
$$6 - 5\sqrt{3}$$

95.
$$\sqrt{3}\left(\sqrt{6} - \sqrt{15}\right) =$$
$$\sqrt{18} - \sqrt{45} =$$
$$\sqrt{9\cdot2} - \sqrt{9\cdot5} =$$
$$3\sqrt{2} - 3\sqrt{5}$$

97.
$$\frac{3\sqrt{5}}{2\sqrt{20}} = \frac{3}{2\sqrt{4}} = \frac{3}{2(2)} = \frac{3}{4}$$

99.
$$\frac{6\sqrt{18}}{8\sqrt{2}} = \frac{3\sqrt{3}}{4\sqrt{2}}$$
$$\text{or } \frac{3\sqrt{3}}{4\sqrt{2}}\cdot\frac{\sqrt{2}}{\sqrt{2}} = \frac{3\sqrt{6}}{4(2)} = \frac{3\sqrt{6}}{8}$$

101.
$$\frac{5\sqrt{48}}{20\sqrt{20}} = \frac{\sqrt{12}}{4\sqrt{5}} = \frac{\sqrt{4\cdot3}}{4\sqrt{5}}$$
$$= \frac{2\sqrt{3}}{4\sqrt{5}} = \frac{\sqrt{3}}{2\sqrt{5}}$$
$$\text{or } \frac{\sqrt{3}}{2\sqrt{5}}\cdot\frac{\sqrt{5}}{\sqrt{5}} = \frac{\sqrt{15}}{10}$$

103.
$$\frac{\sqrt{3y^3}}{\sqrt{y^3}} = \sqrt{3}$$

105.
$$\left(\sqrt{\frac{9}{16}}\right)^2 = \left(\frac{3}{4}\right)^2 = \frac{9}{16}$$

107.
$$\frac{5}{\sqrt{17}} = \frac{5}{\sqrt{17}}\cdot\frac{\sqrt{17}}{\sqrt{17}} = \frac{5\sqrt{17}}{17}$$

109.
$$\frac{\sqrt{7}}{\sqrt{12}} = \frac{\sqrt{7}}{\sqrt{4\cdot3}} = \frac{\sqrt{7}}{2\sqrt{3}} = \frac{\sqrt{7}}{2\sqrt{3}}\cdot\frac{\sqrt{3}}{\sqrt{3}}$$
$$= \frac{\sqrt{21}}{2(3)} = \frac{\sqrt{21}}{6}$$

111.
$$\frac{\sqrt{3}}{\sqrt{8}} = \frac{\sqrt{3}}{\sqrt{8}}\cdot\frac{\sqrt{2}}{\sqrt{2}} = \frac{\sqrt{6}}{\sqrt{16}} = \frac{\sqrt{6}}{4}$$

113.
$$\frac{5\sqrt{3}}{\sqrt{24}} = \frac{5\sqrt{3}}{\sqrt{3\cdot8}} = \frac{5\sqrt{3}}{\sqrt{3\cdot4\cdot2}} = \frac{5\cdot\sqrt{2}}{2\sqrt{2}\cdot\sqrt{2}} = \frac{5\sqrt{2}}{2\sqrt{4}} = \frac{5\sqrt{2}}{2\cdot2} = \frac{5\sqrt{2}}{4}$$

115.
$$\sqrt{-100} = \sqrt{100\cdot-1} = 10i$$

117.
$$\pm\sqrt{-24y^7} = \pm\sqrt{4\cdot6}\sqrt{-1}\sqrt{y^6\cdot y}$$
$$= \pm\left(2\sqrt{6}\right)(i)\left(y^3\sqrt{y}\right)$$
$$= \pm2y^3i\sqrt{6y}$$

119. $i^{14} = \left(i^4\right)^3 \cdot i^2$

   $= (1)^3 \cdot (-1)$

   $= -1$

121. $i^{77} = \left(i^4\right)^{19} \cdot i$

   $= 1 \cdot i$

   $= i$

123. $15i = 0 + 15i$

125. $-12i^5 = -12i^4 \cdot i$

   $= -12i$

   $= 0 - 12i$

127. $(5 + 3i) + (2 - 7i)$

   $5 + 3i + 2 - 7i$

   $(5 + 2) + (3i - 7i)$

   $7 - 4i$

129. $\left(7 - \sqrt{-9}\right) + \left(4 + \sqrt{-16}\right)$

   $(7 - 3i) + (4 + 4i)$

   $7 - 3i + 4 + 4i$

   $(7 + 4) + (-3i + 4i)$

   $11 + i$

131. $x^2 - 36 = 0$

   $x^2 = 0 + 36$

   $x^2 = 36$

   $x = \pm\sqrt{36}$

   $x = \pm 6$

133. $x^2 - 4 = 0$

   $x^2 = 0 + 4$

   $x^2 = 4$

   $x = \pm\sqrt{4}$

   $x = \pm 2$

135. $x^2 + 4 = 0$

   $x^2 = -4$

   $x = \pm\sqrt{-4}$

   $x = \pm 2i$ or

   no real solutions

137. $18 = 2x^2$

   $\dfrac{18}{2} = \dfrac{2x^2}{2}$

   $9 = x^2$

   $\pm\sqrt{9} = x$

   $\pm 3 = x$

   $x = \pm 3$

139. $\sqrt{\dfrac{27}{2}} = x$

   $x = \sqrt{\dfrac{27}{2}} = \dfrac{\sqrt{27}}{\sqrt{2}} = \dfrac{\sqrt{9 \cdot 3}}{\sqrt{2}} = \dfrac{3\sqrt{3}}{\sqrt{2}} \cdot \dfrac{\sqrt{2}}{\sqrt{2}}$

   $x = \dfrac{3\sqrt{6}}{2}$

   or

   $x = 3.674$

141. $\sqrt{q + 3} = 7$

   $\left(\sqrt{q + 3}\right)^2 = 7^2$

   $q + 3 = 49$

   $q = 49 - 3$

   $q = 46$

143. $\sqrt{1.3x^2} = 11.7$

   $\left(\sqrt{1.3x^2}\right)^2 = (11.7)^2$

   $1.3x^2 = 136.89$

   $\dfrac{1.3x^2}{1.3} = \dfrac{136.89}{1.3}$

   $x^2 = 105.3$

   $x = \pm\sqrt{105.3}$

   $x = \pm 10.262$

145. $\sqrt{x^2 + 2} = 9$

   $\left(\sqrt{x^2 + 2}\right)^2 = 9^2$

   $x^2 + 2 = 81$

   $x^2 = 81 - 2$

   $x^2 = 79$

   $x = \pm\sqrt{79}$

   or

   $x = \pm 8.888$

147. $\sqrt{Q^2 - 1} = 0$

   $\left(\sqrt{Q^2 - 1}\right)^2 = 0^2$

   $Q^2 - 1 = 0$

   $Q^2 = 0 + 1$

   $Q^2 = 1$

   $Q = \pm\sqrt{1}$

   $Q = \pm 1$

149. $\sqrt{2 + y^2} = 8$

   $\left(\sqrt{2 + y^2}\right)^2 = 8^2$

   $2 + y^2 = 64$

   $y^2 = 64 - 2$

   $y^2 = 62$

   $y = \pm\sqrt{62}$

   or

   $y = \pm 7.874$

151.
$a = 9$ in.

$b = 12$ in.

$c = ?$

$c^2 = a^2 + b^2$

$c^2 = 9^2 + 12^2$

$c^2 = 81 + 144$

$c^2 = 225$

$c = \sqrt{225}$

$c = 15$ in.

153.
$a = 7$ ft

$b = ?$

$c = 10$ ft

$c^2 = a^2 + b^2$

$10^2 = 7^2 + b^2$

$100 = 49 + b^2$

$100 - 49 = b^2$

$51 = b^2$

$\sqrt{51} = b$

$b = \sqrt{51}$ ft

or

$b = 7.141$ ft

155.
$a = ?$

$b = 15$ yd

$c = 17$ yd

$c^2 = a^2 + b^2$

$17^2 = a^2 + 15^2$

$289 = a^2 + 225$

$289 - 225 = a^2$

$64 = a^2$

$\sqrt{64} = a$

$a = 8$ yd

157.
$a = 11$ mi

$b = 17$ mi

$c = ?$

$c^2 = a^2 + b^2$

$c^2 = 11^2 + 17^2$

$c^2 = 121 + 289$

$c^2 = 410$

$c = \sqrt{410}$

$c = \sqrt{410}$ mi

or

$c = 20.248$ mi

159.
$a = ?$

$b = 40$ cm

$c = 50$ cm

$c^2 = a^2 + b^2$

$50^2 = a^2 + 40^2$

$2500 = a^2 + 1600$

$2500 - 1600 = a^2$

$900 = a^2$

$\sqrt{900} = a$

$a = 30$ cm

161.
$c^2 = a^2 + b^2$

$c^2 = 12^2 + 18^2$

$c^2 = 144 + 324$

$c^2 = 468$

$c = \sqrt{468}$

$c = 6\sqrt{13}$ in.

or

$c = 21.633$ in.

163.

$c^2 = a^2 + b^2$

$c^2 = 3^2 + 3^2$

$c^2 = 9 + 9$

$c^2 = 18$

$c = \sqrt{18}$

$c = 3\sqrt{2}$ in.

or

$c = 4.243$ in.

165.
$5i(3 - 4i) = 5i(3) - 5i(4i)$

$= 15i - 20i^2$

$= 15i - 20(-1)$

$= 15i + 20$

$= 20 + 15i$

Chapter 11 Trial Test

1. $2\sqrt{7} \cdot 3\sqrt{2} = 6\sqrt{14}$

3. $4\sqrt{3} + 2\sqrt{3} = 6\sqrt{3}$

5. $\dfrac{4\sqrt{2}}{\sqrt{3}} = \dfrac{4\sqrt{2}}{\sqrt{3}} \cdot \dfrac{\sqrt{3}}{\sqrt{3}} = \dfrac{4\sqrt{6}}{\sqrt{9}} = \dfrac{4\sqrt{6}}{3}$

rationalize the denominator

7. $\dfrac{6\sqrt{8}}{2\sqrt{3}} = \dfrac{3\sqrt{8}}{\sqrt{3}} = \dfrac{3\sqrt{4\cdot 2}}{\sqrt{3}} = \dfrac{3\left(2\sqrt{2}\right)}{\sqrt{3}} = \dfrac{6\sqrt{2}}{\sqrt{3}}$

$\qquad = \dfrac{6\sqrt{2}}{\sqrt{3}} \cdot \dfrac{\sqrt{3}}{\sqrt{3}} = \dfrac{6\sqrt{6}}{\sqrt{9}} = \dfrac{6\sqrt{6}}{3} = 2\sqrt{6}$

9. $\dfrac{3\sqrt{5}}{2} \cdot \dfrac{7}{\sqrt{3x}} = \dfrac{21\sqrt{5}}{2\sqrt{3x}} = \dfrac{21\sqrt{5}}{2\sqrt{3x}} \cdot \dfrac{\sqrt{3x}}{\sqrt{3x}} = \dfrac{21\sqrt{15x}}{2\sqrt{9x^2}}$

$\qquad = \dfrac{21\sqrt{15x}}{2\left(3x\right)} = \dfrac{21\sqrt{15x}}{6x} = \dfrac{7\sqrt{15x}}{2x}$

11. $\sqrt{5-x^2} = 2$

$\left(\sqrt{5-x^2}\right)^2 = 2^2$

$5 - x^2 = 4$

$-x^2 = 4 - 5$

$-x^2 = -1$

$x^2 = 1$

$\sqrt{x^2} = \sqrt{1}$

$x = \pm 1$

13. $7 = \sqrt{Q}$

$7^2 = \left(\sqrt{Q}\right)^2$

$49 = Q$

$Q = 49$

15. $\sqrt{\dfrac{6}{y}} = \sqrt{\dfrac{2}{3}}$

$\left(\sqrt{\dfrac{6}{y}}\right)^2 = \left(\sqrt{\dfrac{2}{3}}\right)^2$

$\dfrac{6}{y} = \dfrac{2}{3}$

$2y = 18$

$\dfrac{2y}{2} = \dfrac{18}{2}$

$y = 9$

17. $x^2 + 49 = 0$

$x^2 = 0 - 49$

$x^2 = -49$

$x = \sqrt{-49} = \sqrt{49(-1)}$

$x = \pm 7i$ or

no real solutions

19. $\sqrt[3]{27x^{15}} = 27^{1/3}\, x^{15/3}$

$\qquad = \left(3^3\right)^{1/3} x^5$

$\qquad = 3^1 x^5$

$\qquad = 3x^5$

21. $\sqrt[5]{x^{10} y^{15} z^{30}} = x^{10/5} y^{15/5} z^{30/5}$

$\qquad = x^2 y^3 z^6$

23. $\left(125x^{1/2} y^6\right)^{1/3} = 125^{1/3}\left(x^{1/2}\right)^{1/3}\left(y^6\right)^{1/3}$

$\qquad = 5x^{1/6} y^2$

25. $\dfrac{12x^{3/5}}{6x^{-2/5}} = 2x^{3/5-(-2/5)}$

$\qquad = 2x^{5/5} = 2x^1 = 2x$

27. $i^{23} = \left(i^4\right)^5 \cdot i^3$

$\qquad = 1 \cdot -i$

$\qquad = -i$

29. $\left(5+3i\right) - \left(8-2i\right)$

$5 + 3i - 8 + 2i$

$5 - 8 + 3i + 2i$

$-3 + 5i$

31. $\sqrt{7}(5-4) =$

$\sqrt{35} - 4\sqrt{7}$

33. $a = 5$ $c^2 = a^2 + b^2$

$b = 12$ $c^2 = 5^2 + 12^2$

$c = ?$ $c^2 = 25 + 144$

$c^2 = 169$

$c = 13$

35. $a = 8$ $c^2 = a^2 + b^2$

$b = ?$ $10^2 = 8^2 + b^2$

$c = 10$ $100 = 64 + b^2$

$100 - 64 = b^2$

$36 = b^2$

$6 = b$

$b = 6$

37. $a = 8$ $c^2 = a^2 + b^2$

$b = 15$ $c^2 = 8^2 + 15^2$

$c = ?$ $c^2 = 64 + 225$

$c^2 = 289$

$c = 17$ in.

chapter 12 Formulas and Applications

ASSIGNMENT EXERCISES

1. $R = 30\%$
$B = \$2.70$

$$P = \frac{RB}{100}$$
$$= \frac{30(2.70)}{100}$$
$$= \$0.81$$

3. $P = \dfrac{RB}{100}$ $\qquad P = 12 \text{ kg}, B = 125 \text{ kg}$

$$12 = \frac{R(125)}{100}$$
$$\frac{12}{1} = \frac{125R}{100}$$
$$125R = 1200$$
$$\frac{125R}{125} = \frac{1200}{125}$$
$$R = 9.6\%$$

5. $R = \dfrac{100P}{B}$ $\qquad R = 12\%, B = 90$

$$12 = \frac{100P}{90}$$
$$\frac{12}{1} = \frac{100P}{90}$$
$$100P = 1,080$$
$$\frac{100P}{100} = \frac{1,080}{100}$$
$$P = 10.8$$

7. $I = PRT$ $\qquad P = \$440, R = 16\%, T = 2\dfrac{3}{4} \text{ yrs}$
$$I = (440)(0.16)(2.75)$$
$$I = \$193.60$$

9. $I = PRT$ $\qquad I = \$387.50, P = \$1,550, R = 12.5\%$
$$387.50 = 1,550(0.125)T$$
$$387.50 = 193.75T$$
$$\frac{387.50}{193.75} = \frac{193.75T}{193.75}$$
$$2 \text{ yrs} = T$$

11.

$$P = 2(l+w) \qquad P = 160 \text{ in., } w = 30 \text{ in.}$$
$$160 = 2(l+30)$$
$$160 = 2l+60$$
$$160-60 = 2l$$
$$100 = 2l$$
$$\frac{100}{2} = \frac{2l}{2}$$
$$50 = l$$
$$l = 50 \text{ in.}$$

13.

$$M = S - C \qquad M = \$25.75, \ S = \$115.25$$
$$25.75 = 115.25 - C$$
$$25.75 - 115.25 = -C$$
$$\frac{-89.50}{-1} = \frac{-C}{-1}$$
$$\$89.50 = C$$

15.

$$A = \pi r^2 \qquad r = 5.5 \text{ in.}$$
$$A = \pi (5.5)^2$$
$$A = \pi (30.25)$$
$$A = 95.0 \text{ in}^2$$

17.

$$E = IR$$
$$220 = I(80)$$
$$\frac{220}{80} = \frac{I(80)}{80}$$
$$2.75 = I$$
$$I = 2.75 \text{ amps}$$

19.

$$\frac{V_1}{V_2} = \frac{P_2}{P_1}$$
$$\frac{30}{V_2} = \frac{225}{75}$$
$$225V_2 = 2,250$$
$$\frac{225V_2}{225} = \frac{2,250}{225}$$
$$V_2 = 10 \text{ ft}^3$$

21.

$$P = I^2 R$$
$$80 = I^2(8)$$
$$\frac{80}{8} = \frac{I^2(8)}{8}$$
$$10 = I^2$$
$$\sqrt{10} = \sqrt{I^2}$$
$$I = 3.2 \text{ amps}$$

23.

$s = $ speed of driven pulley

$S = 600$ rpm (speed of driving pulley)

$d = 3$ in. (diameter of driven pulley)

$D = 7$ in. (diameter of driving pulley)

$$s = \frac{DS}{d}$$
$$s = \frac{7(600)}{3}$$
$$s = 1,400 \text{ rpm}$$

25.

$$H = \frac{D^2 N}{2.5}$$
$$5 = \frac{(2.5)^2 N}{2.5}$$
$$5 = \frac{6.25N}{2.5}$$
$$(2.5) \, 5 = (2.5)\frac{6.25N}{2.5}$$
$$12.5 = 6.25N$$
$$\frac{12.5}{6.25} = \frac{6.25N}{6.25}$$
$$2 = N$$
$$N = 2 \text{ cylinders}$$

27. $C(x) = 3.48x + 10,000$

    (a) $C(100) = 3.48(100) + 10,000$

                    $= 348 + 10,000$

                    $= \$10,348$

    (b) $C(1,000) = 3.48(1,000) + 10,000$

                    $= 3,480 + 10,000$

                    $= \$13,480$

    (c) $C(10,000) = 3.48(10,000) + 10,000$

                    $= 34,800 + 10,000$

                    $= \$44,800$

29. $R(x) = 40x$

    (a) $R(100) = 40(100)$

               $= \$4,000$

    (b) $R(1,000) = 40(1,000)$

               $= \$40,000$

    (c) $R(10,000) = 40(10,000)$

               $= \$400,000$

31. $A(x) = \dfrac{P(x)}{x} = \dfrac{R(x) - C(x)}{x}$

    (a) $A(100) = \dfrac{4,000 - 10,348}{100}$

              $= \dfrac{-6,348}{100} = -\$63.48$

    (b) $A(1,000) = \dfrac{40,000 - 13,480}{1,000}$

               $= \dfrac{26,520}{1,000} = \$26.52$

    (c) $A(10,000) = \dfrac{400,000 - 44,800}{10,000}$

               $= \dfrac{355,200}{10,000}$

               $= \$35.52$

33. $V = lwh \quad \text{for } w$

$$\frac{V}{lh} = \frac{\cancel{lwh}}{\cancel{lh}}$$

$$\frac{V}{lh} = w$$

$$w = \frac{V}{lh}$$

35. $B = cr^2 x \quad \text{for } r$

$$\frac{B}{cx} = \frac{\cancel{cr^2 x}}{\cancel{cx}}$$

$$\frac{B}{cx} = r^2$$

$$\sqrt{\frac{B}{cx}} = r$$

37. $PB = A \quad \text{for } B$

$$\frac{\cancel{P}B}{\cancel{P}} = \frac{A}{P}$$

$$B = \frac{A}{P}$$

39. $I = Prt \quad \text{for } r$

$$\frac{I}{Pt} = \frac{Prt}{Pt}$$

$$\frac{I}{Pt} = r$$

$$r = \frac{I}{Pt}$$

41. $s = r - d \quad \text{for } r$

$$s + d = r$$

$$r = s + d$$

43. $v = v_0 - 32t \quad \text{for } t$

$$v - v_0 = -32t$$

$$\frac{v - v_0}{-32} = \frac{-32t}{-32}$$

$$\frac{v - v_0}{-32} = t \ \text{ or }\ \frac{v_0 - v}{32} = t$$

$$t = \frac{v_0 - v}{32}$$

45. $A = P(1 + rt)$ for t

$A = P + Prt$

$A - P = Prt$

$$\frac{A - P}{Pr} = \frac{Prt}{Pr}$$

$$\frac{A - P}{Pr} = t$$

$$t = \frac{A - P}{Pr}$$

also acceptable: $t = \dfrac{\frac{A}{P} - 1}{r}$ or $t = \dfrac{A}{Pr} - \dfrac{1}{r}$

47. $S = P - D$ for P

$S + D = P$

$P = S + D$

49. $TSA = ph + 2B$

$TSA = (27.8)(20) + 2(30)$

$TSA = 556 + 60$

$TSA = 616 \text{ cm}^2$

$p = 9 + 6.8 + 12$

$p = 27.8 \text{ cm}$

$B = \dfrac{1}{2}bh$

$B = \dfrac{1}{2}(12)(5)$

$B = 30 \text{ cm}^2$

$2B = 60 \text{ cm}^2$

51. $TSA = ph + 2B$

$TSA = (94.24777961)(14) + 2(706.8583471)$

$\quad = 1,319.469 + 1,413.717$

$\quad = 2,733.1865609$

$\quad = 2,733.186 \text{ cm}^2$

$p = C$

$C = 2\pi r$

$C = 2\pi(15)$

$C = 94.24777961 \text{ cm}$

$B = \pi r^2$

$\quad = \pi(15)^2$

$\quad = 706.8583471 \text{ cm}^2$

53. hexagonal $\rightarrow$ 6 sides

$$\frac{6 \text{ in.}}{1} \times \frac{1 \text{ ft}}{12 \text{ in.}} = 0.5 \text{ ft}$$

$p = 6(0.5 \text{ ft}) = 3 \text{ ft}$

$LSA = ph$

$\quad = (3)(20)$

$\quad = 60 \text{ ft}^2$

55. cylinder, volume

diameter $= 18$ in.

$$= \frac{18}{12} \text{ ft} = 1.5 \text{ ft}$$

height $= 5 \text{ mi} = \dfrac{5 \text{ mi}}{1}\left(\dfrac{5,280 \text{ ft}}{1 \text{ mi}}\right) = 26,400 \text{ ft}$

$LSA = ph \qquad p = \pi d$

$\quad = \pi dh$

$\quad = \pi(1.5)(26,400)$

$\quad = 124,407 \text{ ft}^2$

57. $V = \dfrac{1}{3}Bh$

$= \dfrac{1}{3}(12)(12)(36)$

$= 1,728 \text{ m}^3$

59. $\dfrac{1}{3} \cdot 6 \cdot \left(5.375^2 + 3.625^2 + \sqrt{5.375^2 \cdot 3.625^2}\right)$

$= 2\left(\left(5\dfrac{3}{8}\right)^2 + \left(3\dfrac{5}{8}\right)^2 + \sqrt{\left(5\dfrac{3}{8}\right)^2 + \left(3\dfrac{5}{8}\right)^2}\right)$

$= 2\left(\left(\dfrac{43}{8}\right)^2 + \left(\dfrac{29}{8}\right)^2 + \sqrt{\left(\dfrac{43}{8}\right)^2 + \left(\dfrac{29}{8}\right)^2}\right)$

$= 2\left(\dfrac{1,849}{64} + \dfrac{841}{64} + \dfrac{1,247}{64}\right)$

$= 2\left(\dfrac{3,937}{64}\right)$

$= \dfrac{3,937}{32}$

$= 123 \text{ ft}^3$

61. $TSA = 4\pi r^2$

$= 4\pi (9)^2$

$= 1,017.9 \text{ m}^2$

63. $V = \dfrac{4\pi r^3}{3}$

$= \dfrac{4\pi (12)^3}{3}$

$= \dfrac{4\pi (1,728)}{3}$

$= 7,238.2 \text{ ft}^3$

65. $LSA = \pi rs$

$= \pi (6)(9)$

$= 169.6 \text{ cm}^2$

67. $V = \dfrac{\pi r^2 h}{3}$

$= \dfrac{\pi (6)^2 (10)}{3}$

$= 377.0 \text{ in}^3$

69. $TSA = \pi rs + \pi r^2$

$= \pi (9)(12) + \pi (9)^2$

$= 339.3 + 254.5$

$= 593.8 \text{ ft}^2$

$\dfrac{593.8 \ \cancel{\text{ft}^2}}{1}\left(\dfrac{1 \text{ gal}}{350 \ \cancel{\text{ft}^2}}\right) = 2 \text{ gallons}$

71.

$s = ?$

12

3

6

$c^2 = a^2 + b^2$

$c^2 = 3^2 + 12^2$

$c^2 = 9 + 144$

$c^2 = 153$

$c = \sqrt{153}$

$c = 12.36931688 = s$

$LSA = \pi rs$

$= \pi (3)(12.36931688)$

$= 116.6 \text{ ft}^2$

73. $TSA = 4\pi r^2$

$= 4\pi (4.4)^2$

$= 243.3 \text{ in}^2$

diameter = 8.8 in.

radius $= \dfrac{1}{2}d = \dfrac{1}{2}(8.8) = 4.4$ in.

75. diameter = 20 ft

radius $= \dfrac{1}{2}d = \dfrac{1}{2}(20) = 10$ ft

$V = \dfrac{4\pi r^3}{3}$

$= \dfrac{4\pi (10)^3}{3}$

$= 4,188.8 \text{ ft}^3$

$\dfrac{1}{2}(4,188.8 \text{ ft}^3) = 2,094 \text{ ft}^3$

77. Formula rearrangement allows us to use only arithmetic rather than algebra in solving an equation. $D = RT$. Find R if distance $D = 300$ miles and time $T = 5$ hours.

with rearrangement:

$$\frac{D}{T} = \frac{R\cancel{T}}{\cancel{T}} \qquad \text{then} \qquad R = \frac{300}{5}$$

$$R = \frac{D}{T} \qquad\qquad\qquad R = 60 \text{ mph}$$

Answers may vary.

Chapter 12 Trial Test

1. $R = \dfrac{PL}{A}$

$(A)\, R = (A)\dfrac{PL}{A}$

$AR = PL$

$\dfrac{AR}{P} = \dfrac{PL}{\cancel{P}}$

$\dfrac{AR}{P} = L$

$L = \dfrac{AR}{P}$

3. $d = \pi r^2 sn$

$\dfrac{d}{\pi sn} = \dfrac{\cancel{\pi} r^2 s\cancel{n}}{\cancel{\pi} s\cancel{n}}$

$\dfrac{d}{\pi sn} = r^2$

$\sqrt{\dfrac{d}{\pi sn}} = \sqrt{r^2}$

$r = \sqrt{\dfrac{d}{\pi sn}}$

5. $LSA = ph$

$LSA = (5)(10)$ pentagon, 5 sides, 1 in. each

$LSA = 50 \text{ in}^2$ perimeter $p = 5$ in.

7. $TSA = ph + 2B$

$C = \pi d = 12\pi$

$C = 37.69911184$

$B = \pi (6)^2 = 113.0973355$

$2B = 226.194671$

$TSA = 37.69911184(15) + 226.194671$

$TSA = 791.6813487 \text{ ft}^2$

$= 791.7 \text{ ft}^2$

9. $V = \dfrac{4\pi r^3}{3}$

$V = \dfrac{4\pi (6)^3}{3}$ where $d = 12$ ft

$V = 904.8 \text{ ft}^3$ $r = \dfrac{1}{2}d = \dfrac{1}{2}(12) = 6$ ft

$\dfrac{904.8 \ \cancel{\text{ft}^3}}{1}\left(\dfrac{7.48 \text{ gal}}{1 \ \cancel{\text{ft}^3}}\right) = 6,768 \text{ gal}$

11. $V = \dfrac{\pi r^2 h}{3}$

$V = \dfrac{\pi (17.5)^2 (12)}{3}$ where $d = 35$ ft

$V = 3,848.5 \text{ ft}^3$ $r = \dfrac{1}{2}d \dfrac{1}{2}(35) = 17.5$ ft

13. $TSA = \pi rs + \pi r^2$

$TSA = \pi (15)(29.15475947) + \pi (15)^2$

$TSA = 1,373.885673 + 706.8583471$

$TSA = 2,080.74402 \text{ cm}^2$

$TSA = 2,080.7 \text{ cm}^2$

$c^2 = a^2 + b^2$

$c^2 = 15^2 + 25^2$

$c^2 = 225 + 625$

$c^2 = 850$

$c = \sqrt{850}$

$c = 29.15475947$

15. $20 \text{ in.} = \dfrac{20 \text{ in.}}{1}\left(\dfrac{1 \text{ ft}}{12 \text{ in.}}\right) = \dfrac{5}{3} \text{ ft}$

diameter is $\dfrac{5}{3}$ ft

$LSA = ph \qquad\qquad p = \pi d$

$ = \pi dh$

$ = \pi\left(\dfrac{5}{3}\right)(5)$

$ = 26.17993878$

$ = 26.2 \text{ ft}^2$

17.

$P = \dfrac{1.27F}{D^2}$

$180 = \dfrac{1.27F}{(3.25)^2}$

$\dfrac{180}{1} = \dfrac{1.27F}{10.5625}$

$1.27F = 1,901.25$

$\dfrac{1.27F}{1.27} = \dfrac{1,901.25}{1.27}$

$F = 1,497.047244$

$F = 1,497.05 \text{ lb}$

19.

$E = \dfrac{I - P}{I}$

$0.70 = \dfrac{40,000 - P}{40,000}$

$\dfrac{0.70}{1} = \dfrac{40,000 - P}{40,000}$

$40,000 - P = 28,000$

$-P = 28,000 - 40,000$

$-P = -12,000$

$\dfrac{-P}{-1} = \dfrac{-12,000}{-1}$

$P = 12,000 \text{ calories}$

21. $v = \dfrac{1}{3}h\left(B_1 + B_2 + \sqrt{B_1 B_2}\right)$

$ = \dfrac{1}{3}(9)\left(8^2 + 12^2 + \sqrt{(8^2)(12^2)}\right)$

$ = 3\left(64 + 144 + \sqrt{64(144)}\right)$

$ = 3(208 + 96)$

$ = 3(304)$

$ = 912 \text{ m}^3$

ASSIGNMENT EXERCISES

1. $5x + 5y = 5\left(\dfrac{5x}{5} + \dfrac{5y}{5}\right) = 5(x+y)$

3. $12m^2 - 8n^2 = 4\left(\dfrac{12m^2}{4} - \dfrac{8n^2}{4}\right)$
$= 4(3m^2 - 2n^2)$

5. $2a^3 - 14a^2 - 2a = 2a\left(\dfrac{2a^3}{2a} - \dfrac{14a^2}{2a} - \dfrac{2a}{2a}\right)$
$= 2a(a^2 - 7a - 1)$

7. $15x^3 - 5x^2 - 20x = 5x\left(\dfrac{15x^3}{5x} - \dfrac{5x^2}{5x} - \dfrac{20x}{5x}\right)$
$= 5x(3x^2 - x - 4)$

9. $18a^3 + 12a^2 = 6a^2\left(\dfrac{18a^3}{6a^2} + \dfrac{12a^2}{6a^2}\right)$
$= 6a^2(3a + 2)$

11. $-6x^2 - 10x = -2x\left(\dfrac{-6x^2}{-2x} - \dfrac{10x}{-2x}\right)$
$= -2x(3x + 5)$

13.
$$\overset{F\quad L}{(x+7)\,(x+4)} = x^2 + 4x + 7x + 28$$
$$= x^2 + 11x + 28$$

15.
$$\overset{F\quad L}{(m+3)\,(m-7)} = m^2 - 7m + 3m - 21$$
$$= m^2 - 4m - 21$$

17.
$$\overset{F\quad L}{(4r-5)\,(3r+2)} = 12r^2 + 8r - 15r - 10$$
$$= 12r^2 - 7r - 10$$

19.
$$(4-2m)(1-3m) = 4 - 12m - 2m + 6m^2$$
$$= 4 - 14m + 6m^2$$

21.
$$(x+3)(2x-5) = 2x^2 - 5x + 6x - 15$$
$$= 2x^2 + 1x - 15$$
$$= 2x^2 + x - 15$$

23.
$$(2a+3b)(7a-b) = 14a^2 - 2ab + 21ab - 3b^2$$
$$= 14a^2 + 19ab - 3b^2$$

25.
$$\overset{\text{F\quad O\quad I\quad L}}{(9x-2y)(3x+4y)} = 27x^2+36xy-6xy-8y^2$$
$$= 27x^2+30xy-8y^2$$

27.
$$\overset{\text{F\quad O\quad I\quad L}}{(7m-2n)(3m+5n)} = 21m^2+35mn-6mn-10n^2$$
$$= 21m^2+29mn-10n^2$$

29. $(6x-5)(6x+5)=36x^2-25$
        square, minus, square

31. $(7y+11)(7y-11)=49y^2-121$

33. $(8a-5b)(8a+5b)=64a^2-25b^2$
        square, minus, square

35. $\left(\sqrt{8}+2\right)\left(\sqrt{8}-2\right)=8-4=4$

37. $(3+i)(3-i)=9-i^2=9-(-1)=10$
        square, minus, square

39. $(x+9)^2=x^2+18x+81$

41. $(x-3)^2=x^2-6x+9$
        square, double product, square

43. $(4x-15)^2=16x^2-120x+225$

45. $(8+7m)^2=64+112m+49m^2$
        square, double product, square

47. $(4x-11)^2=16x^2-88x+121$

49. $(g-h)(g^2+gh+h^2)=g^3-h^3$
        cube, minus, cube

51. $(2H-3T)(4H^2+6HT+9T^2)=8H^3-27T^3$

53. $(6+i)(36-6i+i^2)=216+i^3=216-i$
        cube, plus, cube

55. $(z+2t)(z^2-2zt+4t^2)=z^3+8t^3$

57. $(7T+2)(49T^2-14T+4)=343T^3+8$
        cube, plus, cube

59.
$$x-9\;\overline{)\,x^2-11x+18}$$
$$\quad x-2$$
$$\underline{x^2-\ 9x}\qquad\text{subtract}$$
$$-2x+18$$
$$\underline{-2x+18}\qquad\text{subtract}$$
$$0$$

61.
$$5x+2\;\overline{)\,15x^2-4x-4}$$
$$\quad 3x-2$$
$$\underline{15x^2+6x}\qquad\text{subtract}$$
$$-10x-4$$
$$\underline{-10x-4}\qquad\text{subtract}$$
$$0$$

63.
$$x-5\;\overline{)\,x^3-4x^2-10x+25}$$
$$\quad x^2+x-5$$
$$\underline{x^3-5x^2}\qquad\text{subtract}$$
$$1x^2-10x$$
$$\underline{x^2-5x}\qquad\text{subtract}$$
$$-5x+25$$
$$\underline{-5x+25}\qquad\text{subtract}$$
$$0$$

65.
$$2x^2-x-1\;\overline{)\,6x^3-x^2-4x-1}$$
$$\quad 3x+1$$
$$\underline{6x^3-3x^2-3x}\qquad\text{subtract}$$
$$2x^2-x-1$$
$$\underline{2x^2-x-1}\qquad\text{subtract}$$
$$0$$

67. $64+4a^2$ No; this is a *sum*, not a difference.

69. H^2-G^2 Yes

71. $64b^2-49$ Yes

73. $-9x^2 + 12x + 4$ No; the first term is negative.

75. $9t^2 - 24tp + 16p^2$ Yes

77. $j^2 + 10j + 25$ Yes

79. $125a^3 - 8b^3$ Yes, difference

81. $8z^3 - 125$ Yes, difference

83. $64w^3 + 27$ Yes, sum

85. $25y^2 - 4$
$(5y + 2)(5y - 2)$

87. $a^2b^2 + 49$ NSP; this is a *sum*,
not a difference.

89. $a^2 + 2a + 1$ square root, middle sign, square root, square
$(a + 1)^2$

91. $16c^2 - 24bc + 9b^2$
$(4c - 3b)^2$

93. $n^2 + 169 - 26n$
$n^2 - 26n + 169$
$(n - 13)^2$

95. $36a^2 + 84ab + 49b^2$
$(6a + 7b)^2$

97. $49 - 14x + x^2$
$(7 - x)^2$

99. $64 + 25x^2$ NSP; this is a *sum*,
not a difference.

101. $16x^2 + 24x + 9y^2$
NSP, missing y factor in middle term

103. $49 - 81y^2$
$(7 + 9y)(7 - 9y)$

105. $9x^2 - 100y^2$
$(3x + 10y)(3x - 10y)$

107. $9x^2 - 6xy + y^2$
$(3x - y)^2$

109. $9x^2y^2 - z^2$
$(3xy + z)(3xy - z)$

111. $x^2 + 4x + 4$
$(x + 2)^2$

113. $\dfrac{4}{25}x^2 - \dfrac{1}{16}y^2$
$\left(\dfrac{2}{5}x + \dfrac{1}{4}y\right)\left(\dfrac{2}{5}x - \dfrac{1}{4}y\right)$

115. $T^3 - 8$
$(T - 2)(T^2 + 2T + 4)$

117. $d^3 + 729$
$(d + 9)(d^2 - 9d + 81)$

119. $27k^3 + 64$
$(3k + 4)(9k^2 - 12k + 16)$

121. $x^2 + 11x + 24$
$(x + \ )(x + \ )$
$(x + 3)(x + 8)$

24
$1 \cdot 24$
$2 \cdot 12$
$3 \cdot 8$ ★ $+3 + 8 = +11$
$4 \cdot 6$

123. $x^2 + 13x + 30$
$(x + \ )(x + \ )$
$(x + 3)(x + 10)$

30
$1 \cdot 30$
$2 \cdot 15$
$3 \cdot 10$ ★ $+3 + 10 = +30$
$5 \cdot 6$

125. $x^2 - 9x + 8$
$(x - \ )(x - \ )$
$(x - 1)(x - 8)$

8
$1 \cdot 8$ ★ $-1 - 8 = -9$
$2 \cdot 4$

127. $x^2 - 11x - 26$
$(x + \ )(x - \ )$
$(x + 2)(x - 13)$

26
$1 \cdot 26$
$2 \cdot 13$ ★ $+2 - 13 = -11$

129.

$x^2 + 5x - 24$

$(x+\ \ )(x-\ \ )$

$(x+8)(x-3)$

$$\frac{24}{1 \cdot 24}$$
$2 \cdot 12$
$3 \cdot 8$ ★ $-3 + 8 = +5$
$4 \cdot 6$

131.

$6x^2 + 25x + 4$

$\dfrac{(6x+\ \ )(6x+\ \ )}{6}$

$\dfrac{(6x+1)(6x+24)}{6}$

$\dfrac{(6x+1)(\cancel{6})(x+4)}{\cancel{6}}$

$(6x+1)(x+4)$

$6 \cdot 4 = \dfrac{24}{1 \cdot 24}$
$2 \cdot 12$
$3 \cdot 8$
$4 \cdot 6$

★ $+1 + 24 = +25$

133.

$5x^2 - 34x + 24$

$\dfrac{(5x-\ \ )(5x-\ \ )}{5}$

$\dfrac{(5x-4)(5x-30)}{5}$

$\dfrac{(5x-4)(\cancel{5})(x-6)}{\cancel{5}}$

$(5x-4)(x-6)$

$5 \cdot 24 = \dfrac{120}{1 \cdot 120}$
$2 \cdot 60$
$3 \cdot 40$
$4 \cdot 30$ ★ $-4 - 30 = -34$
$5 \cdot 24$
$6 \cdot 20$
$8 \cdot 15$
$10 \cdot 12$

135.

$6x^2 - x - 35$

$\dfrac{(6x+\ \ )(6x-\ \ )}{6}$

$\dfrac{(6x+14)(6x-15)}{6} =$

$\dfrac{(\cancel{2})(3x+7)(\cancel{3})(2x-5)}{\cancel{6}} =$

$(3x+7)(2x-5)$

$6 \cdot 35 = \dfrac{210}{1 \cdot 210}$
$2 \cdot 105$
$3 \cdot 70$
$5 \cdot 42$
$6 \cdot 35$
$7 \cdot 30$
$10 \cdot 21$
$14 \cdot 15$ ★ $+14 - 15 = -1$

137.

$7x^2 - 13x - 24$

$\dfrac{(7x+\ \ )(7x-\ \ )}{7}$

$\dfrac{(7x+8)(7x-21)}{7} =$

$\dfrac{(7x+8)(\cancel{7})(x-3)}{\cancel{7}} =$

$(7x+8)(x-3)$

$7 \cdot 24 = \dfrac{168}{1 \cdot 168}$
$2 \cdot 84$
$3 \cdot 56$
$4 \cdot 42$
$6 \cdot 28$
$7 \cdot 24$
$8 \cdot 21$ ★ $+8 - 21 = -13$
$12 \cdot 14$

139. $9a^2 - 100 =$
$(3a+10)(3a-10)$

141. $2x^2 - 3x - 2$ $2 \cdot 2 = \underline{\quad 4 \quad}$
$\dfrac{(2x+)(2x-)}{2}$ $1 \cdot 4 \quad \bigstar +1-4 = -3$
$\dfrac{(2x+1)(2x-4)}{2} =$ $2 \cdot 2$
$\dfrac{(2x+1)(\cancel{2})(x-2)}{\cancel{2}} =$
$(2x+1)(x-2)$

143. $a^2 - 81 =$
$(a+9)(a-9)$

145. $y^2 - 14y + 49$
$(y-7)^2$

147. $b^2 + 8b + 15$ $\underline{\quad 15 \quad}$
$(b+)(b+)$ $1 \cdot 15$
$(b+3)(b+5)$ $3 \cdot 5 \quad \bigstar +3+5 = +8$

149. $169 - m^2 =$
$(13+m)(13-m)$

151. $x^2 - 4x - 32$ $\underline{\quad 32 \quad}$
$(x+)(x-)$ $1 \cdot 32$
$(x+4)(x-8)$ $2 \cdot 16$
                    $4 \cdot 8 \quad \bigstar +4-8 = -4$

153. $x^2 + 19x - 20$ $\underline{\quad 20 \quad}$
$(x+)(x-)$ $1 \cdot 20 \quad \bigstar -1+20 = +19$
$(x+20)(x-1)$ $2 \cdot 10$
                    $4 \cdot 5$

155. $2x^2 - 4x - 16$
$2\left(\dfrac{2x^2}{2} - \dfrac{4x}{2} - \dfrac{16}{2} \right)$
$2(x^2 - 2x - 8)$ $\underline{\quad 8 \quad}$
$2(x+)(x-)$ $1 \cdot 8$
$2(x+2)(x-4)$ $2 \cdot 4 \quad \bigstar +2-4 = -2$

157. $2x^3 - 10x^2 - 12x$
$2x\left(\dfrac{2x^3}{2x} - \dfrac{10x^2}{2x} - \dfrac{12x}{2x} \right)$
$2x(x^2 - 5x - 6)$ $\underline{\quad 6 \quad}$
$2x(x+)(x-)$ $1 \cdot 6 \quad \bigstar +1-6 = -5$
$2x(x+1)(x-6)$ $2 \cdot 3$

159. Recognizing special products makes our work faster and easier.

161. Surface Area $= 375 \text{ ft}^2$

$y = x$
$SA = (25+x)(15+x)$
$SA = 375 + 40x + x^2$

163. Yes; decrease size by 5, or –5, using formula (b) with negative variable.
$SA = 375 + 40x + x^2$
$ = 375 + 40(-5) + (-5)^2$
$ = 375 - 200 + 25 = 200$

check: $SA = lw$
$ = 20(10)$
$ = 200 \text{ ft}^2$

Answers will vary.

Chapter 13 Trial Test

1. $(m-7)(m+7) = m^2 - 49$

square, minus, square

3. $(a+3)^2 = a^2 + 6a + 9$

5. $\overset{\text{F O I L}}{(x-3)(2x-5)} = 2x^2 - 5x - 6x + 15$

$= 2x^2 - 11x + 15$

7. $(x-2)(x^2 + 2x + 4) = x^3 + 2x^2 + 4x$

$\underline{ -2x^2 - 4x - 8}$

$x^3 - 8$

9. $(5a-3)(25a^2 + 15a + 9) = 125a^3 - 27$

cube, minus, cube

11.

$$x-3 \overline{\smash{\big)}\, 2x^2 + x - 21} \quad \overset{2x+7}{}$$

$\underline{2x^2 - 6x}$ subtract

$7x - 21$

$\underline{7x - 21}$ subtract

0

13. $7x^2 + 8x = x\left(\dfrac{7x^2}{x} + \dfrac{8x}{x}\right)$

$= x(7x+8)$

15. $7a^2b - 14ab = 7ab\left(\dfrac{7a^2b}{7ab} - \dfrac{14ab}{7ab}\right)$

$= 7ab(a-2)$

17. $9x^2 - 25 = (3x+5)(3x-5)$

19. $8y^3 + 27x^3 = (2y+3x)(4y^2 - 6xy + 9x^2)$

21. $x^2 - 18x + 81 = (x-9)^2$

23. $x^2 - 12x + 36 = (x-6)(x-6)$

$= (x-6)^2$

25. $6x^2 - 5x - 6$

$\dfrac{(6x+)(6x-)}{6}$

$\dfrac{(6x+4)(6x-9)}{6}$

$\dfrac{(\cancel{2})(3x+2)(\cancel{3})(2x-3)}{\cancel{6}}$

$(3x+2)(2x-3)$

$6 \cdot 6 = \quad \underline{36}$

$1 \cdot 36$

$2 \cdot 18$

$3 \cdot 12$

$4 \cdot 9 \quad \bigstar \quad +4-9 = -5$

$6 \cdot 6$

27. $a^2 + 16ab + 64b^2 =$

$(a+8b)^2$

29. $b^2 - 3b - 10$

$(b+)(b-)$

$(b+2)(b-5)$

$\underline{10}$

$1 \cdot 10$

$2 \cdot 5 \quad \bigstar \quad +2-5 = -3$

31. $3x^2 + 23x + 30$

$\dfrac{(3x+)(3x+)}{3}$

$\dfrac{(3x+5)(3x+18)}{3} =$

$\dfrac{(3x+5)(\cancel{3})(x+6)}{\cancel{3}} =$

$(3x+5)(x+6)$

$3 \cdot 30 = \quad \underline{90}$

$1 \cdot 90$

$2 \cdot 45$

$3 \cdot 30$

$5 \cdot 18 \quad \bigstar \quad +5+18 = +23$

$6 \cdot 15$

$9 \cdot 10$

33. $3m^2 - 5m + 2$

$\dfrac{(3m- \quad)(3m- \quad)}{3}$

$\dfrac{(3m-2)(3m-3)}{3} =$

$\dfrac{(3m-2)(\cancel{3})(m-1)}{\cancel{3}} =$

$(3m-2)(m-1)$

$3 \cdot 2 = \dfrac{6}{1 \cdot 6}$

$2 \cdot 3 \quad \bigstar \quad -2-3 = -5$

35. $3x^2 - 11x + 6$

$\dfrac{(3x- \quad)(3x- \quad)}{3}$

$\dfrac{(3x-2)(3x-9)}{3} =$

$\dfrac{(3x-2)\cancel{3}(x-3)}{\cancel{3}} =$

$(3x-2)(x-3)$

$3(6) = \dfrac{18}{1 \cdot 18}$

$\bigstar \quad 2 \cdot 9$

$3 \cdot 6$

37. $3x^3 - 24 =$

$3(x^3 - 8) =$

$3(x-2)(x^2 + 2x + 4)$

39. $5x^2 - 20 =$

$5(x^2 - 4) =$

$5(x+2)(x-2)$

41. $3x^2 + 12x + 12 =$

$3(x^2 + 4x + 4) =$

$3(x+2)^2$

ASSIGNMENT EXERCISES

1. $\dfrac{18}{24} = \dfrac{3 \cdot \cancel{6}}{4 \cdot \cancel{6}} = \dfrac{3}{4}$

3. $\dfrac{5a^2b^3c}{10a^3bc^2} = \dfrac{\cancel{5}\,\cancel{a^2}\,\cancel{b^3}^{\,b^2}\,\cancel{c}}{\cancel{10}_{2}\,\cancel{a^3}_{a}\,\cancel{b}\,\cancel{c^2}_{c}} = \dfrac{b^2}{2ac}$

5. $\dfrac{4xy(x-3)}{8xy(x+3)} = \dfrac{\cancel{4}\,\cancel{xy}\,(x-3)}{\cancel{8}_{2}\,\cancel{xy}\,(x+3)} = \dfrac{x-3}{2(x+3)}$

7. $\dfrac{(x-4)(x+2)}{(x+2)(4-x)} = \dfrac{(x-4)\,\cancel{(x+2)}}{\cancel{(x+2)}\,(4-x)} = \dfrac{x-4}{4-x} = -1$

9. $\dfrac{m^2-n^2}{m^2+n^2}$

11. $\dfrac{x}{x+xy} = \dfrac{x}{x(1+y)} = \dfrac{\cancel{x}}{\cancel{x}(1+y)} = \dfrac{1}{1+y}$

13. $\dfrac{5x+15}{x+3} = \dfrac{5(x+3)}{x+3} = \dfrac{5\cancel{(x+3)}}{\cancel{x+3}} = 5$

15. $\dfrac{y^2+2y+1}{y+1} = \dfrac{(y+1)^2}{y+1} = \dfrac{(y+1)^{\cancel{2}^{\,1}}}{\cancel{y+1}} = y+1$

17. $\dfrac{2x-6}{x^2+3x-18} = \dfrac{2(x-3)}{(x+6)(x-3)} = \dfrac{2\cancel{(x-3)}}{(x+6)\cancel{(x-3)}} = \dfrac{2}{x+6}$

19. $\dfrac{3x-9}{x-3} = \dfrac{3(x-3)}{x-3} = \dfrac{3\cancel{(x-3)}}{\cancel{x-3}} = 3$

21. $\dfrac{3x^2}{2y} \cdot \dfrac{5x}{6y} = \dfrac{\cancel{3}^{\,1}x^2}{2y} \cdot \dfrac{5x}{\cancel{6}_{2}y} = \dfrac{5x^3}{4y^2}$

23. $\dfrac{\cancel{9}^{\,3}}{x+b} \cdot \dfrac{5x+5b}{\cancel{3}} = \dfrac{3}{\cancel{x+b}} \cdot \dfrac{5\cancel{(x+b)}}{1} = 3 \cdot 5 = 15$

25. $\dfrac{4y^2-4y+1}{6y-6}\cdot\dfrac{24}{2y-1}=\dfrac{(2y-1)^2}{6(y-1)}\cdot\dfrac{24}{2y-1}$

$\qquad\qquad=\dfrac{(2y-1)^{\cancel{2}^{1}}}{\cancel{6}(y-1)}\cdot\dfrac{\cancel{24}^{4}}{\cancel{2y-1}}$

$\qquad\qquad=\dfrac{4(2y-1)}{y-1}$

27. $\dfrac{5-x}{x-5}\cdot\dfrac{x-1}{1-x}=\dfrac{\cancel{5-x}^{-1}}{\cancel{x-5}}\cdot\dfrac{\cancel{x-1}^{-1}}{\cancel{1-x}}$

$\qquad\qquad=1$

29. $\dfrac{x^2+6x+9}{x^2-4}\cdot\dfrac{x-2}{x+3}=\dfrac{(x+3)^2}{(x+2)(x-2)}\cdot\dfrac{x-2}{x+3}$

$\qquad\qquad=\dfrac{(x+3)^{\cancel{2}^{1}}}{(x+2)\cancel{(x-2)}}\cdot\dfrac{\cancel{x-2}}{\cancel{x+3}}$

$\qquad\qquad=\dfrac{x+3}{x+2}$

31. $\dfrac{2a+b}{8}\div\dfrac{2a+b}{2}=\dfrac{2a+b}{8}\cdot\dfrac{2}{2a+b}$

$\qquad\qquad=\dfrac{\cancel{2a+b}}{\underset{4}{\cancel{8}}}\cdot\dfrac{\cancel{2}}{\cancel{2a+b}}$

$\qquad\qquad=\dfrac{1}{4}$

33. $\dfrac{y^2-2y+1}{y}\div\dfrac{1}{y-1}=\dfrac{(y-1)^2}{y}\cdot\dfrac{y-1}{1}$

$\qquad\qquad=\dfrac{(y-1)^3}{y}$

35. $\dfrac{y^2+6y+9}{y^2+4y+4}\div\dfrac{y+3}{y+2}=\dfrac{y^2+6y+9}{y^2+4y+4}\cdot\dfrac{y+2}{y+3}$

$\qquad\qquad=\dfrac{(y+3)^2}{(y+2)^2}\cdot\dfrac{y+2}{y+3}$

$\qquad\qquad=\dfrac{(y+3)^{\cancel{2}^{1}}}{(y+2)^{\cancel{2}^{1}}}\cdot\dfrac{\cancel{y+2}}{\cancel{y+3}}$

$\qquad\qquad=\dfrac{y+3}{y+2}$

37. $\dfrac{3x^2+6x}{x}\div\dfrac{2x+4}{x^2}=\dfrac{3x^2+6x}{x}\cdot\dfrac{x^2}{2x+4}$

$\qquad\qquad=\dfrac{3x(x+2)}{x}\cdot\dfrac{x^2}{2(x+2)}$

$\qquad\qquad=\dfrac{3\cancel{x}\,\cancel{(x+2)}}{\cancel{x}}\cdot\dfrac{x^2}{2\cancel{(x+2)}}$

$\qquad\qquad=\dfrac{3x^2}{2}$

39. $\dfrac{y^2-16}{y+3}\div\dfrac{y-4}{y^2-9}=\dfrac{(y+4)(y-4)}{y+3}\cdot\dfrac{(y+3)(y-3)}{y-4}$

$\qquad\qquad=\dfrac{(y+4)\cancel{(y-4)}}{\cancel{y+3}}\cdot\dfrac{\cancel{(y+3)}(y-3)}{\cancel{y-4}}$

$\qquad\qquad=(y+4)(y-3)$

41. $\dfrac{\frac{5}{x-3}}{4} = \dfrac{5}{x-3} \cdot \dfrac{1}{4} = \dfrac{5}{4(x-3)} = \dfrac{5}{4x-12}$

43. $\dfrac{\frac{x^2-4x}{6x}}{\frac{x-4}{8x^2}} = \dfrac{x^2-4x}{6x} \cdot \dfrac{8x^2}{x-4} = \dfrac{x(x-4)}{6x} \cdot \dfrac{8x^2}{x-4}$

$= \dfrac{\cancel{x}\,(x-4)}{\cancel{6}\,\cancel{x}} \cdot \dfrac{\overset{4}{\cancel{8}}\,x^2}{\cancel{x-4}}$

$= \dfrac{4x^2}{3}$

45. $\dfrac{12}{6-\sqrt{5}} = \dfrac{12}{\left(6-\sqrt{5}\right)} \cdot \dfrac{\left(6+\sqrt{5}\right)}{\left(6+\sqrt{5}\right)} = \dfrac{72+12\sqrt{5}}{36-5}$

$= \dfrac{72+12\sqrt{5}}{31}$

47. $\dfrac{7+\sqrt{3}}{7-\sqrt{3}} = \dfrac{\left(7+\sqrt{3}\right)}{\left(7-\sqrt{3}\right)} \cdot \dfrac{\left(7+\sqrt{3}\right)}{\left(7+\sqrt{3}\right)} = \dfrac{49+7\sqrt{3}+7\sqrt{3}+3}{49-3}$

$= \dfrac{52+14\sqrt{3}}{46} = \dfrac{2\left(26+7\sqrt{3}\right)}{46}$

$= \dfrac{26+7\sqrt{3}}{23}$

49. $\dfrac{5+\sqrt{2}}{7-3\sqrt{5}} = \dfrac{\left(5+\sqrt{2}\right)}{\left(7-3\sqrt{5}\right)} \cdot \dfrac{\left(7+3\sqrt{5}\right)}{\left(7+3\sqrt{5}\right)}$

$= \dfrac{35+15\sqrt{5}+7\sqrt{2}+3\sqrt{10}}{49-45}$

$= \dfrac{35+15\sqrt{5}+7\sqrt{2}+3\sqrt{10}}{4}$

51. $\dfrac{8+2\sqrt{3}}{5} = \dfrac{\left(8+2\sqrt{3}\right)}{5} \cdot \dfrac{\left(8-2\sqrt{3}\right)}{\left(8-2\sqrt{3}\right)}$

$= \dfrac{64-12}{40-10\sqrt{3}} = \dfrac{52}{2\left(20-5\sqrt{3}\right)}$

$= \dfrac{26}{20-5\sqrt{3}}$

53. $\dfrac{4-\sqrt{13}}{12} = \dfrac{\left(4-\sqrt{13}\right)}{12} \cdot \dfrac{\left(4+\sqrt{13}\right)}{\left(4+\sqrt{13}\right)}$

$= \dfrac{16-13}{48+12\sqrt{13}} = \dfrac{3}{3\left(16+4\sqrt{13}\right)}$

$= \dfrac{1}{16+4\sqrt{13}}$

55. $\dfrac{5-\sqrt{7}}{16} = \dfrac{\left(5-\sqrt{7}\right)}{16} \cdot \dfrac{\left(5+\sqrt{7}\right)}{\left(5+\sqrt{7}\right)}$

$= \dfrac{25-7}{16\left(5+\sqrt{7}\right)} = \dfrac{18}{16\left(5+\sqrt{7}\right)}$

$= \dfrac{9}{8\left(5+\sqrt{7}\right)}$ or $\dfrac{9}{40+8\sqrt{7}}$

57. $\dfrac{2}{9}+\dfrac{4}{9}=\dfrac{6}{9}=\dfrac{2\cdot\cancel{3}}{3\cdot\cancel{3}}=\dfrac{2}{3}$

59. $\dfrac{3x}{7}+\dfrac{2x}{14}=\dfrac{3x(2)}{7(2)}+\dfrac{2x}{14}$

$$=\dfrac{6x}{14}+\dfrac{2x}{14}$$

$$=\dfrac{8x}{14}=\dfrac{2(4x)}{2(7)}$$

$$=\dfrac{\cancel{2}(4x)}{\cancel{2}(7)}$$

$$=\dfrac{4x}{7}$$

61. $\dfrac{3x}{4}+\dfrac{5x}{6}=\dfrac{3x(3)}{4(3)}+\dfrac{5x(2)}{6(2)}$

$$=\dfrac{9x}{12}+\dfrac{10}{12}$$

$$=\dfrac{19x}{12}$$

63. $\dfrac{5}{x}-\dfrac{7}{3}=\dfrac{(3)(5)}{(3)x}-\dfrac{7(x)}{3(x)}$

$$=\dfrac{15}{3x}-\dfrac{7x}{3x}$$

$$=\dfrac{15-7x}{3x}$$

65. $\dfrac{3}{4x}+\dfrac{2}{x}+\dfrac{3}{6x}=\dfrac{3(3)}{3(4x)}+\dfrac{12(2)}{12(x)}+\dfrac{2(3)}{2(6x)}$

$$=\dfrac{9}{12}+\dfrac{24}{12x}+\dfrac{6}{12x}$$

$$=\dfrac{39}{12x}$$

$$=\dfrac{13}{4x}$$

67. $\dfrac{7}{x-3}+\dfrac{3}{x+2}=\dfrac{7(x+2)}{(x-3)(x+2)}+\dfrac{3(x-3)}{(x-3)(x+2)}$

$$=\dfrac{7x+14+3x-9}{(x-3)(x+2)}$$

$$=\dfrac{10x+5}{(x-3)(x+2)}$$

$$\text{or}$$

$$=\dfrac{5(2x+1)}{(x-3)(x+2)}$$

69. $\dfrac{8}{x+3}-\dfrac{2}{x-4}=\dfrac{8(x-4)}{(x+3)(x-4)}-\dfrac{2(x+3)}{(x+3)(x-4)}$

$$=\dfrac{8x-32-2x-6}{(x+3)(x-4)}$$

$$=\dfrac{6x-38}{(x+3)(x-4)}$$

$$\text{or}$$

$$=\dfrac{2(3x-19)}{(x+3)(x-4)}$$

71. $\dfrac{x}{x-5}-\dfrac{3}{5-x}=\dfrac{x}{x-5}-\dfrac{3(-1)}{x-5}$

$$=\dfrac{x+3}{x-5}$$

73.

$$\frac{\frac{5}{x}-\frac{3}{4x}}{\frac{2}{3x}+\frac{2}{x}}=\frac{\frac{5(4)}{4x}-\frac{3}{4x}}{\frac{1}{3x}+\frac{2(3)}{3x}}=$$

$$\frac{\frac{20}{4x}-\frac{3}{4x}}{\frac{1}{3x}+\frac{6}{3x}}=\frac{\frac{17}{4x}}{\frac{7}{3x}}$$

$$=\frac{17}{4x}\cdot\frac{3x}{7}=\frac{17}{4x}\cdot\frac{3x}{7}$$

$$=\frac{51}{28}$$

75.

$$\frac{\frac{3x}{6}-\frac{5}{x}}{\frac{x}{3}+\frac{4}{2x}}=\frac{\frac{3x(x)}{6x}-\frac{5(6)}{6x}}{\frac{x(2x)}{6x}+\frac{4(3)}{6x}}$$

$$=\frac{\frac{3x^2-30}{6x}}{\frac{2x^2+12}{6x}}$$

$$=\frac{3x^2-30}{6x}\cdot\frac{6x}{2x^2+12}$$

$$=\frac{3(x^2-10)}{6x}\cdot\frac{6x}{2(x^2+6)}$$

$$=\frac{3(x^2-10)}{2(x^2+6)}$$

$$=\frac{3x^2-30}{2x^2+12}$$

77.

$$\frac{4}{x}=\frac{3}{x-2}$$

LCD: $x(x-2)$

$$x(x-2)\neq 0$$

$$x\neq 0 \quad x-2\neq 0$$

$$x\neq 2$$

79.

$$\frac{5x}{2x-1}-6=\frac{4}{3x}$$

LCD: $3x(2x-1)$

$$3x(2x-1)\neq 0$$

$$3x\neq 0 \quad 2x-1\neq 0$$

$$\frac{3x}{3}\neq\frac{0}{3} \quad 2x\neq 1$$

$$x\neq 0 \quad \frac{2x}{2}\neq\frac{1}{2}$$

$$x\neq\frac{1}{2}$$

81.

$$\frac{4}{x}=\frac{1}{x+5}$$

$$4(x+5)=1(x)$$

$$4x+20=x$$

$$20=x-4x$$

$$20=-3x$$

$$\frac{20}{-3}=\frac{-3x}{-3}$$

$$x=-\frac{20}{3}$$

83.

$$\frac{-4x}{x+1}=3-\frac{4}{x+1}$$

$$(x+1)\frac{-4x}{x+1}=(x+1)3-(x+1)\frac{4}{x+1}$$

$$(x+1)\frac{-4x}{x+1}=(x+1)3-(x+1)\frac{4}{x+1}$$

$$-4x=3x+3-4$$

$$-4x=3x-1$$

$$-4x-3x=-1$$

$$-7x=-1$$

$$\frac{-7x}{-7}=\frac{-1}{-7}$$

$$x=\frac{1}{7}$$

85.

x students
y price per person

$$4(y-10)=120$$

$$4y-40=120$$

$$4y=160$$

$$\frac{4y}{4}=\frac{160}{4}$$

$$y=40$$

$$x(40)=120$$

$$\frac{x(40)}{40}=\frac{120}{40}$$

$$x=3 \text{ original students}$$

87.
$$\frac{1}{5}(3) + \frac{1}{x}(3) = 1$$

$$\frac{3}{5} + \frac{3}{x} = 1$$

$$5x\left(\frac{3}{5}\right) + 5x\left(\frac{3}{x}\right) = 5x(1)$$

$$3x + 15 = 5x$$

$$15 = 5x - 3x$$

$$15 = 2x$$

$$\frac{15}{2} = \frac{2x}{2}$$

$$x = 7\frac{1}{2} \text{ hours alone}$$

Chapter 14 Trial Test

1.
$$\frac{x-3}{2x-6} = \frac{x-3}{2(x-3)} = \frac{\cancel{x-3}}{2\cancel{(x-3)}} = \frac{1}{2}$$

3.
$$\frac{6x^2 - 11x + 4}{2x^2 + 5x - 3} = \frac{\frac{(6x-\ )(6x-\ )}{6}}{\frac{(2x+\ )(2x-\ )}{2}}$$

$$6 \cdot 4 = \frac{24}{3 \cdot 8} \quad -3 - 8 = -11$$

$$2 \cdot 3 = \frac{6}{1 \cdot 6} \quad -1 + 6 = 5$$

$$= \frac{\frac{(6x-3)(6x-8)}{6}}{\frac{(2x+6)(2x-1)}{2}}$$

$$= \frac{\frac{\cancel{(3)}(2x-1)\cancel{(2)}(3x-4)}{\cancel{6}}}{\frac{\cancel{(2)}(x+3)(2x-1)}{\cancel{2}}}$$

$$= \frac{(2x-1)(3x-4)}{(x+3)(2x-1)} = \frac{\cancel{(2x-1)}(3x-4)}{(x+3)\cancel{(2x-1)}}$$

$$= \frac{3x-4}{x+3}$$

5.
$$\frac{(x-2)(x-4)}{(4-x)(x+2)} = \frac{(x-2)\cancel{(x-4)}}{-\cancel{(x-4)}(x+2)} = -\frac{x-2}{x+2}$$

7.
$$\frac{6xy}{ab} \cdot \frac{a^2b}{2xy^2} = \frac{\cancel{6}^{3}\,\cancel{x}y}{\cancel{ab}} \cdot \frac{\cancel{a^2}^{a}\,\cancel{b}}{\cancel{2}\cancel{x}\,\cancel{y^2}_{y}} = \frac{3a}{y}$$

9.
$$\frac{x-2y}{x^3-3x^2y} \div \frac{x^2-4y^2}{x-3y} = \frac{x-2y}{x^3-3x^2y} \cdot \frac{x-3y}{x^2-4y^2}$$

$$= \frac{x-2y}{x^2(x-3y)} \cdot \frac{x-3y}{(x+2y)(x-2y)}$$

$$= \frac{\cancel{x-2y}}{x^2\cancel{(x-3y)}} \cdot \frac{\cancel{x-3y}}{(x+2y)\cancel{(x-2y)}}$$

$$= \frac{1}{x^2(x+2y)}$$

11.
$$\frac{2x^2+3x+1}{x} \div \frac{x+1}{1} = \frac{2x^2+3x+1}{x} \cdot \frac{1}{x+1}$$

$$= \frac{(2x+1)(x+1)}{x} \cdot \frac{1}{x+1}$$

$$= \frac{(2x+1)\cancel{(x+1)}}{x} \cdot \frac{1}{\cancel{x+1}}$$

$$= \frac{2x+1}{x}$$

13.
$$\frac{1}{x+2} - \frac{1}{x-3} = \frac{1(x-3)}{(x+2)(x-3)} - \frac{1(x+2)}{(x+2)(x-3)}$$

$$= \frac{x-3-x-2}{(x+2)(x-3)}$$

$$= \frac{-5}{(x+2)(x-3)} \text{ or } -\frac{5}{(x+2)(x-3)}$$

15.
$$\frac{3}{x} + \frac{1}{4} = \frac{3(4)}{4x} + \frac{1(x)}{4x}$$

$$= \frac{12+x}{4x}$$

17.
$$\frac{5}{3x-2} + \frac{7}{2-3x} = \frac{5}{3x-2} + \frac{7}{-3x+2}$$

$$= \frac{5}{3x-2} + \frac{7}{-1(3x-2)}$$

$$= \frac{5}{3x-2} - \frac{7}{3x-2}$$

$$= -\frac{2}{3x-2} \text{ or } \frac{2}{2-3x}$$

19.
$$\frac{x-2y}{x^2-4y^2} = \frac{x-2y}{(x+2y)(x-2y)}$$

$$= \frac{\cancel{x-2y}}{(x+2y)\cancel{(x-2y)}}$$

$$= \frac{1}{x+2y}$$

21.
$$\frac{2x}{1-\frac{3}{x}} = \frac{2x}{\frac{x}{x}-\frac{3}{x}} = \frac{2x}{\frac{x-3}{x}}$$

$$= \frac{2x}{1} \cdot \frac{x}{x-3} = \frac{2x^2}{x-3}$$

23.
$$\frac{5}{x} = \frac{2}{x+3}$$
LCD: $x(x+3)$

$$x \neq 0 \quad x+3 \neq 0$$

$$x \neq -3$$

25.

$$\frac{3x}{x-2}+4=\frac{3}{x-2}$$

$$(x-2)\frac{3x}{x-2}+(x-2)4=(x-2)\frac{3}{x-2}$$

$$3x+4(x-2)=3$$

$$3x+4x-8=3$$

$$7x-8=3$$

$$7x=3+8$$

$$7x=11$$

$$\frac{7x}{7}=\frac{11}{7}$$

$$x=\frac{11}{7}$$

Check:

$$\frac{3\left(\frac{11}{7}\right)}{\frac{11}{7}-2}+4=\frac{3}{\frac{11}{7}-2}$$

$$\frac{\frac{33}{7}}{\frac{11}{7}-\frac{14}{7}}+4=\frac{3}{\frac{11}{7}-\frac{14}{7}}$$

$$\frac{\frac{33}{7}}{-\frac{3}{7}}+4=\frac{3}{-\frac{3}{7}}$$

$$\frac{\overset{11}{\cancel{33}}}{\cancel{7}}\left(-\frac{\cancel{7}}{\cancel{3}}\right)+4=\frac{\cancel{3}}{1}\left(-\frac{7}{\cancel{3}}\right)$$

$$-11+4=-7$$

$$-7=-7$$

27.

$$\frac{5}{x-2}=\frac{-4}{x+1}$$

$$5(x+1)=-4(x-2)$$

$$5x+5=-4x+8$$

$$5x+4x=8-5$$

$$9x=3$$

$$\frac{9x}{9}=\frac{3}{9}$$

$$x=\frac{3}{9}$$

$$x=\frac{1}{3}$$

29.

$x=$ people in group

$y=$ cost per person

$xy=100,000$ thus $x=\dfrac{100,000}{y}$

$$(x+5)\left(\frac{100,000}{x}-10,000\right)=100,000$$

$$100,000-10,000x+\frac{500,000}{x}-50,000=100,000$$

$$0=10,000x+50,000-\frac{500,000}{x}$$

$$0=x(10,000x)+x(50,000)-x\left(\frac{500,000}{x}\right)$$

$$0=10,000x^2+50,000x-500,000$$

$$0=10,000(x^2+5x-50)$$

$$0=10,000(x+10)(x-5)$$

$$x=5 \text{ people}$$

$$(2x)(y-10,000)=100,000$$

$$2\left(\frac{100,000}{y}\right)(y-10,000)=100,000$$

$$y\left[\frac{200,000}{y}(y-10,000)\right]=100,000y$$

$$200,000(y-10,000)=100,000y$$

$$200,000y-2,000,000,000=100,000y$$

$$200,000y-100,000y=2,000,000,000$$

$$100,000y=2,000,000,000$$

$$y=20,000$$

$$x=\frac{100,000}{20,000}$$

$$x=5 \text{ original people}$$

chapter 15

Quadratic and Higher-Degree Equations

ASSIGNMENT EXERCISES

1. $x^2 = 49$
$x^2 - 49 = 0$
$a = 1 \quad c = -49$
pure

3. $5x^2 - 45 = 0$
$a = 5 \quad c = -45$
pure

5. $8x^2 + 6x = 0$
$a = 8 \quad b = 6$
incomplete

7. $x^2 - 32 = 0$
$a = 1 \quad c = -32$
pure

9. $3x^2 + 6x + 1 = 0$
$a = 3 \quad b = 6 \quad c = 1$
complete

11. $2x^2 - 5 = 8x$
$2x^2 - 8x - 5 = 0 \quad$ standard form

13. $5 + x^2 - 7x = 0$
$x^2 - 7x + 5 = 0 \quad$ standard form

15. $3x = 1 - 4x^2$
$4x^2 + 3x - 1 = 0 \quad$ standard form

17. $x^2 = 100$
$\sqrt{x} = \pm\sqrt{100}$
$x = \pm 10$

19. $4x^2 = 9$
$\dfrac{4x^2}{4} = \dfrac{9}{4}$
$x^2 = \dfrac{9}{4}$
$x = \pm\sqrt{\dfrac{9}{4}}$
$x = \pm\dfrac{\sqrt{9}}{\sqrt{4}}$
$x = \pm\dfrac{3}{2} \text{ or } \pm 1.5$

21. $0.36y^2 = 1.09$
$\dfrac{0.36y^2}{0.36} = \dfrac{1.09}{0.36}$
$y^2 = 3.028$
$y = \pm\sqrt{3.028}$
$y = \pm 1.740$

23. $5x^2 = 40$
$\dfrac{5x^2}{5} = \dfrac{40}{5}$
$x^2 = 8$
$x = \pm\sqrt{8}$
$x = \pm 2\sqrt{2}$
or
$x = \pm 2.828$

25.
$$6x^2 + 4 = 34$$
$$6x^2 = 34 - 4$$
$$6x^2 = 30$$
$$\frac{6x^2}{6} = \frac{30}{6}$$
$$x^2 = 5$$
$$x = \pm\sqrt{5}$$
or
$$x = \pm 2.236$$

27.
$$3x^2 = 12$$
$$\frac{3x^2}{3} = \frac{12}{3}$$
$$x^2 = 4$$
$$x = \pm\sqrt{4}$$
$$x = \pm 2$$

29.
$$2x^2 = 34$$
$$\frac{2x^2}{2} = \frac{34}{2}$$
$$x^2 = 17$$
$$x = \pm\sqrt{17}$$
or
$$x = \pm 4.123$$

31.
$$3y^2 - 36 = -8$$
$$3y^2 = -8 + 36$$
$$3y^2 = 28$$
$$\frac{3y^2}{3} = \frac{28}{3}$$
$$y^2 = 9.333$$
$$y = \pm\sqrt{9.333}$$
$$y = \pm 3.055$$

33.
$$\frac{1}{2}x^2 = 8$$
$$(2)\frac{1}{2}x^2 = (2)8$$
$$x^2 = 16$$
$$x = \pm\sqrt{16}$$
$$x = \pm 4$$

35.
$$\frac{1}{4}x^2 - 1 = 15$$
$$\frac{1}{4}x^2 = 15 + 1$$
$$\frac{1}{4}x^2 = 16$$
$$(4)\frac{1}{4}x^2 = (4)16$$
$$x^2 = 64$$
$$x = \pm\sqrt{64}$$
$$x = \pm 8$$

37.
$$\pi r^2 = A$$
$$\pi(r^2) = 845$$
$$r^2 = \frac{845}{\pi} = 268.97$$
$$r = \pm\sqrt{268.97}$$
$$r = 16.4 \text{ cm}$$

39.
$$x^2 - 5x = 0$$
$$x(x-5) = 0$$
$$x = 0 \quad x - 5 = 0$$
$$x = 5$$

41.
$$6x^2 - 12x = 0$$
$$6x(x-2) = 0$$
$$6x = 0 \quad x - 2 = 0$$
$$\frac{6x}{6} = \frac{0}{6} \quad x = 2$$
$$x = 0$$

43.
$$10x^2 + 5x = 0$$
$$5x(2x+1) = 0$$
$$5x = 0 \quad 2x + 1 = 0$$
$$\frac{5x}{5} = \frac{0}{5} \quad 2x = -1$$
$$x = 0 \quad \frac{2x}{2} = \frac{-1}{2}$$
$$x = \frac{-1}{2} \text{ or } -\frac{1}{2}$$

45.
$$y^2 - 5y = 0$$
$$y(y-5) = 0$$
$$y = 0 \quad y - 5 = 0$$
$$y = 5$$

47.
$$12x^2 + 8x = 0$$
$$4x(3x+2) = 0$$
$$4x = 0 \quad 3x + 2 = 0$$
$$\frac{4x}{4} = \frac{0}{4} \quad 3x = -2$$
$$x = 0 \quad \frac{3x}{3} = \frac{-2}{3}$$
$$x = \frac{-2}{3} \text{ or } -\frac{2}{3}$$

49.
$$x^2 + 3x = 0$$
$$x(x+3) = 0$$
$$x = 0 \quad x + 3 = 0$$
$$x = -3$$

51. $5x^2 = 45x$

$5x^2 - 45x = 0$

$5x(x-9) = 0$

$5x = 0 \quad x - 9 = 0$

$\dfrac{5x}{5} = \dfrac{0}{5} \quad x = 9$

$x = 0$

53. $y^2 + 8y = 0$

$y(y+8) = 0$

$y = 0 \quad y + 8 = 0$

$y = -8$

55. $3m^2 - 5m = 0$

$m(3m-5) = 0$

$m = 0 \quad 3m - 5 = 0$

$3m = 5$

$\dfrac{3m}{3} = \dfrac{5}{3}$

$m = \dfrac{5}{3}$

57. $2x^2 = x$

$2x^2 - x = 0$

$x(2x-1) = 0$

$x = 0 \quad 2x - 1 = 0$

$2x = 1$

$\dfrac{2x}{2} = \dfrac{1}{2}$

$x = \dfrac{1}{2}$

59. $3x^2 = 12x$

$3x^2 - 12x = 0$

$3x(x-4) = 0 \qquad x - 4 = 0$

$3x = 0 \qquad\qquad x = 4$

$\dfrac{3x}{3} = \dfrac{0}{3}$

$x = 0$

61. $x^2 - 4x + 3 = 0$

$(x-3)(x-1) = 0$

$x - 3 = 0 \quad x - 1 = 0$

$x = 3 \qquad x = 1$

63. $x^2 + 3x = 10$

$x^2 + 3x - 10 = 0$

$(x+5)(x-2) = 0$

$x + 5 = 0 \quad x - 2 = 0$

$x = -5 \qquad x = 2$

65. $x^2 + 7x = -6$

$x^2 + 7x + 6 = 0$

$(x+1)(x+6) = 0$

$x + 1 = 0 \quad x + 6 = 0$

$x = -1 \qquad x = -6$

67. $x^2 - 6x + 8 = 0$

$(x-2)(x-4) = 0$

$x - 2 = 0 \quad x - 4 = 0$

$x = 2 \qquad x = 4$

69. $6y^2 - 5y - 6 = 0$

$\dfrac{(6y -)(6y +)}{6} = 0 \qquad 6 \cdot 6 = \underline{\begin{array}{c} 36 \\ 4 \cdot 9 \end{array}} \quad \bigstar \; (+4 - 9 = -5)$

$\dfrac{(6y-9)(6y+4)}{6} = 0$

$\dfrac{\cancel{(3)}\,(2y-3)\,\cancel{(2)}\,(3y+2)}{\cancel{6}} = 0$

$(2y-3)(3y+2) = 0$

$2y - 3 = 0 \quad 3y + 2 = 0$

$2y = 3 \qquad 3y = -2$

$\dfrac{2y}{2} = \dfrac{3}{2} \qquad \dfrac{3y}{3} = \dfrac{-2}{3}$

$y = \dfrac{3}{2} \qquad y = -\dfrac{2}{3}$

71. $10y^2 - 21y - 10 = 0$

$$\frac{(10y+\ )(10y-\ )}{10} = 0$$

$$\frac{(10y+4)(10y-25)}{10} = 0$$

$$\frac{\cancel{(2)}(5y+2)\cancel{(5)}(2y-5)}{\cancel{10}} = 0$$

$$(5y+2)(2y-5) = 0$$

$10 \cdot 10 = \dfrac{100}{4 \cdot 25}$ ★ $(+4-25 = -21)$

$5y+2 = 0$	$2y-5 = 0$
$5y = -2$	$2y = 5$
$\dfrac{5y}{5} = \dfrac{-2}{5}$	$\dfrac{2y}{2} = \dfrac{5}{2}$
$y = -\dfrac{2}{5}$	$y = \dfrac{5}{2}$

73. $4x^2 + 7x + 3 = 0$

$$\frac{(4x+\ )(4x+\ )}{4} = 0$$

$$\frac{(4x+3)(4x+4)}{4} = 0$$

$$\frac{(4x+3)\,\cancel{(4)}\,(x+1)}{\cancel{4}} = 0$$

$$(4x+3)(x+1) = 0$$

$4 \cdot 3 = \dfrac{12}{3 \cdot 4}$ ★ $(3+4 = 7)$

$4x+3 = 0$	$x+1 = 0$
$4x = -3$	$x = -1$
$\dfrac{4x}{4} = \dfrac{-3}{4}$	
$x = \dfrac{-3}{4} = -\dfrac{3}{4}$	

75. $12y^2 - 5y - 3 = 0$

$$\frac{(12y+\ )(12y-\ )}{12} = 0$$

$$\frac{(12y+4)(12y-9)}{12} = 0$$

$$\frac{\cancel{(4)}(3y+1)\cancel{(3)}(4y-3)}{\cancel{12}} = 0$$

$$(3y+1)(4y-3) = 0$$

$12 \cdot 3 = \dfrac{36}{4 \cdot 9}$ ★ $(+4-9 = -5)$

$3y+1 = 0$	$4y-3 = 0$
$3y = -1$	$4y = 3$
$\dfrac{3y}{3} = \dfrac{-1}{3}$	$\dfrac{4y}{4} = \dfrac{3}{4}$
$y = -\dfrac{1}{3}$	$y = \dfrac{3}{4}$

77. $x^2 + 19x = 42$

$x^2 + 19x - 42 = 0$

$(x-2)(x+21) = 0$

$x-2=0 \quad x+21=0$

$x=2 \qquad x=-21$

79. $3y^2 + y - 2 = 0$

$$\frac{(3y+)(3y-)}{3} = 0$$

$$\frac{(3y+3)(3y-2)}{3} = 0$$

$$\frac{\cancel{(3)}(y+1)(3y-2)}{\cancel{3}} = 0$$

$(y+1)(3y-2) = 0$

$y+1=0 \quad 3y-2=0$

$y=-1 \qquad 3y=2$

$$\frac{3y}{3} = \frac{2}{3}$$

$$y = \frac{2}{3}$$

$3 \cdot 2 = \dfrac{6}{2 \cdot 3}$ ★ $(-2+3=1)$

81. $2x^2 - 10x + 12 = 0$

$2(x^2 - 5x + 6) = 0$

$2(x-2)(x-3) = 0$

$x-2=0 \quad x-3=0$

$x=2 \qquad x=3$

83. $x^2 - 3x - 18 = 0$

$(x-6)(x+3) = 0$

$x-6=0 \quad x+3=0$

$x=6 \qquad x=-3$

85. $2y^2 + 22y + 60 = 0$

$2(y^2 + 11y + 30) = 0$

$2(y+5)(y+6) = 0$

$y+5=0 \quad y+6=0$

$y=-5 \qquad y=-6$

87. $x^2 + 7x - 18 = 0$

$(x+9)(x-2) = 0$

$x+9=0 \quad x-2=0$

$x=-9 \qquad x=2$

89. $A = lw;\ l = w+7$

$A = (w+7)w$

$228 = w^2 + 7w$

$0 = w^2 + 7w - 228$

$0 = (w+19)(w-12)$

$w+19=0 \qquad\qquad w-12=0$

$w=-19 \qquad\qquad\quad w=12 \text{ ft}$

Disregard negative root. $l = w+7$

$l = 12+7$

$l = 19 \text{ ft}$

91. $x^2 - 4x + 4 = 0$

$x^2 - 4x = -4$

$x^2 - 4x + \left(\dfrac{4}{2}\right)^2 = -4 + \left(\dfrac{4}{2}\right)^2$

$x^2 - 4x + 4 = -4 + 4$

$x^2 - 4x + 4 = 0$

$(x-2)^2 = 0$

$x-2=0 \quad x-2=0$

$x=2 \qquad x=2$ double root

93. $x^2 - 8x + 12 = 0$

$x^2 - 8x = -12$

$x^2 - 8x + (4)^2 = -12 + (4)^2$

$x^2 - 8x + 16 = -12 + 16$

$(x-4)^2 = 4$

$x - 4 = \pm 2$

$x - 4 = 2 \quad x - 4 = -2$

$\quad x = 6 \qquad x = 2$

95. $x^2 - 8x + 14 = 0$

$x^2 - 8x = -14$

$x^2 - 8x + (4)^2 = -14 + (4)^2$

$x^2 - 8x + 16 = -14 + 16$

$(x-4)^2 = 2$

$x - 4 = \pm\sqrt{2}$

$x = 4 + \sqrt{2} \quad x = 4 - \sqrt{2}$

97. $x^2 - 6x + 12 = 0$

$x^2 - 6x = -12$

$x^2 - 6x + (3)^2 = -12 + (3)^2$

$x^2 - 6x + 9 = -12 + 9$

$(x-3)^2 = -3$

$x - 3 = \pm\sqrt{-3}$

$x = 3 \pm i\sqrt{3}$

$x = 3 + i\sqrt{3} \quad x = 3 - i\sqrt{3}$

or no real roots

99. $x^2 - 5x + 4 = 0$

$x^2 - 5x = -4$

$x^2 - 5x + \left(\dfrac{5}{2}\right)^2 = -4 + \left(\dfrac{5}{2}\right)^2$

$x^2 - 5x + \dfrac{25}{4} = -4 + \dfrac{25}{4}$

$\left(x - \dfrac{5}{2}\right)^2 = \dfrac{-16}{4} + \dfrac{25}{4}$

$\left(x - \dfrac{5}{2}\right)^2 = \dfrac{9}{4}$

$x - \dfrac{5}{2} = \pm\dfrac{3}{2}$

$x = \dfrac{5}{2} + \dfrac{3}{2} \quad x = \dfrac{5}{2} - \dfrac{3}{2}$

$x = \dfrac{8}{2} = 4 \quad x = \dfrac{2}{2} = 1$

101. $x^2 - 3x - 7 = 0$

$x^2 - 3x = 7$

$x^2 - 3x + \left(\dfrac{3}{2}\right)^2 = 7 + \left(\dfrac{3}{2}\right)^2$

$x^2 - 3x + \dfrac{9}{4} = 7 + \dfrac{9}{4}$

$\left(x - \dfrac{3}{2}\right)^2 = \dfrac{28}{4} + \dfrac{9}{4}$

$\left(x - \dfrac{3}{2}\right)^2 = \dfrac{37}{4}$

$x - \dfrac{3}{2} = \pm\sqrt{\dfrac{37}{4}}$

$x = \dfrac{3}{2} \pm \dfrac{\sqrt{37}}{2}$

$x = \dfrac{3 + \sqrt{37}}{2} \quad x = \dfrac{3 - \sqrt{37}}{2}$

103. $x^2 - 2x = 8$

$x^2 - 2x - 8 = 0$

$a = 1 \quad b = -2 \quad c = -8$

105. $x^2 + 3x = 4$

$x^2 + 3x - 4 = 0$

$a = 1 \quad b = 3 \quad c = -4$

107. $x^2 - 3x = -2$

$x^2 - 3x + 2 = 0$

$a = 1 \quad b = -3 \quad c = 2$

109.
$$x^2 - 8x - 9 = 0$$
$$a = 1 \quad b = -8 \quad c = -9$$
$$x = \frac{-b \pm \sqrt{b^2 - 4ac}}{2a}$$
$$x = \frac{-(-8) \pm \sqrt{(-8)^2 - 4(1)(-9)}}{2(1)}$$
$$x = \frac{8 \pm \sqrt{64 + 36}}{2}$$
$$x = \frac{8 \pm \sqrt{100}}{2} = \frac{8 \pm 10}{2}$$
$$x = \frac{8 + 10}{2} = \frac{18}{2} = 9$$
$$x = \frac{8 - 10}{2} = \frac{-2}{2} = -1$$
$$x = 9, -1$$

111.
$$x^2 + 2x = 8$$
$$x^2 + 2x - 8 = 0$$
$$a = 1 \quad b = 2 \quad c = -8$$
$$x = \frac{-b \pm \sqrt{b^2 - 4ac}}{2a} = \frac{-2 \pm \sqrt{(2)^2 - 4(1)(-8)}}{2(1)}$$
$$x = \frac{-2 \pm \sqrt{4 + 32}}{2}$$
$$x = \frac{-2 \pm \sqrt{36}}{2} = \frac{-2 \pm 6}{2}$$
$$x = \frac{-2 + 6}{2} = \frac{4}{2} = 2$$
$$x = \frac{-2 - 6}{2} = \frac{-8}{2} = -4$$
$$x = 2, -4$$

113.
$$2x^2 - 3x - 2 = 0$$
$$a = 2 \quad b = -3 \quad c = -2$$
$$x = \frac{-b \pm \sqrt{b^2 - 4ac}}{2a}$$
$$x = \frac{-(-3) \pm \sqrt{(-3)^2 - 4(2)(-2)}}{2(2)}$$
$$x = \frac{3 \pm \sqrt{9 + 16}}{4}$$
$$x = \frac{3 \pm \sqrt{25}}{4}$$
$$x = \frac{3 \pm 5}{4}$$
$$x = \frac{3 + 5}{4} = \frac{8}{4} = 2$$
$$x = \frac{3 - 5}{4} = \frac{-2}{4} = \frac{-1}{2}$$
$$x = 2, -\frac{1}{2}$$

115.
$$2x^2 - 3x - 1 = 0$$
$$a = 2 \quad b = -3 \quad c = -1$$
$$x = \frac{-b \pm \sqrt{b^2 - 4ac}}{2a}$$
$$x = \frac{-(-3) \pm \sqrt{(-3)^2 - 4(2)(-1)}}{2(2)}$$
$$x = \frac{3 \pm \sqrt{9 + 8}}{4}$$
$$x = \frac{3 \pm \sqrt{17}}{4}$$
$$x = \frac{3 \pm 4.123105626}{4}$$
$$x = \frac{3 + 4.123105626}{4} = \frac{7.123105626}{4} = 1.78$$
$$x = \frac{3 - 4.123105626}{4} = \frac{-1.123105626}{4} = -0.28$$
$$x = 1.78, -0.28$$

117.

$$3x^2 + 5x + 1 = 0$$

$$a = 3 \quad b = 5 \quad c = 1$$

$$x = \frac{-b \pm \sqrt{b^2 - 4ac}}{2a}$$

$$x = \frac{-5 \pm \sqrt{5^2 - 4(3)(1)}}{2(3)}$$

$$x = \frac{-5 \pm \sqrt{25 - 12}}{6}$$

$$x = \frac{-5 \pm \sqrt{13}}{6}$$

$$x = \frac{-5 \pm 3.605551275}{6}$$

$$x = \frac{-5 + 3.605551275}{6} = \frac{-1.394448725}{6} = -0.23$$

$$x = \frac{-5 - 3.605551275}{6} = \frac{-8.605551275}{6} = -1.43$$

$$x = -0.23, \, -1.43$$

119.

$$l = 2w$$

$$A = lw$$

$$A = (2w)(w)$$

$$A = 2w^2$$

$$240 = 2w^2$$

$$0 = 2w^2 - 240$$

$$a = 2 \quad b = 0 \quad c = -240$$

$$w = \frac{-b \pm \sqrt{b^2 - 4ac}}{2a}$$

$$= \frac{-(0) \pm \sqrt{(0)^2 - 4(2)(-240)}}{2^2}$$

$$= \frac{0 \pm \sqrt{0 + 1920}}{4} = \frac{0 \pm \sqrt{1920}}{4}$$

$$= \frac{0 \pm 43.8178046}{4} = \frac{0 + 43.8178046}{4} = \frac{43.8178046}{4} = 11 \text{ ft}$$

$$= \frac{0 - 43.8178046}{4} = \frac{-43.8178046}{4} = -11 \text{ ft} \quad \text{not reasonable}$$

$$w = 11 \text{ ft (rounded)}$$

$$l = 2w = 2(11) = 22 \text{ ft}$$

121.
$$l = 3w$$
$$A = lw$$
$$A = (3w)(w)$$
$$591 = 3w^2$$
$$0 = 3w^2 - 591$$
$$a = 3 \quad b = 0 \quad c = -591$$
$$w = \frac{-b \pm \sqrt{b^2 - 4ac}}{2a} = \frac{-0 \pm \sqrt{0^2 - 4(3)(-591)}}{2(3)}$$
$$w = \frac{0 \pm \sqrt{0 + 7092}}{6} = \frac{0 \pm 84.21401309}{6}$$
$$w = \frac{0 + 84.21401309}{6} = \frac{84.21401309}{6} = 14$$
$$w = \frac{0 - 84.21401309}{6} = \frac{-84.21401309}{6} = -14 \quad \text{not reasonable}$$
$$w = 14 \text{ in.}$$
$$l = 3w = 3(14) = 42 \text{ in.}$$

123.
$$x^2 + 8x + 16 = 0$$
$$a = 1 \quad b = 8 \quad c = 16$$
$$b^2 - 4ac = 8^2 - 4(1)(16)$$
$$= 64 - 64$$
$$= 0$$
real, rational, equal (1 root)

125.
$$5x^2 - 100 = 0$$
$$a = 5 \quad b = 0 \quad c = -100$$
$$b^2 - 4ac = 0^2 - 4(5)(-100)$$
$$= 0 + 2,000$$
$$= 2,000$$
real, irrational, unequal (2 roots)

127.
$$2x = 5x^2 - 3$$
$$0 = 5x^2 - 2x - 3$$
$$a = 5 \quad b = -2 \quad c = -3$$
$$b^2 - 4ac = (-2)^2 - 4(5)(-3)$$
$$= 4 + 60$$
$$= 64 \text{ perfect square}$$
real, rational, unequal (2 roots)

129.
$$3x - 2x^3 + 8 = 0$$
$$0 = 2x^3 - 3x - 8$$
3rd degree

131.
$$6 - 3x - 3 = 2x + 4$$
$$0 = 5x + 1$$
1st degree

133.
$$5y^8 + 2y^3 - 6 = y^2$$
$$5y^8 + 2y^3 + y^2 - 6 = 0$$
8th degree

135.
$$2x(3x - 2)(x - 2) = 0$$
$$2x = 0 \quad 3x - 2 = 0 \quad x - 2 = 0$$
$$\frac{2x}{2} = \frac{0}{2} \quad 3x = 2 \quad x = 2$$
$$x = 0 \quad \frac{3x}{3} = \frac{2}{3}$$
$$x = \frac{2}{3}$$

137.
$$2x^3 + 10x^2 + 12x = 0$$
$$2x(x^2 + 5x + 6) = 0$$
$$2x(x + 2)(x + 3) = 0$$
$$2x = 0 \quad x + 2 = 0 \quad x + 3 = 0$$
$$\frac{2x}{2} = \frac{0}{2} \quad x = -2 \quad x = -3$$
$$x = 0$$

139.
$$2x^3 + 9x^2 = 5x$$
$$2x^3 + 9x^2 - 5x = 0$$
$$x(2x^2 + 9x - 5) = 0 \quad \text{Factor trinomial.}$$
$$2x^2 + 9x - 5 = 0$$
$$\frac{(2x +)(2x -)}{2} = 0$$
$$\frac{(2x + 10)(2x - 1)}{2} = 0$$
$$\frac{\cancel{2}(x + 5)(2x - 1)}{\cancel{2}} = (x + 5)(2x - 1) = 0$$
$$x(x + 5)(2x - 1) = 0 \quad \text{Use all three factors.}$$
$$x = 0 \quad x + 5 = 0 \quad 2x - 1 = 0$$
$$ \quad x = -5 \quad 2x = 1$$
$$\frac{2x}{2} = \frac{1}{2}$$
$$x = \frac{1}{2}$$

$$2 \cdot 5 = \frac{10}{1 \cdot 10} \quad \bigstar \quad (-1 + 10 = 9)$$

141.
$$3x^3 - 6x^2 = 0$$
$$3x^2(x - 2) = 0$$
$$3x^2 = 0 \qquad x - 2 = 0$$
$$\frac{3x^2}{3} = \frac{0}{3} \qquad x = 2$$
$$x^2 = 0$$
$$\sqrt{x^2} = \sqrt{0}$$
$$x = 0$$

143.
$$x^3 + 6x^2 + 8x = 0$$
$$x(x^2 + 6x + 8) = 0$$
$$x(x + 2)(x + 4) = 0$$
$$x = 0 \quad x + 2 = 0 \quad x + 4 = 0$$
$$ \quad x = -2 \qquad x = -4$$

145.
$$x^3 - x^2 - 20x = 0$$
$$x(x^2 - x - 20) = 0$$
$$x(x + 4)(x - 5) = 0$$
$$x = 0 \quad x + 4 = 0 \quad x - 5 = 0$$
$$ \quad x = -4 \qquad x = 5$$

147.
$$y^3 - 6y^2 + 7y = 0$$
$$y(y^2 - 6y + 7) = 0$$
$$a = 1 \quad b = -6 \quad c = 7$$
$$y = \frac{-b \pm \sqrt{b^2 - 4ac}}{2a}$$
$$y = 0 \quad y = \frac{-(-6) \pm \sqrt{36 - 4(1)(7)}}{2(1)}$$
$$y = \frac{6 \pm \sqrt{8}}{2}$$
$$y = \frac{6 \pm 2\sqrt{2}}{2}$$
$$y = \frac{\cancel{2}(3 \pm \sqrt{2})}{\cancel{2}}$$
$$y = 3 \pm \sqrt{2}$$
$$y = 3 \pm 1.414$$
$$y = 4.414 \text{ or } y = 1.586$$

149.

$$x^3 - 3x^2 - 4x = 0$$
$$x(x^2 - 3x - 4) = 0$$
$$x(x+1)(x-4) = 0$$
$$x = 0 \quad x+1 = 0 \quad x-4 = 0$$
$$x = -1 \quad\quad x = 4$$

151.

$$2y^3 + 6y^2 + 4y = 0$$
$$2y(y^2 + 3y + 2) = 0$$
$$2y(y+2)(y+1) = 0$$
$$2y = 0 \quad y+2 = 0 \quad y+1 = 0$$
$$y = 0 \quad\quad y = -2 \quad\quad y = -1$$

153.

$$51x = 3x^3$$
$$0 = 3x^3 - 51x$$
$$0 = 3x(x^2 - 17)$$
$$3x = 0 \quad x^2 - 17 = 0$$
$$\frac{3x}{3} = \frac{0}{3} \quad\quad x^2 = 17$$
$$x = 0 \quad\quad x = \pm\sqrt{17}$$
$$x = \pm 4.123$$

Chapter 15 Trial Test

1.

$$3x^2 = 42$$
$$3x^2 - 42 = 0$$
$$a = 3 \quad c = -42$$
pure

3.

$$5x^2 = 7x$$
$$5x^2 - 7x = 0$$
$$a = 5 \quad b = -7$$
incomplete

5.

$$x^2 = 81$$
$$x = \pm\sqrt{81}$$
$$x = \pm 9$$

7.

$$9x^2 = 16$$
$$\frac{9x^2}{9} = \frac{16}{9}$$
$$x^2 = \frac{16}{9}$$
$$x^2 = \pm\sqrt{\frac{16}{9}}$$
$$x = \pm\frac{\sqrt{16}}{\sqrt{9}}$$
$$x = \pm\frac{4}{3}$$
or ± 1.333

9.

$$0.09x^2 = 0.49$$
$$\frac{0.09x^2}{0.09} = \frac{0.49}{0.09}$$
$$x^2 = 5.444$$
$$x = \pm\sqrt{5.444}$$
$$x = \pm 2.333$$
or
$$x = \pm 2\frac{1}{3}$$

11.

$$3x^2 - 6x = 0$$
$$3x(x-2) = 0$$
$$3x = 0 \quad x-2 = 0$$
$$\frac{3x}{3} = \frac{0}{3} \quad\quad x = 2$$
$$x = 0$$

13.

$$x^2 - 5x + 6 = 0$$
$$(x-2)(x-3) = 0$$
$$x-2 = 0 \quad x-3 = 0$$
$$x = 2 \quad\quad x = 3$$

15.
$$2x^2 + 12 = 11x$$
$$2x^2 - 11x + 12 = 0$$
$$\frac{(2x-\quad)(2x-\quad)}{2} = 0$$
$$\frac{(2x-3)(2x-8)}{2} = 0$$
$$\frac{(2x-3)(\cancel{2})(x-4)}{\cancel{2}} = 0$$
$$(2x-3)(x-4) = 0$$
$$2x-3=0 \quad x-4=0$$
$$2x=3 \qquad x=4$$
$$x = \frac{3}{2}$$

$$2 \cdot 12 = \underline{\quad 24 \quad}$$
$$1 \cdot 24$$
$$2 \cdot 12$$
$$\star \, 3 \cdot 8$$
$$4 \cdot 6$$

17.
$$R = \frac{KL}{d^2}$$
$$1.314 = \frac{(10.4)(3,642.5)}{d^2}$$
$$1.314(d^2) = (\cancel{d^2})\frac{(10.4)(3,642.5)}{\cancel{d^2}}$$
$$1.314\,d^2 = 37,882$$
$$\frac{1.314\,d^2}{1.314} = \frac{37,882}{1.314}$$
$$d^2 = 28,829.53$$
$$d = \sqrt{28,829.53}$$
$$d = 169.79 \text{ mils}$$

19.
$$R = \frac{W}{I^2}$$
$$52.29 = \frac{205}{I^2}$$
$$(I^2)52.29 = (\cancel{I^2})\frac{205}{\cancel{I^2}}$$
$$52.29 I^2 = 205$$
$$\frac{52.29 I^2}{52.29} = \frac{205}{52.29}$$
$$I^2 = 3.92$$
$$I = \sqrt{3.92}$$
$$I = 1.98 \text{ amps}$$

21.
$$E = 0.5mv^2$$
$$180 = 0.5(10)v^2$$
$$180 = 5v^2$$
$$\frac{180}{5} = \frac{5v^2}{5}$$
$$36 = v^2$$
$$\sqrt{36} = v$$
$$v = 6$$

23.
$$6x^3 + 21x^2 = 45x$$
$$6x^3 + 21x^2 - 45x = 0$$
$$3x(2x^2 + 7x - 15) = 0$$
$$\frac{3x(2x+\quad)(2x-\quad)}{2}$$
$$\frac{3x(2x+10)(2x-3)}{2} = 0$$
$$\frac{3x(\cancel{2})(x+5)(2x-3)}{\cancel{2}} = 0$$
$$3x(x+5)(2x-3) = 0$$
$$3x=0 \quad x+5=0 \quad 2x-3=0$$
$$\frac{3x}{3} = \frac{0}{3} \qquad x=-5 \qquad 2x=3$$
$$x=0$$
$$\frac{2x}{2} = \frac{3}{2}$$
$$x = \frac{3}{2}$$

$$2 \cdot 15 = \underline{\quad 30 \quad}$$
$$3 \cdot 10 \quad \star \quad (-3+10 = +7)$$

25.
$$6x^3 - 18x^2 = 0$$
$$6x^2(x-3) = 0$$
$$6x^2 = 0 \qquad x-3=0$$
$$x^2 = \frac{0}{6} \qquad x=3$$
$$x^2 = 0$$
$$\sqrt{x^2} = \sqrt{0}$$
$$x = 0$$

Exponential and Logarithmic Equations

ASSIGNMENT EXERCISES

1. $5^x = 5^8$
$x = 8$

3. $3^x = 3^{-2}$
$x = -2$

5. $4^{x-2} = 4^2$
$x - 2 = 2$
$x = 2 + 2$
$x = 4$

7. $6^{3x+2} = 6^{-3}$
$3x + 2 = -3$
$3x = -3 - 2$
$3x = -5$
$\dfrac{3x}{3} = \dfrac{-5}{3}$
$x = -\dfrac{5}{3}$ or $-1\dfrac{2}{3}$

9. $3^x = 81$
$3^x = 3^4$
$x = 4$

11. $2^x = \dfrac{1}{32}$
$2^x = 2^{-5}$
$x = -5$

13. $5^{3x} = 125$
$5^{3x} = 5^3$
$3x = 3$
$\dfrac{3x}{3} = \dfrac{3}{3}$
$x = 1$

15. $6^{2-x} = \dfrac{1}{36}$
$6^{2-x} = 6^{-2}$
$2 - x = -2$
$-x = -2 - 2$
$-x = -4$
$\dfrac{-x}{-1} = \dfrac{-4}{-1}$
$x = 4$

17. $e^{-4} = 0.01831563889$

some calculators: $\boxed{e^x}\, 4\, \boxed{+/-}\ \boxed{=}$

other calculators: $\boxed{e^x}\ \boxed{(-)}\ 4\ \boxed{\text{ENT}}$

19. $e^{-10} = 0.00004539992976$

some calculators: $\boxed{e^x}$ 10 $\boxed{+/-}$ $\boxed{=}$;

other calculators: 10 $\boxed{+/-}$ $\boxed{e^x}$ or $\boxed{e^x}$ $\boxed{(-)}$ 10 $\boxed{\text{ENTER}}$

21. $I = P(1+R)^N - P$ $\qquad$ $P = \$1,600$

$I = 1,600(1+0.13)^3 - 1,600$ $\qquad$ $R = 0.13$

$I = 1,600(1.13)^3 - 1,600$ $\qquad$ $N = 3$

$I = 1,600(1.442897) - 1,600$

$I = 2,308.6352 - 1,600$

$I = \$708.64$

Calculator: 1600 $\boxed{(}$ 1 $\boxed{.}$ 13 $\boxed{)}$ $\boxed{\wedge}$ 3 $\boxed{-}$ 1600 $\boxed{\text{ENTER}}$ $\Rightarrow$ 708.6352

23. $I = P(1+R)^N - P$ $\qquad$ $P = \$2,000$

$I = 2,000(1+0.06)^4 - 2,000$ $\qquad$ $R = \dfrac{0.12}{12} = 0.06$

$I = 2,000(1.06)^4 - 2,000$ $\qquad$ $N = 2(2) = 4$

$I = 2,000(1.26247696) - 2,000$

$I = 2,524.95392 - 2,000$

$I = \$524.95$

Calculator: 2000 $\boxed{(}$ 1 $\boxed{.}$ 06 $\boxed{)}$ $\boxed{\wedge}$ 4 $\boxed{-}$ 2000 $\boxed{\text{ENTER}}$ $\Rightarrow$ 524.95392

25. $A = P(1+R)^N$ $\qquad$ $P = \$3,000$

$A = 3,000(1+0.06)^{10}$ $\qquad$ $R = \dfrac{0.12}{2} = 0.06$

$A = 3,000(1.06)^{10}$ $\qquad$ $N = 5(2) = 10$

$A = 3,000(1.790847697)$

$A = \$5,372.54$ Rounding could differ slightly from text answer.

27. $I = P(1+R)^N - P$ $\qquad$ $P = \$10,000$

$I = 10,000(1+0.02)^{10} - 10,000$ $\qquad$ $R = \dfrac{0.04}{2} = 0.02$

$I = 10,000(1.02)^{10} - 10,000$ $\qquad$ $N = 5(2) = 10$

$I = 10,000(1.21899442) - 10,000$

$I = 12,189.9442 - 10,000$

$I = \$2,189.94$ Rounding could differ slightly from text answer.

29. $FV = PV(1+R)^N$ $\qquad$ $PV = \$8,000$

$FV = \$8,000(1+0.02)^{28}$ $\qquad$ $R = \dfrac{0.08}{4} = 0.02$

$FV = 8,000(1.02)^{28}$ $\qquad$ $N = 7(4) = 28$

$FV = 8,000(1.741024206)$

$FV = \$13,928.19$ Rounding may differ slightly from text answer.

31.

$A = Pe^{rt}$ $P = \$5,000$

$A = 5,000e^{(0.12)2}$ $t = 2$ years

$A = 5,000e^{0.24}$ $r = 0.12$

$A = 5,000(1.27124915)$

$A = \$6,356.25$

$I = A - P$

$I = \$6,356.25 - \$5,000 = \$1,356.25$

33.

$E = \left(1 + \dfrac{r}{n}\right)^{n} - 1$

$E = \left(1 + \dfrac{0.08}{4}\right)^{4} - 1$

$E = (1 + 0.02)^{4} - 1$

$E = (1.02)^{4} - 1$

$E = 0.08243216$

$E = 8.24\%$

35.

$I = P(1 + R)^{N} - P$ $P = \$1,500$

$I = 1,500(1 + 0.0025)^{48} - 1,500$ $R = \dfrac{0.03}{12} = 0.0025$

$I = 1,500(1.0025)^{48} - 1,500$ $N = 4(12) = 48$

$I = 1,500(1.127328021) - 1,500$

$I = 1,690.9920316 - 1,500$

$I = \$190.99$

37.

$PV = \dfrac{FV}{(1 + R)^{N}}$ $FV = \$4,000$

$PV = \dfrac{4,000}{(1 + 0.02)^{16}}$ $R = \dfrac{0.08}{4} = 0.02$

$PV = \dfrac{4,000}{(1.02)^{16}}$ $N = 4(4) = 16$

$PV = \dfrac{4,000}{1.372785705}$

$PV = \$2,913.78$

39.

$PV = \dfrac{FV}{(1 + R)^{N}}$ $FV = \$11,000$

$PV = \dfrac{11,000}{(1 + 0.01)^{18}}$ $R = \dfrac{0.12}{12} = 0.01$

$PV = \dfrac{11,000}{(1.01)^{18}}$ $N = 1.5(12) = 18$

$PV = \dfrac{11,000}{1.196147476}$

$PV = \$9,196.19$ The collector should sell the painting to an individual for
     $11,000 to be paid in 18 months. Its present value is $9,196.19, which is more than $8,000.

41.

$$PV = \frac{FV}{(1+R)^N} \qquad FV = \$7,000$$

$$PV = \frac{7,000}{(1+0.1)^4} \qquad R = 0.1$$

$$PV = \frac{7,000}{(1.1)^4} \qquad N = 4$$

$$PV = \frac{7,000}{1.4641}$$

$$PV = \$4,781.09$$

43.

$$FV = P\left(\frac{(1+R)^N - 1}{R}\right) \qquad P = \$2,000$$

$$FV = 2,000\left(\frac{(1+0.06)^{10} - 1}{0.06}\right) \qquad R = \frac{0.12}{2} = 0.06$$

$$FV = 2,000\left(\frac{(1.06)^{10} - 1}{0.06}\right) \qquad N = 5(2) = 10$$

$$FV = 2,000\left(\frac{0.7908476965}{0.06}\right)$$

$$FV = \$2,000(13.18079494)$$

$$FV = \$26,361.59$$

45.

$$P = FV\left[\frac{R}{(1+R)^N - 1}\right] \qquad FV = \$155,000$$

$$P = 155,000\left[\frac{0.04}{(1+0.04)^{16} - 1}\right] \qquad R = \frac{0.08}{2} = 0.04$$

$$P = 155,000\left[\frac{0.04}{(1.04)^{16} - 1}\right] \qquad N = 8(2) = 16$$

$$P = 155,000\left[\frac{0.04}{1.872981246}\right]$$

$$P = 155,000\,[0.0458199992]$$

$$P = \$7,102.10$$

Calculator: 155000 $\boxed{(}$ $\boxed{.}$ 04 $\boxed{\div}$ $\boxed{(}$ $\boxed{(}$ 1 $\boxed{+}$ $\boxed{.}$ 04 $\boxed{)}$ $\boxed{\wedge}$ 16 $\boxed{-}$ 1 $\boxed{)}$ $\boxed{)}$ $\boxed{\text{ENTER}}$

47. $P = FV\left[\dfrac{R}{(1+R)^N - 1}\right]$ $FV = \$45{,}000$

$P = 45{,}000\left[\dfrac{0.01}{(1+0.01)^{18} - 1}\right]$ $R = \dfrac{0.12}{12} = 0.01$

$P = 45{,}000\left[\dfrac{0.01}{(1.01)^{18} - 1}\right]$ $N = 1.5(12) = 18$

$P = 45{,}000\left[\dfrac{0.01}{1.196147476 - 1}\right]$

$P = 45{,}000\left[\dfrac{0.01}{0.196147476}\right]$

$P = 45{,}000\,[0.0509820479]$

$P = \$2{,}294.19$

49. $P = FV\left[\dfrac{R}{(1+R)^N - 1}\right]$ $FV = \$75{,}000$

$P = 75{,}000\left[\dfrac{0.02}{(1+0.02)^{12} - 1}\right]$ $R = \dfrac{0.08}{4} = 0.02$

$P = 75{,}000\left[\dfrac{0.02}{(1.02)^{12} - 1}\right]$ $N = 3(4) = 12$

$P = 75{,}000\left[\dfrac{0.02}{1.268241795 - 1}\right]$

$P = 75{,}000\left[\dfrac{0.02}{0.268241795}\right]$

$P = 75{,}000\,[0.0745595966]$

$P = \$5{,}591.97$

51. $P = FV\left[\dfrac{R}{(1+R)^N - 1}\right]$ $FV = \$25{,}000$

$P = 25{,}000\left[\dfrac{0.08}{(1+0.08)^6 - 1}\right]$ $R = 0.08$

$P = 25{,}000\left[\dfrac{0.08}{(1.08)^6 - 1}\right]$ $N = 6$

$P = 25{,}000\left[\dfrac{0.08}{1.586874323 - 1}\right]$

$P = 25{,}000\left[\dfrac{0.08}{0.5868743229}\right]$

$P = 25{,}000\,[0.1363153862]$

$P = \$3{,}407.88$

53.

$$M = P\left(\frac{R}{1-(1+R)^{-N}}\right)$$

$P = \$238,000$

$R = \dfrac{0.075}{12} = 0.00625$

$$M = 238,000\left(\frac{0.00625}{1-(1+0.00625)^{-240}}\right)$$

$N = 20(12) = 240$

$$M = 238,000\left(\frac{0.00625}{1-(1.00625)^{-240}}\right)$$

$$M = 238,000\left(\frac{0.00625}{1-(0.22417418)}\right)$$

$$M = 238,000\left(\frac{0.00625}{0.77582582}\right)$$

$$M = 238,000(0.0080559319)$$

$$M = \$1,917.31$$

55.

$I = 1.50e^{-200t}$ $t = 0.07$ sec

$I = 1.50e^{-200(0.07)}$

$I = 1.50e^{-14}$

$I = 0.000001247293079$ Calculator display: 1.247293079**E-6**

$I = 1.25 \times 10^{-6}$

57.

$I = 1.50e^{-200t}$ $t = 0.4$ sec

$I = 1.50e^{-200(0.4)}$

$I = 1.50e^{-80}$

$I = 2.70727708 \times 10^{-35}$ Calculator display: 2.70727708**E-35**

$I = 2.71 \times 10^{-35}$

59. $2^3 = 8$

$\log_2 8 = 3$

If $x = b^y$ then $\log_b x = y$.

61. $3^4 = 81$

$\log_3 81 = 4$

If $x = b^y$ then $\log_b x = y$

63. $27^{1/3} = 3$

$\log_{27} 3 = \dfrac{1}{3}$

65. $4^{-3} = \dfrac{1}{64}$

$\log_4 \dfrac{1}{64} = -3$

67. $9^{-1/2} = \dfrac{1}{3}$

$\log_9 \dfrac{1}{3} = -\dfrac{1}{2}$

69. $12^{-2} = \dfrac{1}{144}$

$\log_{12} \dfrac{1}{144} = -2$

71. $\log_{11} 121 = 2$

$11^2 = 121$

$\log_b x = y$ converts to $x = b^y$.

73. $\log_{15} 1 = 0$

$15^0 = 1$

75. $\log_7 7 = 1$

$7^1 = 7$ or $7 = 7$

77. $\log_4 \dfrac{1}{16} = -2$

$4^{-2} = \dfrac{1}{16}$

79. $\log_9 \dfrac{1}{3} = -0.5$

$9^{-0.5} = \dfrac{1}{3}$

81. $\log_{10} 1,000 = 3$ **83.** $\log 5 = 0.6990$ **85.** $\log 180 = 2.2553$

$10^3 = 1,000$ calculator: $\boxed{\log}$ 5 $\boxed{\text{ENTER}}$ calculator: $\boxed{\log}$ 180 $\boxed{\text{ENTER}}$

$1,000 = 1,000$

87. $\log 0.4 = -0.3979$ **89.** $\ln 270 = 5.5984$

calculator: $\boxed{\log}$ 0.4 $\boxed{\text{ENTER}}$ calculator: $\boxed{\ln}$ 270 $\boxed{\text{ENTER}}$

91. $\ln 0.8 = -0.2231$ **93.** $\log_5 30 = \dfrac{\log 30}{\log 5} = \dfrac{1.4771}{0.6990} = 2.1133$

calculator: $\boxed{\ln}$ 0.8 $\boxed{\text{ENTER}}$

95. $\log_4 16 = x$ **97.** $\log_7 x = 3$ **99.** $\log_6 \dfrac{1}{36} = x$

$4^x = 16$ $7^3 = x$

$4^x = 4^2$ $343 = x$ $6^x = \dfrac{1}{36}$

$x = 2$ $6^x = 6^{-2}$

$x = -2$

101. Richter scale rating $= \log \dfrac{I}{I_0}$

(a) $\quad R = \log \dfrac{100 I_0}{I_0}$ (b) $\quad R = \log \dfrac{10,000 I_0}{I_0}$ (c) $\quad R = \log \dfrac{150,000,000 I_0}{I_0}$

$= \log 100$ $= \log 10,000$ $= \log 150,000,000$

$= 2$ $= 4$ $= 8.1761$ (rounded)

103. $\log_2 9 = \log_2 3^2$ **105.** $t = \dfrac{\ln A - \ln P}{r}$ $A = \$150,000$

$= 2\left(\log_2 3\right)$ $P = \$100,000$

$= 2\left(1.585\right)$ $t = \dfrac{\ln 150,000 - \ln 100,000}{0.041}$ $r = 4.1\%$

$= 3.17$ $t = \dfrac{11.91839057 - 11.51292546}{0.041}$

$t = \dfrac{0.405465105}{0.041}$

$t = 9.889$ years

107. (a) $C_t = 72,000,000(0.65)^x$

(b) 60 days = 2 30-day periods, so $x = 2$

$$C = 72,000,000(0.65)^2$$
$$= 72,000,000(0.4225)$$
$$= 30,420,000 \text{ units per cubic meter after 60 days}$$

150 days = 5 30-day periods, so $x = 5$

$$C = 72,000,000(0.65)^5$$
$$= 72,000,000(0.1160290625)$$
$$= 8,354,092.5 \text{ units per cubic meter after 150 days}$$

(c)
$$C_t = C_c(0.65)^x$$
$$C_t = 72,000,000(0.65)^x$$
$$\frac{60,000}{72,000,000} = \frac{72,000,000(0.65)^x}{72,000,000}$$
$$8.33 \times 10^{-4} = 0.65^x$$
$$\log(8.33 \times 10^{-4}) = \log 0.65^x$$
$$\frac{\log(8.33 \times 10^{-4})}{\log(0.65)} = \frac{x \cancel{\log(0.65)}}{\cancel{\log(0.65)}}$$
$$16.5 = x$$

16.5 30-day periods, or 495 days.
Generally, we can say approximately 500 days or 16 to 17 months.

Chapter 16 Trial Test

1. $1.2^{45} = 3657.26199$

calculator: 1.2 $\boxed{y^x}$ 45 $\boxed{=}$

or 1.2 $\boxed{\wedge}$ 45 $\boxed{\text{ENTER}}$

3. $15^{3/2} = 58.09475019$

calculator: 15 $\boxed{y^x}$ 3 $\boxed{b/a_c}$ 2 $\boxed{=}$

or 15 $\boxed{\wedge}$ $\boxed{(}$ 3 $\boxed{\div}$ 2 $\boxed{)}$ $\boxed{\text{ENTER}}$

5. $12^5 = 248,832$

calculator: 12 $\boxed{y^x}$ 5 $\boxed{=}$

or 12 $\boxed{\wedge}$ 5 $\boxed{\text{ENTER}}$

7.
$$2^{x-4} = 2^5$$
$$x - 4 = 5$$
$$x = 5 + 4$$
$$x = 9$$

9.
$$2^{2x-1} = 8$$
$$2^{2x-1} = 2^3$$
$$2x - 1 = 3$$
$$2x = 3 + 1$$
$$2x = 4$$
$$\frac{2x}{2} = \frac{4}{2}$$
$$x = 2$$

11.
$$4^{-1/2} = \frac{1}{2}$$
$$\log_4 \frac{1}{2} = -\frac{1}{2}$$

13. $\log_3 \dfrac{1}{27} = -3$

$3^{-3} = \dfrac{1}{27}$

15. $\ln 32 = 3.4657$

calculator: $\boxed{\ln}$ 32 $\boxed{\text{ENTER}}$

17. $\log_6 216 = x$

$6^x = 216$

$6^x = 6^3$

$x = 3$

19. $\log_8 21 = \dfrac{\log 21}{\log 8}$

$\log_8 21 = \dfrac{1.3222}{0.9031}$

$\log_8 21 = 1.4641$

21.
$$S = 125 + 83\log(5t+1)$$
$$= 125 + 83\log(5(3)+1)$$
$$= 125 + 83\log(16)$$
$$= 125 + 83(1.20412)$$
$$= 125 + 99.94$$
$$= \$224.94 \text{ thousands}$$

23. $A = p\left(1 + \dfrac{r}{n}\right)^{nt}$

$p = \$5,000, r = 5.8\%, t = 2 \text{ yrs}, n = 1$

$A = 5,000\left(1 + \dfrac{0.058}{1}\right)^{1(2)}$

$A = 5,000(1.058)^2$

$A = 5,000(1.119364)$

$A = \$5,596.82$

25. $FV = P\left(\dfrac{(1+R)^N - 1}{R}\right)$

$P = \$9,000$

$R = 0.15$

$N = 2$

$FV = 9,000\left(\dfrac{(1+0.15)^2 - 1}{0.15}\right)$

$FV = 9,000\left(\dfrac{(1.15)^2 - 1}{0.15}\right)$

$FV = 9,000\left(\dfrac{1.3225 - 1}{0.15}\right)$

$FV = 9,000\left(\dfrac{0.3225}{0.15}\right)$

$FV = \$9,000(2.15)$

$FV = \$19,350$

27.

$$P = FV\left[\dfrac{R}{(1+R)^N - 1}\right]$$

$$P = 125,000\left[\dfrac{0.04}{(1+0.04)^{16} - 1}\right]$$

$$P = 125,000\left[\dfrac{0.04}{(1.04)^{16} - 1}\right]$$

$$P = 125,000\left[\dfrac{0.04}{1.872981246 - 1}\right]$$

$$P = 125,000\left[\dfrac{0.04}{0.872981246}\right]$$

$$P = 125,000\,[0.0458199992]$$

$$P = \$5,727.50$$

$FV = \$125,000$

$R = 0.04$

$N = 16$

29.

$$E = \left(1 + \dfrac{r}{n}\right)^n - 1$$

$$E = \left(1 + \dfrac{0.12}{4}\right)^4 - 1$$

$$E = (1 + 0.03)^4 - 1$$

$$E = (1.03)^4 - 1$$

$$E = 0.12550881$$

$$E = 12.55\%$$

$r = 0.12$

$n = 4$

31.

$$A = P(1+R)^N$$

$$A = 600(1 + 0.01)^{12}$$

$$A = 600(1.01)^{12}$$

$$A = 600(1.12682503)$$

$$A = \$676.10$$

$P = \$600$

$R = \dfrac{0.12}{12} = 0.01$

$N = 12$

$680 in 1 year is slightly better than accepting $600 now and investing it for 1 year.

33. Option 1

$$A = P(1+R)^N$$

$$A = 2,000(1 + 0.02)^{16}$$

$$A = 2,000(1.02)^{16}$$

$$A = 2,000(1.372785705)$$

$$A = \$2,745.57$$

$P = \$2,000$

$R = \dfrac{0.08}{4} = 0.02$

$N = 4(4) = 16$

Option 2

$$A = P(1+R)^N$$

$$A = 2,000(1 + 0.0825)^4$$

$$A = 2,000(1.0825)^4$$

$$A = 2,000(1.373129888)$$

$$A = \$2,746.26$$

$P = \$2,000$

$R = 0.0825$

$N = 4$

Option 2 yields slightly more interest.

35. $A = Pe^{rt}$ $P = \$1,000$

$A = 1,000e^{(0.04)20}$ $t = 20$ years

$A = 1,000e^{0.8}$ $r = 0.04$

$A = 1,000(2.225540928)$

$A = \$2,225.54$

37. $PV = \dfrac{FV}{(1+R)^N}$ $FV = \$15,000$

$R = 0.104$

$PV = \dfrac{15,000}{(1+0.104)^1}$ $N = 1$

$PV = \dfrac{15,000}{(1.104)^1}$

$PV = \$13,586.96$

chapter 17 — Inequalities and Absolute Values

ASSIGNMENT EXERCISES

1. The empty set is a set containing no elements.
$\{\ \}$ or ϕ

3. $5 \in W$

5. $x > -7$

-7
$(-7, \infty)$

7. $-4 \le x < 2$

-4 2
$[-4, 2)$

9. $-2 < x$
or
$x > -2$

-2
$(-2, \infty)$

11. $42 > 8m - 2m$
$42 > 6m$
$\dfrac{42}{6} > \dfrac{6m}{6}$
$7 > m$
$m < 7$

7
$(-\infty, 7)$

13. $0 < 2x - x$
$0 < x$
$x > 0$

0
$(0, \infty)$

15. $10 - 2x \ge 4$
$-2x \ge 4 - 10$
$-2x \ge -6$
$\dfrac{-2x}{-2} \ge \dfrac{-6}{-2}$
$x \le 3$

3
$(-\infty, 3]$

17. $10x + 18 > 8x$
$18 > 8x - 10x$
$18 > -2x$
$\dfrac{18}{-2} > \dfrac{-2x}{-2}$
$-9 < x$
$x > -9$

-9
$(-9, \infty)$

19. $12 + 5x > 6 - x$
$5x + x > 6 - 12$
$6x > -6$
$\dfrac{6x}{6} > \dfrac{-6}{6}$
$x > -1$

-1
$(-1, \infty)$

21. $15 \ge 5(2 - y)$
$15 \ge 10 - 5y$
$15 - 10 \ge -5y$
$5 \ge -5y$
$\dfrac{5}{-5} \ge \dfrac{-5y}{-5}$
$-1 \le y$
$y \ge -1$

-1
$[-1, \infty)$

23.
$$6x - 2(x - 3) \leq 30$$
$$6x - 2x + 6 \leq 30$$
$$4x + 6 \leq 30$$
$$4x \leq 30 - 6$$
$$4x \leq 24$$
$$\frac{4x}{4} \leq \frac{24}{4}$$
$$x \leq 6$$

$$6$$
$$(-\infty, 6]$$

25.
$$D = P + \$5.60$$
$$2D + 12P \leq \$59.80$$
$$2(P + 5.60) + 12P \leq 59.80$$
$$2P + 11.20 + 12P \leq 59.80$$
$$14P + 11.20 \leq 59.80$$
$$14P \leq 59.80 - 11.20$$
$$14P \leq 48.60$$
$$\frac{14P}{14} \leq \frac{48.60}{14}$$
$$P \leq \$3.47$$
$$D \leq 3.47 + 5.60$$
$$D \leq \$9.07$$

27. $A \cap B$ intersection: set that includes all elements that appear in *both* sets   **29.** $A \cap D$
  $\{\ \}$ no elements in common, empty set $\{-1\}$

31.
$$(A \cup C)'$$
$$A \cup C = \{-2, -1, 0, 1, 2, 3, 4\}$$
$$(A \cup C)' = \{5\}\, 4$$

33.
$$x + 4 > 2$$
$$x > 2 - 4$$
$$x > -2$$

$$-2$$
$$(-2, \infty)$$

35.
$$3x - 2 \leq 4x + 1$$
$$3x - 4x \leq 1 + 2$$
$$-x \leq 3$$
$$\frac{-x}{-1} \leq \frac{3}{-1}$$
$$x \geq -3$$

$$-3$$
$$[-3, \infty)$$

37.
$$-3 < 2x - 4 < 5$$
$$-3 < 2x - 4 \qquad 2x - 4 < 5$$
$$-3 + 4 < 2x \qquad 2x < 5 + 4$$
$$1 < 2x \qquad\qquad 2x < 9$$
$$\frac{1}{2} < \frac{2x}{2} \qquad\qquad \frac{2x}{2} < \frac{9}{2}$$
$$\frac{1}{2} < x \qquad\qquad x < 4\frac{1}{2} \ \text{or} \ \frac{9}{2}$$
$$\frac{1}{2} < x < 4\frac{1}{2}$$

$$\frac{1}{2}\, 1 \qquad 4\frac{1}{2}\, 5$$
$$\left(\frac{1}{2}, 4\frac{1}{2}\right)$$

39.
$$x + 1 < 5 < 2x + 1$$
$$x + 1 < 5 \qquad\quad 5 < 2x + 1$$
$$x < 5 - 1 \quad 5 - 1 < 2x$$
$$x < 4 \qquad\quad 4 < 2x$$
$$\frac{4}{2} < \frac{2x}{2}$$
$$2 < x$$
$$2 < x < 4$$

$$2 \qquad 4$$
$$(2, 4)$$

41.
$$x + 2 < 7 < 2x - 15$$
$$x + 2 < 7 \qquad\qquad 7 < 2x - 15$$
$$x < 7 - 2 \quad 7 + 15 < 2x$$
$$x < 5 \qquad\qquad 22 < 2x$$
$$\frac{22}{2} < \frac{2x}{2}$$
$$11 < x$$
$$11 < x < 5$$
NO SOLUTION

43. $2x+3 < 15 < 3x+9$

$2x+3 < 15 \qquad 15 < 3x+9$

$\quad 2x < 15-3 \qquad 15-9 < 3x$

$\quad 2x < 12 \qquad\qquad 6 < 3x$

$\quad \dfrac{2x}{2} < \dfrac{12}{2} \qquad \dfrac{6}{3} < \dfrac{3x}{3}$

$\quad x < 6 \qquad\qquad 2 < x$

$2 < x < 6$

$(2, 6)$

45. $-5 \le -3x+1 < 10$

$\quad -5 \le -3x+1 \qquad -3x+1 < 10$

$\quad -5-1 \le -3x \qquad\quad -3x < 10-1$

$\quad -6 \le -3x \qquad\qquad -3x < 9$

$\quad \dfrac{-6}{-3} \le \dfrac{-3x}{-3} \qquad \dfrac{-3x}{-3} < \dfrac{9}{-3}$

$\quad 2 \ge x \qquad\qquad\quad x > -3$

$-3 < x \le 2$

$(-3, 2]$

47. $-3 \le 4x+5 \le 2$

$\quad -3 \le 4x+5 \qquad 4x+5 \le 2$

$\quad -3-5 \le 4x \qquad\quad 4x \le 2-5$

$\quad -8 \le 4x \qquad\qquad 4x \le -3$

$\quad \dfrac{-8}{4} \le \dfrac{4x}{4} \qquad\quad \dfrac{4x}{4} \le \dfrac{-3}{4}$

$\quad -2 \le x \qquad\qquad\quad x \le \dfrac{-3}{4}$

$-2 \le x \le \dfrac{-3}{4}$

$\left[-2, -\dfrac{3}{4}\right]$

49.

$x+3 < 5 \quad$ or $\quad x > 8$

$x < 2 \quad$ or $\quad x > 8$

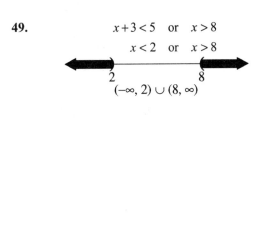

$(-\infty, 2) \cup (8, \infty)$

51. $x-3 < -12 \qquad$ or $\qquad x+1 > 9$

$\quad x < -12+3 \qquad\qquad x > 9-1$

$\quad x < -9 \qquad$ or $\qquad x > 8$

$(-\infty, -9) \cup (8, \infty)$

53. $x(1,365+199) > 15,000$

$\quad x(1,564) > 15,000$

$\quad x > \dfrac{15,000}{1,564} = 9.6$ or 10

or

$x(1,365+199) < 30,000$

$\quad x(1,564) < 30,000$

$\quad x < \dfrac{30,000}{1,564} = 19.2$ or 19

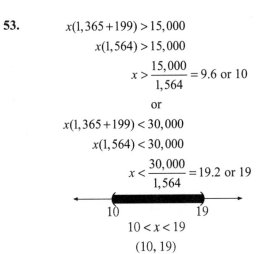

$10 < x < 19$

$(10, 19)$

55. $(x-5)(x-2) > 0$

critical values:

$x - 5 = 0 \qquad x - 2 = 0$

$\quad x = 5 \qquad\qquad x = 2$

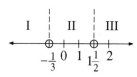

Region I	Region II	Region III
$x < 2$	$2 < x < 5$	$x > 5$
let $x = 1$	let $x = 3$	let $x = 6$
$(1-5)(1-2) > 0$	$(3-5)(3-2) > 0$	$(6-5)(6-2) > 0$
$(-4)(-1) > 0$	$(-2)(1) > 0$	$(1)(4) > 0$
$4 > 0$	$-2 > 0$	$4 > 0$
true	false	true

$-x < 2 \text{ or } x > 5$

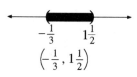

$(-\infty, 2) \cup (5, \infty)$

57. $(3x+1)(2x-3) < 0$

critical values: $3x + 1 = 0 \qquad\qquad 2x - 3 = 0$

$\qquad\qquad\qquad 3x = -1 \qquad\qquad\quad 2x = 3$

$\qquad\qquad\qquad \dfrac{3x}{3} = \dfrac{-1}{3} \qquad\qquad \dfrac{2x}{2} = \dfrac{3}{2}$

$\qquad\qquad\qquad\quad x = \dfrac{-1}{3} \qquad\qquad x = 1\dfrac{1}{2} \text{ or } \dfrac{3}{2}$

Region I	Region II	Region III
$x < -\dfrac{1}{3}$	$-\dfrac{1}{3} < x < 1\dfrac{1}{2}$	$x > 1\dfrac{1}{2}$
let $x = -1$	let $x = 0$	let $x = 2$
$(3 \cdot -1 + 1)(2 \cdot -1 - 3) < 0$	$(3 \cdot 0 + 1)(2 \cdot 0 - 3) < 0$	$(3 \cdot 2 + 1)(2 \cdot 2 - 3) < 0$
$(-3+1)(-2-3) < 0$	$(0+1)(0-3) < 0$	$(6+1)(4-3) < 0$
$(-2)(-5) < 0$	$(1)(-3) < 0$	$(7)(1) < 0$
$10 < 0$	$-3 < 0$	$7 < 0$
false	true	false

$-\dfrac{1}{3} < x < 1\dfrac{1}{2}$

$\left(-\dfrac{1}{3}, 1\dfrac{1}{2}\right)$

59. $(x+1)(x-2) \le 0$

critical values: $\quad x+1=0 \quad\quad x-2=0$

$$x=-1 \quad\quad x=2$$

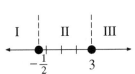

Region I	Region II	Region III
$x \le -1$	$-1 \le x \le 2$	$x \ge 2$
let $x=-2$	let $x=0$	let $x=3$
$(-2+1)(-2-2) \le 0$	$(0+1)(0-2) \le 0$	$(3+1)(3-2) \le 0$
$(-1)(-4) \le 0$	$(1)(-2) \le 0$	$(4)(1) \le 0$
$4 \le 0$	$-2 \le 0$	$4 \le 0$
false	true	false

$$-1 < x \le 2$$

$$[-1, 2]$$

61. $2x^2 \le 5x+3$

$2x^2 - 5x - 3 \le 0$

$\dfrac{(2x+\quad)(2x-\quad)}{2}$ $\qquad$ $2 \cdot 3 = \dfrac{6}{1 \cdot 6} \qquad +1-6=-5$

$\dfrac{(2x+1)(2x-6)}{2} \le 0$

$\dfrac{(2x+1)\,\cancel{(2)}\,(x-3)}{\cancel{2}} \le 0$

$(2x+1)(x-3) \le 0$

critical values: $\quad 2x+1=0 \quad\quad x-3=0$

$$2x=-1 \quad\quad x=3$$

$$x=\dfrac{-1}{2}$$

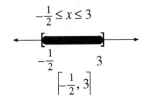

Region I	Region II	Region III
$x \le -\dfrac{1}{2}$	$-\dfrac{1}{2} \le x \le 3$	$x \ge 3$
let $x=-1$	let $x=0$	let $x=4$
$2(-1)^2 \le 5(-1)+3$	$2(0)^2 \le 5(0)+3$	$2(4)^2 \le 5(4)+3$
$2(1) \le -5+3$	$2(0) \le 0+3$	$2(16) \le 20+3$
$2 \le -2$ false	$0 \le 3$ true	$32 \le 23$ false

$$-\dfrac{1}{2} \le x \le 3$$

$$\left[-\dfrac{1}{2}, 3\right]$$

63. $2x^2 + 7x - 15 < 0$ $2 \cdot 15 = \underline{30}$ critical values:

$\dfrac{(2x+\ \ )(2x-\ \ )}{2}$ $1 \cdot 30$ $x + 5 = 0 \qquad 2x - 3 = 0$

$\dfrac{(2x+10)(2x-3)}{2} < 0$ $2 \cdot 15$ $\qquad\qquad x = -5 \qquad 2x = 3$

$\dfrac{\cancel{(2)}(x+5)\ (2x-3)}{\cancel{2}} < 0$ $3 \cdot 10 \quad \bigstar \ -3 + 10 = 7$ $\dfrac{2x}{2} = \dfrac{3}{2}$

$(x+5)(2x-3) < 0$ $x = 1\dfrac{1}{2} \ \text{ or } \ \dfrac{3}{2}$

$$
\begin{array}{ccc}
\text{I} & \text{II} & \text{III}
\end{array}
$$

（number line with open circles at -5 and $1\frac{1}{2}$）

Region I	Region II	Region III
$x < -5$	$-5 < x < 1\dfrac{1}{2}$	$x > 1\dfrac{1}{2}$
let $x = -6$	let $x = 0$	let $x = 2$
$2(-6)^2 + 7(-6) - 15 < 0$	$2(0)^2 + 7(0) - 15 < 0$	$2(2)^2 + 7(2) - 15 < 0$
$72 - 42 - 15 < 0$	$0 + 0 - 15 < 0$	$8 + 14 - 15 < 0$
$15 < 0$ false	$-15 < 0$ true	$7 < 0$ false

$$-5 < x < 1\dfrac{1}{2}$$

（number line shaded between -5 and $1\frac{1}{2}$）

$$\left(-5,\ 1\dfrac{1}{2}\right)$$

65. $\dfrac{x-7}{x+1} < 0$

critical values: $x - 7 = 0 \qquad x + 1 = 0$

$\qquad\qquad\qquad\quad\ x = 7 \qquad\quad\ x = -1$

$$
\begin{array}{cccc}
\text{I} & \text{II} & x = 7 & \text{III}
\end{array}
$$

（number line with open circles at -1 and 7）

Region I	Region II	Region III
$x < -1$	$-1 < x < 7$	$x > 7$
let $x = -2$	let $x = 0$	let $x = 8$
$\dfrac{-2-7}{-2+1} < 0$	$\dfrac{0-7}{0+1} < 0$	$\dfrac{8-7}{8+1} < 0$
$\dfrac{-9}{-1} < 0$	$\dfrac{-7}{1} < 0$	$\dfrac{1}{9} < 0$ false
$9 < 0$ false	$-7 < 0$ true	

$$-1 < x < 7$$

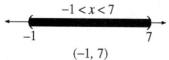

$$(-1,\ 7)$$

67. $\dfrac{x}{x+8} > 0$

critical values: $x = 0$ $x + 8 = 0$

$x = -8$

Region I	Region II	Region III
$x < -8$	$-8 < x < 0$	$x > 0$
let $x = -9$	let $x = -1$	let $x = 1$
$\dfrac{-9}{-9+8} > 0$	$\dfrac{-1}{-1+8} > 0$	$\dfrac{1}{1+8} > 0$
$\dfrac{-9}{-1} > 0$	$\dfrac{-1}{7} > 0$ false	$\dfrac{1}{9} > 0$ true
$9 > 0$ true		

$x < -8 \text{ or } x > 0$

$(-\infty, -8) \cup (0, \infty)$

69. $|x| = 12$
$x = 12$ $-x = 12$
$x = -12$

71. $|x+3| = 7$
$x + 3 = 7$ $-(x+3) = 7$
$x = 7 - 3$ $-x - 3 = 7$
$x = 4$ $-x = 7 + 3$
$-x = 10$
$\dfrac{-x}{-1} = \dfrac{10}{-1}$
$x = -10$

73. $|x-8| = 12$
$x - 8 = 12$ $-(x-8) = 12$
$x = 12 + 8$ $-x + 8 = 12$
$x = 20$ $-x = 12 - 8$
$-x = 4$
$\dfrac{-x}{-1} = \dfrac{4}{-1}$
$x = -4$

75. $|4x - 7| = 17$
$4x - 7 = 17$ $-(4x - 7) = 17$
$4x = 17 + 7$ $-4x + 7 = 17$
$4x = 24$ $-4x = 17 - 7$
$\dfrac{4x}{4} = \dfrac{24}{4}$ $-4x = 10$
$x = 6$ $\dfrac{-4x}{-4} = \dfrac{10}{-4}$
$x = 6$ $x = -2\dfrac{1}{2} \text{ or } -\dfrac{5}{2}$

77. $|7x + 8| = 15$
$7x + 8 = 15$ $-(7x + 8) = 15$
$7x = 15 - 8$ $-7x - 8 = 15$
$7x = 7$ $-7x = 15 + 8$
$\dfrac{7x}{7} = \dfrac{7}{7}$ $-7x = 23$
$x = 1$ $\dfrac{-7x}{-7} = \dfrac{23}{-7}$
$x = -3\dfrac{2}{7} \text{ or } -\dfrac{23}{7}$

79. $|7x - 4| = 17$
$7x - 4 = 17$ $-(7x - 4) = 17$
$7x = 17 + 4$ $-7x + 4 = 17$
$7x = 21$ $-7x = 17 - 4$
$\dfrac{7x}{7} = \dfrac{21}{7}$ $-7x = 13$
$x = 3$ $\dfrac{-7x}{-7} = \dfrac{13}{-7}$
$x = -1\dfrac{6}{7} \text{ or } -\dfrac{13}{7}$

81. $|3x - 9| = 2$
$3x - 9 = 2$ $-(3x - 9) = 2$
$3x = 2 + 9$ $-3x + 9 = 2$
$3x = 11$ $-3x = 2 - 9$
$\dfrac{3x}{3} = \dfrac{11}{3}$ $-3x = -7$
$x = 3\dfrac{2}{3} \text{ or } \dfrac{11}{3}$ $\dfrac{-3x}{-3} = \dfrac{-7}{-3}$
$x = 2\dfrac{1}{3} \text{ or } \dfrac{7}{3}$

83.
$$|x| + 12 = 19$$
$$|x| = 19 - 12$$
$$|x| = 7$$
$$x = 7 \qquad -x = 7$$
$$\frac{-x}{-1} = \frac{7}{-1}$$
$$x = -7$$

85.
$$|x| - 9 = 7$$
$$|x| = 7 + 9$$
$$|x| = 16$$
$$x = 16 \qquad -x = 16$$
$$\frac{-x}{-1} = \frac{16}{-1}$$
$$x = -16$$

87.
$$-5 + |x - 3| = 2$$
$$|x - 3| = 2 + 5$$
$$|x - 3| = 7$$
$$x - 3 = 7 \qquad -(x - 3) = 7$$
$$x = 7 + 3 \qquad -x + 3 = 7$$
$$x = 10 \qquad -x = 7 - 3$$
$$-x = 4$$
$$\frac{-x}{-1} = \frac{4}{-1}$$
$$x = -4$$

89.
$$|4x - 3| - 12 = -7$$
$$|4x - 3| = -7 + 12$$
$$|4x - 3| = 5$$
$$4x - 3 = 5 \qquad -(4x - 3) = 5$$
$$4x = 5 + 3 \qquad -4x + 3 = 5$$
$$4x = 8 \qquad -4x = 5 - 3$$
$$\frac{4x}{4} = \frac{8}{4} \qquad -4x = 2$$
$$x = 2 \qquad \frac{-4x}{-4} = \frac{2}{-4}$$
$$x = -\frac{1}{2}$$

91.
$$|x - 3| < 4$$
$$-4 < x - 3 < 4$$
$$-4 < x - 3 \qquad x - 3 < 4$$
$$-4 + 3 < x \qquad x < 4 + 3$$
$$-1 < x \qquad x < 7$$

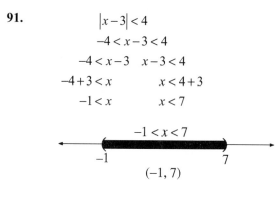

$$-1 < x < 7$$
$$(-1, 7)$$

93.
$$|x - 4| - 3 < 5$$
$$|x - 4| < 5 + 3$$
$$|x - 4| < 8$$
$$-8 < x - 4 < 8$$
$$-8 < x - 4 \qquad x - 4 < 8$$
$$-8 + 4 < x \qquad x < 8 + 4$$
$$-4 < x \qquad x < 12$$

$$-4 < x < 12$$
$$(-4, 12)$$

95.
$$|x - 3| < -4$$
absolute value < negative

(positive)   number

NO SOLUTION

97.
$R =$ Riddle's income
$S =$ Smith's income
$D =$ Duke's income
$$S < R < D$$
$$\$108,000 < R < \$250,000$$

99.
$$8,700 \geq 620x + 300$$
$$8,700 - 300 \geq 620x$$
$$8,400 \geq 620x$$
$$\frac{8,400}{620} \geq x$$
$$x \leq 13.5$$
No more than 13 students can go on the trip.

Chapter 17 Trial Test

1.

$$x \geq -12$$

$$-12$$
$$[-12, \infty)$$

3.

$$3x - 1 > 8$$
$$3x > 8 + 1$$
$$3x > 9$$
$$\frac{3x}{3} > \frac{9}{3}$$
$$x > 3$$

$$3$$
$$(3, \infty)$$

5.

$$10 < 2 + 4x$$
$$10 - 2 < 4x$$
$$8 < 4x$$
$$\frac{8}{4} < \frac{4x}{4}$$
$$2 < x$$
$$x > 2$$

$$2$$
$$(2, \infty)$$

7.

$$\frac{1}{3}x + 5 \leq 3$$
$$(3)\frac{1}{3}x + (3)5 \leq (3)3$$
$$x + 15 \leq 9$$
$$x \leq 9 - 15$$
$$x \leq -6$$

$$-6$$
$$(-\infty, -6]$$

9.

$$5 - 3x < 3 - (2x - 4)$$
$$5 - 3x < 3 - 2x + 4$$
$$5 - 3x < 7 - 2x$$
$$-3x + 2x < 7 - 5$$
$$-x < 2$$
$$\frac{-x}{-1} < \frac{2}{-1}$$
$$x > -2$$

$$-2$$
$$(-2, \infty)$$

11.

$$-5 < x + 3 < 7$$
$$-5 < x + 3 \qquad x + 3 < 7$$
$$-5 - 3 < x \qquad x < 7 - 3$$
$$-8 < x \qquad\qquad x < 4$$
$$-8 < x < 4$$

$$-8 \qquad\qquad 4$$
$$(-8, 4)$$

13.

$$3x - 1 \leq 5 \leq x - 5$$
$$3x - 1 \leq 5 \qquad 5 \leq x - 5$$
$$3x \leq 5 + 1 \qquad 5 + 5 \leq x$$
$$3x \leq 6 \qquad\qquad 10 \leq x$$
$$\frac{3x}{3} \leq \frac{6}{3}$$
$$x \leq 2$$

NO SOLUTION

15. $(2x+3)(x-1) > 0$

critical values: $2x+3 = 0$ $x-1 = 0$

$2x = -3$ $x = 1$

$\dfrac{2x}{2} = \dfrac{-3}{2}$

$x = -1\dfrac{1}{2}$ or $-\dfrac{3}{2}$

Region I	Region II	Region III
$x < -1\dfrac{1}{2}$	$-1\dfrac{1}{2} < x < 1$	$x > 1$
let $x = -2$	let $x = 0$	let $x = 2$
$(2\cdot-2+3)(-2-1) > 0$	$(2\cdot0+3)(0-1) > 0$	$(2\cdot2+3)(2-1) > 0$
$(-1)(-3) > 0$	$(3)(-1) > 0$	$(7)(1) > 0$
$+3 > 0$	$-3 > 0$	$7 > 0$
true	false	true

$x < -1\dfrac{1}{2}$ or $x > 1$

$\left(-\infty, -1\dfrac{1}{2}\right)$ or $(1, \infty)$

17. $2x-3 < 1$ or $x+1 > 7$

$2x < 1+3$ $x+1 > 7$

$2x < 4$ $x > 7-1$

$\dfrac{2x}{2} < \dfrac{4}{2}$ $x > 6$

$x < 2$ or $x > 6$

$(-\infty, 2)$ or $(6, \infty)$

19. $A \cup B$ union: a set that includes all elements that appear in *either* set
$\{1, 2, 3, 4, 5, 6, 7, 8, 9\}$

21. $A \cap B' = \{9\}$

23. $\dfrac{x-2}{x+5} < 0$

$x - 2 = 0 \quad x + 5 = 0$

$x = 2 \qquad x = -5 \quad$ critical values

Region I	Region II	Region III
$x < -5$	$-5 < x < 2$	$x > 2$
let $x = -6$	let $x = 0$	let $x = 3$
$\dfrac{-6-2}{-6+5} < 0$	$\dfrac{0-2}{0+5} < 0$	$\dfrac{3-2}{3+5} < 0$
$\dfrac{-8}{-1} < 0$	$\dfrac{-2}{5} < 0$ true	$\dfrac{1}{8} < 0$ false
$8 < 0$ false		

$(-5, 2)$

25.

$|x| = 15$

$x = 15 \qquad -x = 15$

$\dfrac{-x}{-1} = \dfrac{15}{-1}$

$x = -15$

27.

$|x| + 8 = 10$

$|x| = 10 - 8$

$|x| = 2$

$x = 2 \qquad -x = 2$

$\dfrac{-x}{-1} = \dfrac{2}{-1}$

$x = -2$

29. $|x + 8| > 10$

$x + 8 > 10 \quad$ or $\quad x + 8 < -10$

$x > 10 - 8 \qquad\qquad x < -10 - 8$

$x > 2 \quad$ or $\quad x < -18$

$(-\infty, -18)$ or $(2, \infty)$

31. $96.8 - 0.1 = 96.7$

$96.8 + 0.1 = 96.9$

Range of acceptable measures: $96.7 \le 96.8 \le 96.9$

ASSIGNMENT EXERCISES

Since plotted solutions will vary, check graphs by comparing *x*- and *y*-intercepts.

1.

x	f(x)	2x − 3
−1	−5	2(−1) − 3
1	−1	2(1) − 3
3	3	2(3) − 3

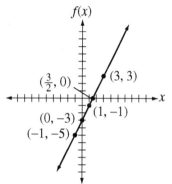

3.

x	f(x)	3x
−1	−3	3(−1)
0	0	3(0)
1	3	3(1)

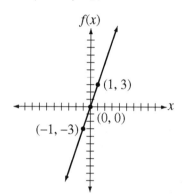

5.

x	f(x)	−3x
−1	3	−3(−1)
0	0	−3(0)
1	−3	−3(1)

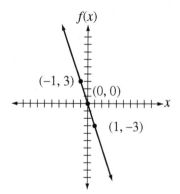

7.

x	f(x)	2x + 1
−1	−1	2(−1) + 1
0	1	2(0) + 1
1	3	2(1) + 1

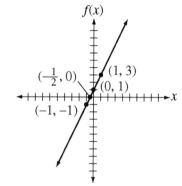

9.

x	$f(x)$	$4x - 2$
-2	-10	$4(-2) - 2$
-1	-6	$4(-1) - 2$
0	-2	$4(0) - 2$
1	2	$4(1) - 2$
2	6	$4(2) - 2$

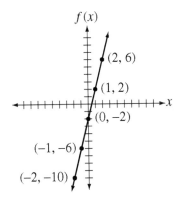

11.

x	$f(x)$	$\frac{1}{2}x - 2$
-2	-3	$\frac{1}{2}(-2) - 2$
-1	$-2\frac{1}{2}$	$\frac{1}{2}(-1) - 2$
0	-2	$\frac{1}{2}(0) - 2$
1	$-1\frac{1}{2}$	$\frac{1}{2}(1) - 2$
2	-1	$\frac{1}{2}(2) - 2$

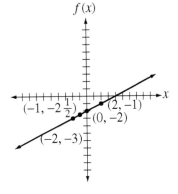

13.
$$2x - 3y = 12 \quad (-2, -3)$$
$$2(-2) - 3(-3) = 12$$
$$-4 + 9 = 5$$
$$5 \neq 12 \quad \text{no}$$

15.
$$2x - 3y = 12 \quad (3, -2)$$
$$2(3) - 3(-2) = 12$$
$$6 + 6 = 12$$
$$12 = 12 \quad \text{yes}$$

17.
$$2x - 3y = 12 \quad (6, 0)$$
$$2(6) - 3(0) = 12$$
$$12 - 0 = 12$$
$$12 = 12 \quad \text{yes}$$

19.
$$x - 3y = 5 \quad x = 8$$
$$8 - 3y = 5$$
$$-3y = -3$$
$$y = 1$$

21. $\quad x = -4y - 1$

x	y
0	$-\frac{1}{4}$
-1	0

$$x = -4y - 1$$
$$0 = -4y - 1$$
$$1 = -4y$$
$$-\frac{1}{4} = y$$

$$x = -4y - 1$$
$$x = -4(0) - 1$$
$$x = 0 - 1$$
$$x = -1$$

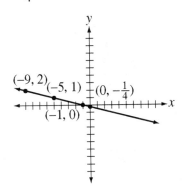

23. $\quad 3x - y = 1$

x	y
0	-1
$\frac{1}{3}$	0

$$3x - y = 1$$
$$3(0) - y = 1$$
$$0 - y = 1$$
$$-y = 1$$
$$y = -1$$

$$3x - y = 1$$
$$3x - 0 = 1$$
$$3x = 1$$
$$x = \frac{1}{3}$$

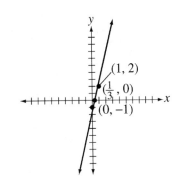

25.
$$\frac{1}{2}x + \frac{1}{3}y = 1$$

x	y
0	3
2	0

Let $x = 0$.

$$\frac{1}{2}(0) + \frac{1}{3}y = 1$$

$$0 + \frac{1}{3}y = 1$$

$$3\left(\frac{1}{3}y\right) = 1(3)$$

$$y = 3$$

Let $y = 0$.

$$\frac{1}{2}x + \frac{1}{3}(0) = 1$$

$$\frac{1}{2}x = 1$$

$$2\left(\frac{1}{2}x\right) = 1(2)$$

$$x = 2$$

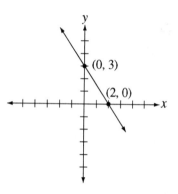

27.
$$y = 5x - 2$$

$$m = \frac{5}{1} \qquad b = -2$$

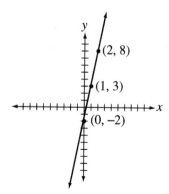

29.
$$y = -3x - 1$$

$$m = \frac{-3}{1} \qquad b = -1$$

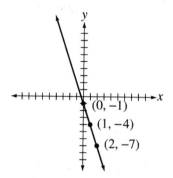

31. $x - y = 4$

$-y = -x + 4$

$\dfrac{-y}{-1} = \dfrac{-x}{-1} + \dfrac{4}{-1}$

$y = x - 4$

$m = \dfrac{1}{1} \qquad b = -4$

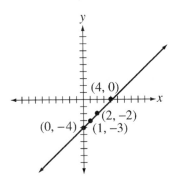

33. $x - 2y = -1$

$-2y = -x - 1$

$\dfrac{-2y}{-2} = \dfrac{-x}{-2} - \dfrac{1}{-2}$

$y = \dfrac{1}{2}x + \dfrac{1}{2}$

$m = \dfrac{1}{2} \qquad b = \dfrac{1}{2}$

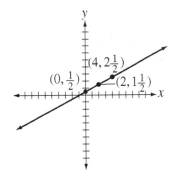

35. $y - 2x = -2$

$y = 2x - 2$

$m = \dfrac{2}{1} \quad b = -2$

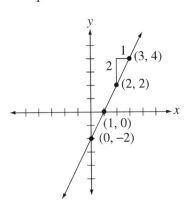

37. $y = 0.5x - 3$

$m = 0.5 = \dfrac{1}{2}$

$b = -3$

39. $y = 20x - 15$

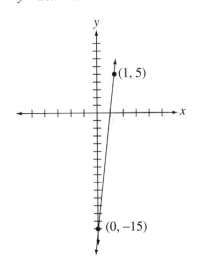

41. $f(x) = 5x + 8,000$

$f(10,000) = 5(10,000) + 8,000$

$= 50,000 + 8,000$

$= 58,000$

$58,000 to make 10,000 widgets

43.
$$x + 2 = 8$$
$$x + 2 - 8 = 0$$
$$x - 6 = 0$$
$$f(x) = x - 6$$

x	$f(x)$	$x - 6$
0	−6	$0 - 6$
3	−3	$3 - 6$
6	0	$6 - 6$

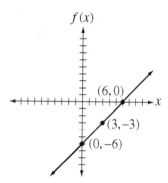

45.
$$2x + 1 = 5x + 7$$
$$0 = 5x - 2x + 7 - 1$$
$$0 = 3x + 6$$
$$f(x) = 3x + 6$$

x	$f(x)$	$3x + 6$
0	6	$3(0) + 6$
−2	0	$3(-2) + 6$
−4	−6	$3(-4) + 6$

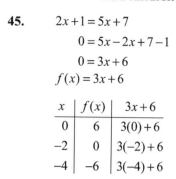

47.
$$5(x + 2) = 3(x + 4)$$
$$5x + 10 = 3x + 12$$
$$5x - 3x + 10 - 12 = 0$$
$$2x - 2 = 0$$
$$f(x) = 2x - 2$$

x	$f(x)$	$2x - 2$
2	2	$2(2) - 2$
0	−2	$2(0) - 2$
−2	−6	$2(2) - 2$

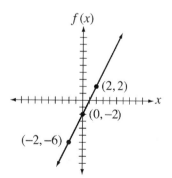

49.
$$4x + y < 2$$
$$y < -4x + 2$$
$$m = -4, \; b = 2$$
dotted line
test: $(0, 0)$
$$4(0) + 0 < 2$$
$$0 + 0 < 2$$
$$0 < 2 \quad \text{true}$$
shade!
test: $(5, 0)$
$$4(5) + 0 < 2$$
$$20 + 0 < 2$$
$$20 < 2 \quad \text{false}$$

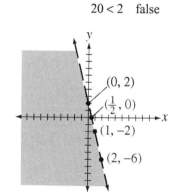

51. $3x + y \leq 2$

$y \leq -3x + 2$

$m = -3, \quad b = 2$

solid line

test: $(0, 0)$

$3(0) + 0 \leq 2$

$0 + 0 \leq 2$

$0 \leq 2$ true

shade!

test: $(5, 0)$

$3(5) + 0 \leq 2$

$15 + 0 \leq 2$

$15 \leq 2$ false

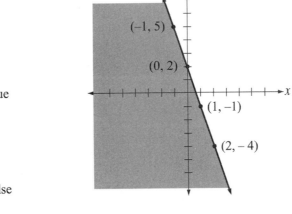

53. $x - 2y < 8$

$-2y < -x + 8$

$\dfrac{-2y}{-2} < \dfrac{-x}{-2} + \dfrac{8}{-2}$

$y > \dfrac{1}{2}x - 4$

$m = \dfrac{1}{2}, \quad b = -4$

dotted line

test: $(0, 0)$

$0 - 2(0) < 8$

$0 - 0 < 8$

$0 < 8$ true

shade!

test: $(0, -5)$

$0 - 2(-5) < 8$

$0 + 10 < 8$

$10 < 8$ false

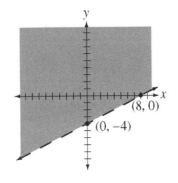

55. $y \geq 3x - 2$

$m = 3, \quad b = -2$

solid line

test: $(0, 0)$

$0 \geq 3(0) - 2$

$0 \geq 0 - 2$

$0 \geq -2$ true

shade!

test: $(5, 0)$

$0 \geq 3(5) - 2$

$0 \geq 15 - 2$

$0 \geq 13$ false

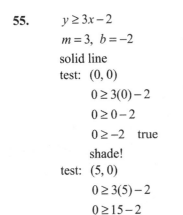

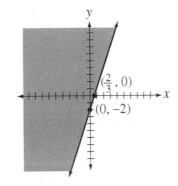

57. $y > \dfrac{2}{3}x - 2$

$m = \dfrac{2}{3}, \; b = -2$

dotted line

test: $(0, 0)$

$0 > \dfrac{2}{3}(0) - 2$

$0 > 0 - 2$

$0 > -2 \quad$ true

shade!

test: $(6, 0)$

$0 > \dfrac{2}{3}(6) - 2$

$0 > 4 - 2$

$0 > 2 \qquad$ false

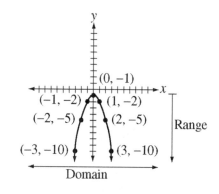

59. $y = -x^2 - 1$

vertex $\quad \dfrac{-b}{2a} = \dfrac{-(0)}{2(-1)} = \dfrac{0}{-2} = 0$

x	y
3	−10
2	−5
1	−2
0	−1
−1	−2
−2	−5
−3	−10

$-(3)^2 - 1 = -9 - 1 = -10$
$-(2)^2 - 1 = -4 - 1 = -5$
$-(1)^2 - 1 = -1 - 1 = -2$
$-(0)^2 - 1 = 0 - 1 = -1$
$-(-1)^2 - 1 = -1 - 1 = -2$
$-(-2)^2 - 1 = -4 - 1 = -5$
$-(-3)^2 - 1 = -9 - 1 = -10$

Domain: $(-\infty, \infty)$

Range: $\quad (-\infty, -1]$

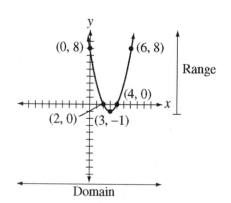

61. $y = x^2 - 6x + 8$

vertex $\quad \dfrac{-b}{2a} = \dfrac{-(-6)}{2(1)} = \dfrac{6}{2} = 3$

x	y
6	8
5	3
4	0
3	−1
2	0
1	3
0	8

$(6)^2 - 6(6) + 8 = 8$
$5^2 - 6(5) + 8 = 3$
$4^2 - 6(4) + 8 = 0$
$3^2 - 6(3) + 8 = -1$
$2^2 - 6(2) + 8 = 0$
$1^2 - 6(1) + 8 = 3$
$0^2 - 6(0) + 8 = 8$

Domain: $(-\infty, \infty)$

Range: $\quad [-1, \infty)$

63. $y = -x^2 + 2x - 1$

vertex $\dfrac{-b}{2a} = \dfrac{-(2)}{2(-1)} = \dfrac{-2}{-2} = 1$

x	y
4	−9
3	−4
2	−1
1	0
0	−1
−1	−4
−2	−9

$-(4)^2 + 2(4) - 1 = -16 + 8 - 1 = -9$
$-(3)^2 + 2(3) - 1 = -9 + 6 - 1 = -4$
$-(2)^2 + 2(2) - 1 = -4 + 4 - 1 = -1$
$-(1)^2 + 2(1) - 1 = -1 + 2 - 1 = 0$
$-(0)^2 + 2(0) - 1 = 0 + 0 - 1 = -1$
$-(-1)^2 + 2(-1) - 1 = -1 - 2 - 1 = -4$
$-(-2)^2 + 2(-2) - 1 = -4 - 4 - 1 = -9$

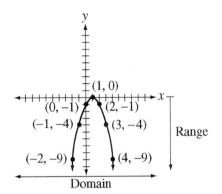

Domain: $(-\infty, \infty)$

Range: $(-\infty, 0)$

65. $y = -x^2 + 4x - 4$

Domain: $(-\infty, \infty)$

Range: $(-\infty, 0)$

vertex $\dfrac{-b}{2a} = \dfrac{-(4)}{2(-1)} = \dfrac{-4}{-2} = 2$

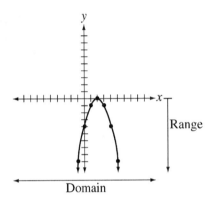

x	y
5	−9
4	−4
3	−1
2	0
1	−1
0	−4
−1	−9

$-(5)^2 + 4(5) - 4 = -25 + 20 - 4 = -9$
$-(4)^2 + 4(4) - 4 = -16 + 16 - 4 = -4$
$-(3)^2 + 4(3) - 4 = -9 + 12 - 4 = -1$
$-(2)^2 + 4(2) - 4 = -4 + 8 - 4 = 0$
$-(1)^2 + 4(1) - 4 = -1 + 4 - 4 = -1$
$-(0)^2 + 4(0) - 4 = 0 + 0 - 4 = -4$
$-(-1)^2 + 4(-1) - 4 = -1 - 4 - 4 = -9$

67. $x^2 - 4x - 12 = 0$

$f(x) = x^2 - 4x - 12$

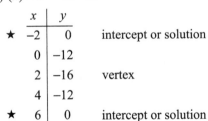

	x	y	
★	−2	0	intercept or solution
	0	−12	
	2	−16	vertex
	4	−12	
★	6	0	intercept or solution

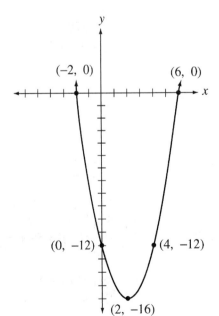

Two solutions: $x = -2$; $x = 6$

69. $x^2 + 8x = -16$

$f(x) = x^2 + 8x + 16$

x	y
-2	4
$\star$ -4	0
-6	4

$(-2)^2 + 8(-2) + 16 = 4 - 16 + 16$

$(-4)^2 + 8(-4) + 16 = 16 - 32 + 16$

$(-6)^2 + 8(-6) + 16 = 36 - 48 + 16$

One solution: $x = -4$

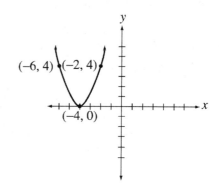

71. $y \geq -2x^2$

vertex $\dfrac{-b}{2a} = \dfrac{-(0)}{2(-2)} = \dfrac{0}{4} = 0$

x	y
2	-8
1	-2
0	0
-1	-2
-2	-8

$-2(2)^2 = -2(4) = -8$

$-2(1)^2 = -2(1) = -2$

$-2(0)^2 = -2(0) = 0$

$-2(-1)^2 = -2(1) = -2$

$-2(2)^2 = -2(4) = -8$

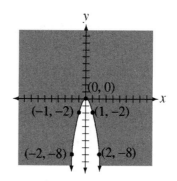

solid parabola

test: $(0, 5)$ outside

$5 \geq -2(0)^2$

$5 \geq -2(0)$

$5 \geq 0$ true

shade!

test: $(0, -5)$ inside

$-5 \geq -2(0)^2$

$-5 \geq -2(0)$

$-5 \geq 0$ false

73. $y = 5x^3$

Domain: $(-\infty, \infty)$;

Range: $(-\infty, \infty)$

x	y	$5x^3$
-2	-40	$5(-2)^3 = 5(-8) = -40$
-1	-5	$5(-1)^3 = 5(-1) = -5$
0	0	$5(0)^3\ \ \ = 5(0) = 0$
1	5	$5(1)^3\ \ \ = 5(1) = 5$
2	40	$5(2)^3\ \ \ = 5(8) = 40$

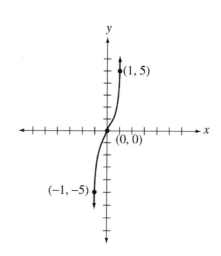

75. $y = 5^x$

Domain: $(-\infty, \infty)$

Range: $(0, \infty]$

x	y
-2	$\dfrac{1}{25}$
-1	$\dfrac{1}{5}$
0	1
1	5
2	25

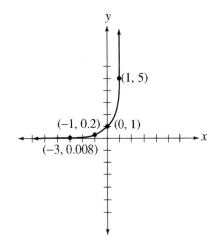

77. $y = \ln\ 4x$

Domain: $(0, \infty)$

Range : $(-\infty, \infty)$

x	y
$\dfrac{1}{4}$	0
$\dfrac{1}{2}$	0.6931471
$\dfrac{3}{4}$	1.0986
$\dfrac{4}{4} = 1$	1.38629
5	2.9957

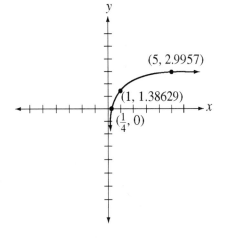

79. $x = -y^3 + 2y^2 + 2y + 3$

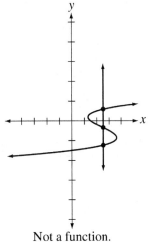

Not a function.

81. $\dfrac{x^2}{25} + \dfrac{y^2}{4} = 1$

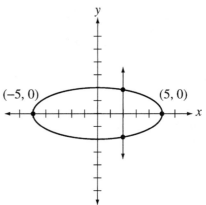

Not a function.

83.

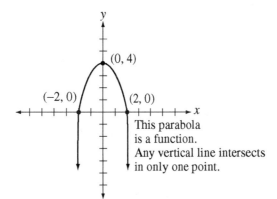

This parabola
is a function.
Any vertical line intersects
in only one point.

85.

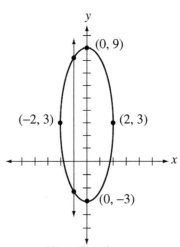

Not a function.

87. (a)

gallons	square feet
x	y
1	400
2	800
3	1200
4	1600
5	2000
6	2400
7	2800
8	3200
9	3600
10	4000
increments of 2	increments of 750

$$\frac{400 \text{ ft}^2}{5{,}500 \text{ ft}^2} = \frac{1 \text{ gal}}{x \text{ gal}}$$

(b)

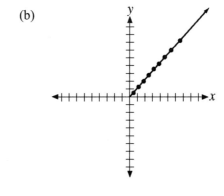

(c)   direct proportion $400x = 5{,}500$

$x = 13.75$ gal; need 14 gallons

(d) $14 \text{ gallons} \times \dfrac{\$19.95}{\text{gal}} = \$279.30$

(e)

$$\frac{R}{100} = \frac{P}{B}$$

$$\frac{8.25}{100} = \frac{P}{279.30}$$

$P = \$23.04$ sales tax

$279.30
$+\ \ 23.04$
$\overline{\$302.34}$ total cost

89.

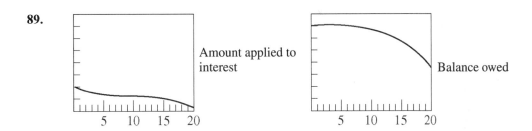

Amount applied to interest

Balance owed

Chapter 18 Trial Test

Since plotted solutions will vary, check graphs by comparing x- and y-intercepts.

1.

x	$f(x)$	$\frac{1}{2}x$
-2	-1	$\frac{1}{2}(-2)$
0	0	$\frac{1}{2}(0)$
2	1	$\frac{1}{2}(2)$

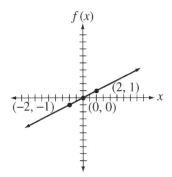

3.

x	$f(x)$	$2x-4$
-1	-6	$2(-1)-4$
0	-4	$2(0)-4$
1	-2	$2(1)-4$
2	0	$2(2)-4$

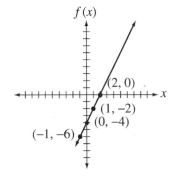

5. $f(x) = 3x - 3$

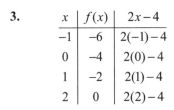

x	$f(x)$	$3x-3$
-1	-6	$3(-1)-3$
0	-3	$3(0)-3$
1	0	$3(1)-3$

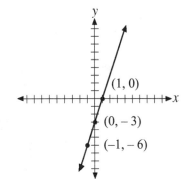

7. $x + y = 7$ if $x = 2$

$2 + y = 7$ $(2, 5)$

$y = 7 - 2$

$y = 5$

9.

x-axis (hp)	y-axis (rpm)
30	500
45	1,000
60	1,500
75	2,000
increments of 15	increments of 500

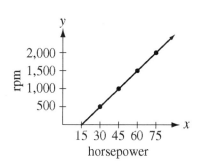

11. $f(x) = 3x - 800$

$f(x) = 3(8000) - 800$

$= 24000 - 800$

$= \$23,200$

13. $x + 2y = 8$

x-intercept	y-intercept
$y = 0$	$x = 0$
$x + 2(0) = 8$	$0 + 2y = 8$
$x + 0 = 8$	$2y = 8$
$x = 8$	$y = 4$
$(8, 0)$	$(0, 4)$

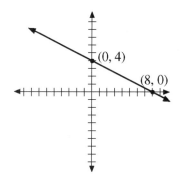

15. $2x + y = -3$

$y = -2x - 3$

$m = \dfrac{-2}{+1}$ y-intercept $= (0, -3)$

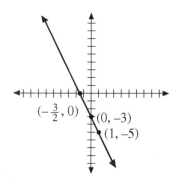

17. $y = x - 5$

$m = 1 \quad y\text{-intercept} = (0, -5)$

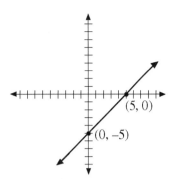

19. $2x - y \leq 2$

$-y \leq -2x + 2$

$\dfrac{-y}{-1} \leq \dfrac{-2x}{-1} + \dfrac{2}{-1}$

$y \geq 2x - 2$

$m = 2, \ b = -2$

solid line

test: $(0, 0)$

$2(0) - 0 \leq 2$

$0 - 0 \leq 2$

$0 \leq 2 \quad$ true

shade!

test: $(5, 0)$

$2(5) - 0 \leq 2$

$10 - 0 \leq 2$

$10 \leq 2 \qquad$ false

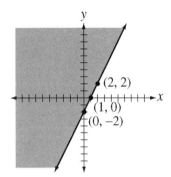

21. $x + y < 1$

$y < -x + 1$

$m = -1, \ b = 1$

dotted line

test: $(0, 0)$

$0 + 0 < 1$

$0 < 1 \quad$ true

shade!

test: $(5, 0)$

$5 + 0 < 1$

$5 < 1 \qquad$ false

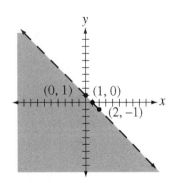

23. $y = x^2 + 2x + 1$

vertex $\dfrac{-b}{2a} = \dfrac{-(2)}{2(1)} = \dfrac{-2}{2} = -1$ $(-1, 0)$

$0 = x^2 + 2x + 1$

$0 = (x + 2)^2$

$x = -1$ solution

$(-1, 0)$ point on graph

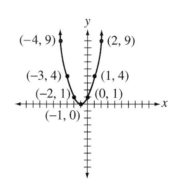

x	y	
2	9	$2^2 + 2(2) + 1 = 4 + 4 + 1 = 9$
1	4	$1^2 + 2(1) + 1 = 1 + 2 + 1 = 4$
0	1	$0^2 + 2(0) + 1 = 0 + 0 + 1 = 1$
−1	0	$(-1)^2 + 2(-1) + 1 = 1 - 2 + 1 = 0$
−2	1	$(-2)^2 + 2(-2) + 1 = 4 - 4 + 1 = 1$
−3	4	$(-3)^2 + 2(-3) + 1 = 9 - 6 + 1 = 4$
−4	9	$(-4)^2 + 2(-4) + 1 = 16 - 8 + 1 = 9$

25. $y \le x^2 - 6x + 8$

vertex $\dfrac{-b}{2a} = \dfrac{-(-6)}{2(1)} = \dfrac{6}{2} = 3$ $(3, -1)$

solid parabola

$0 = x^2 - 6x + 8$

$0 = (x - 2)(x - 4)$

$x = 2, 4$ solutions

$(2, 0)\ (4, 0)$ points on graph

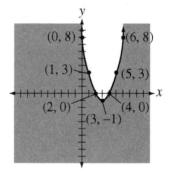

x	y	
6	8	$6^2 - 6(6) + 8 = 36 - 36 + 8 = 8$
5	3	$5^2 - 6(5) + 8 = 25 - 30 + 8 = 3$
4	0	$4^2 - 6(4) + 8 = 16 - 24 + 8 = 0$
3	−1	$3^2 - 6(3) + 8 = 9\ -18 + 8 = -1$
2	0	$2^2 - 6(2) + 8 = 4\ -12 + 8 = 0$
1	3	
0	8	

test: $(0, 0)$ outside

$0 \le 0^2 - 6(0) + 8$

$0 \le 0 - 0 + 8$

$0 \le 8$ true

shade!

test: $(3, 0)$ inside

$0 \le 3^2 - 6(3) + 8$

$0 \le 9 - 18 + 8$

$0 \le -1$ false

27. $y < -\dfrac{1}{2}x^2$

vertex $\dfrac{-b}{2a} = \dfrac{-(0)}{2\left(-\dfrac{1}{2}\right)} = \dfrac{0}{-1} = 0$ $(0, 0)$

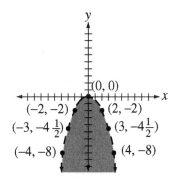

x	y
3	$-4\dfrac{1}{2}$
2	-2
1	$-\dfrac{1}{2}$
0	0
-1	$-\dfrac{1}{2}$
-2	-2
-3	$-4\dfrac{1}{2}$

$-\dfrac{1}{2}\ (3)^2 = -\dfrac{1}{2}\ (9) = -\dfrac{9}{2}$

$-\dfrac{1}{2}\ (2)^2 = -\dfrac{1}{2}\ (4) = -2$

$-\dfrac{1}{2}\ (1)^2 = -\dfrac{1}{2}\ (1) = -\dfrac{1}{2}$

$-\dfrac{1}{2}\ (0)^2 = -\dfrac{1}{2}\ (0) = 0$

$-\dfrac{1}{2}\ (-1)^2 = -\dfrac{1}{2}\ (1) = -\dfrac{1}{2}$

dotted parabola
test: $(0, 6)$ outside

$$6 < -\dfrac{1}{2}(0)^2$$

$$6 < -\dfrac{1}{2}(0)$$

$$6 < 0 \qquad \text{false}$$

test: $(0, -5)$ inside

$$-5 < -\dfrac{1}{2}(0)^2$$

$$-5 < -\dfrac{1}{2}(0)$$

$$-5 < 0 \qquad \text{true}$$

shade!

29. $x = y^3 - 2y^2 - y$
Domain: All real numbers
Range: All real numbers

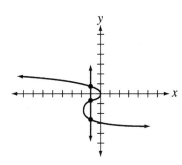

The relation is *not* a function.

chapter 19

Slope and Distance

ASSIGNMENT EXERCISES

1. $(-2, 2)$ and $(1, 3)$

$$m = \frac{y_2 - y_1}{x_2 - x_1} = \frac{3 - 2}{1 - (-2)} = \frac{1}{3}$$

3. $(3, 2)$ and $(5, 6)$

$$m = \frac{y_2 - y_1}{x_2 - x_1} = \frac{6 - 2}{5 - 3} = \frac{4}{2} = 2$$

5. $(4, 3)$ and $(-4, -2)$

$$m = \frac{y_2 - y_1}{x_2 - x_1} = \frac{-2 - 3}{-4 - 4} = \frac{-5}{-8} = \frac{5}{8}$$

7. $(3, -4)$ and $(0, 0)$

$$m = \frac{y_2 - y_1}{x_2 - x_1} = \frac{0 - (-4)}{0 - 3} = \frac{4}{-3} = -\frac{4}{3}$$

9. $(-4, 1)$ and $(-4, 3)$

$$m = \frac{y_2 - y_1}{x_2 - x_1} = \frac{3 - 1}{-4 - (-4)} = \frac{2}{0} = \text{undefined or no slope}$$

11. $(5, 0)$ and $(-2, 4)$

$$m = \frac{y_2 - y_1}{x_2 - x_1} = \frac{4 - 0}{-2 - 5} = \frac{4}{-7} = -\frac{4}{7}$$

13. $(-4, -8)$ and $(-2, -1)$

$$m = \frac{y_2 - y_1}{x_2 - x_1} = \frac{(-1) - (-8)}{(-2) - (-4)} = \frac{7}{2}$$

15. $(5, -3)$ and $(-1, -3)$

$$m = \frac{y_2 - y_1}{x_2 - x_1} = \frac{(-3) - (-3)}{(-1) - 5} = \frac{0}{-6} = 0$$

17. $(-7, 0)$ and $(-7, 5)$

$$m = \frac{y_2 - y_1}{x_2 - x_1} = \frac{5 - 0}{(-7) - (-7)} = \frac{5}{0} = \text{undefined or no slope}$$

19. $(5, 9)$ and $(7, 11)$

$$m = \frac{y_2 - y_1}{x_2 - x_1}$$

$$= \frac{11 - 9}{7 - 5} = \frac{2}{2} = 1$$

21. points on the same horizontal line (slope $m = 0$; thus y_1 and y_2 are same value)

$(3, 5)$ and $(4, 5)$ Answers will vary.

23. $(1{,}998, 1{,}745)$ $(1{,}999, 1{,}702)$

$$m = \frac{y_2 - y_1}{x_2 - x_1}$$

rate of change $= \dfrac{1{,}702 - 1{,}745}{1{,}999 - 1{,}998} = \dfrac{-43}{1} = -43$

Rate of change was a *decrease* of \$43 or $-\$43$.

25. $(1{,}993, 1{,}410)$ $(1{,}994, 1{,}534)$

$$m = \frac{y_2 - y_1}{x_2 - x_1}$$

rate of change $= \dfrac{1{,}534 - 1{,}410}{1{,}994 - 1{,}993} = \dfrac{124}{1} = 124$

Rate of change $= 124$.

27. Explain why the rate of change is different in 24, 25, 26.
The table of values does not represent a perfect linear function, so the rate of change (slope) varies.

29. $(-6, 2)$ and $m = \dfrac{1}{3}$

$y - y_1 = m(x - x_1)$

$y - 2 = \dfrac{1}{3}(x - (-6))$

$y - 2 = \dfrac{1}{3}(x + 6)$

$y - 2 = \dfrac{1}{3}x + 2$

$y = \dfrac{1}{3}x + 2 + 2$

$y = \dfrac{1}{3}x + 4$

31. $(4, 0)$ and $m = \dfrac{3}{4}$

$y - y_1 = m(x - x_1)$

75 $y - 0 = \dfrac{3}{4}(x - 4)$

$y = \dfrac{3}{4}x - 3$

33. $(2, 3)$ and $m = 4$

$y - y_1 = m(x - x_1)$

$y - 3 = 4(x - 2)$

$y - 3 = 4x - 8$

$y = 4x - 8 + 3$

$y = 4x - 5$

35. $(5, -4)$ and $m = \dfrac{-2}{3}$

$y - y_1 = m(x - x_1)$

$y - (-4) = \dfrac{-2}{3}(x - 5)$

$y + 4 = \dfrac{-2}{3}x + \dfrac{10}{3}$

$y = \dfrac{-2}{3}x + \dfrac{10}{3} - 4$

$y = \dfrac{-2}{3}x + \dfrac{10}{3} - \dfrac{12}{3}$

$y = -\dfrac{2}{3}x - \dfrac{2}{3}$

37. $(-5, 2)$ and $(6, 1)$

$m = \dfrac{y_2 - y_1}{x_2 - x_1} = \dfrac{1 - 2}{6 - (-5)} = \dfrac{-1}{11}$

$y - y_1 = m(x - x_1)$

$y - 2 = \dfrac{-1}{11}(x - (-5))$

$y - 2 = \dfrac{-1}{11}(x + 5)$

$y - 2 = \dfrac{-1}{11}x - \dfrac{5}{11}$

$y = \dfrac{-1}{11}x - \dfrac{5}{11} + 2$

$y = \dfrac{-1}{11}x - \dfrac{5}{11} + \dfrac{22}{11}$

$y = -\dfrac{1}{11}x + \dfrac{17}{11}$

39. $(-1, -3)$ and $(3, 4)$

$m = \dfrac{y_2 - y_1}{x_2 - x_1} = \dfrac{4 - (-3)}{3 - (-1)} = \dfrac{7}{4}$

$y - y_1 = m(x - x_1)$

$y - (-3) = \dfrac{7}{4}(x - (-1))$

$y + 3 = \dfrac{7}{4}(x + 1)$

$y + 3 = \dfrac{7}{4}x + \dfrac{7}{4}$

$y = \dfrac{7}{4}x + \dfrac{7}{4} - 3$

$y = \dfrac{7}{4}x + \dfrac{7}{4} - \dfrac{12}{4}$

$y = \dfrac{7}{4}x - \dfrac{5}{4}$

41. $(-2, -3)$ and $(3, 6)$

$$m = \frac{y_2 - y_1}{x_2 - x_1} = \frac{6 - (-3)}{3 - (-2)} = \frac{9}{5}$$

$$y - y_1 = m(x - x_1)$$

$$y - (-3) = \frac{9}{5}(x - (-2))$$

$$y + 3 = \frac{9}{5}(x + 2)$$

$$y + 3 = \frac{9}{5}x + \frac{18}{5}$$

$$y = \frac{9}{5}x + \frac{18}{5} - 3$$

$$y = \frac{9}{5}x + \frac{18}{5} - \frac{15}{5}$$

$$y = \frac{9}{5}x + \frac{3}{5}$$

43. $(5, 2)$ and $(6, 3)$

$$m = \frac{y_2 - y_1}{x_2 - x_1} = \frac{3 - 2}{6 - 5} = \frac{1}{1} = 1$$

$$y - y_1 = m(x - x_1)$$

$$y - 2 = 1(x - 5)$$

$$y - 2 = x - 5$$

$$y = x - 5 + 2$$

$$y = x - 3$$

45. $(-1, -2)$ and $(-3, -4)$

$$m = \frac{y_2 - y_1}{x_2 - x_1} = \frac{-4 - (-2)}{-3 - (-1)} = \frac{-2}{-2} = 1$$

$$y - y_1 = m(x - x_1)$$

$$y - (-2) = 1(x - (-1))$$

$$y + 2 = 1(x + 1)$$

$$y + 2 = x + 1$$

$$y = x + 1 - 2$$

$$y = x - 1$$

47. $(5, -2)$ and $(3, -2)$

$$m = \frac{y_2 - y_1}{x_2 - x_1} = \frac{-2 - (-2)}{3 - 5} = \frac{0}{-2} = 0$$

horizontal line $y = -2$

49. $(80, \$3,800)$
$(120, \$4,200)$

$$m = \frac{y_2 - y_1}{x_2 - x_1}$$

$$m = \frac{4,200 - 3,800}{120 - 80}$$

$$m = \frac{10}{1} = 10$$

$$y - 38,000 = 10(x - 80)$$

$$y - 38,000 = 10x - 800$$

$$y = 10x - 800 + 3,800$$

$$y = 10x + 3,000$$

$$S(x) = 10x + 3,000$$

51. $y = 3x + \frac{1}{4}$

$$m = 3 \quad b = \frac{1}{4}$$

53. $y = -5x + 4$

$m = -5 \quad b = 4$

55. $x = 8$

no slope

no y-intercept

57. $y = \dfrac{x}{8} - 5$

$y = \dfrac{1}{8}x - 5$

$m = \dfrac{1}{8} \quad b = -5$

59. $C(x) = 18x + 5{,}050$

$C(0) = 18(0) + 5{,}050$

$C(0) = 5{,}050$

$y\text{-intercept} = 5{,}550$

The fixed cost is \$5,050.

61. $2x + y = 8$

$y = -2x + 8$

$m = -2 \quad b = 8$

63. $3x - 2y = 6$

$-2y = -3x + 6$

$\dfrac{-2y}{-2} = \dfrac{-3x}{-2} + \dfrac{6}{-2}$

$y = \dfrac{3}{2}x - 3$

$m = \dfrac{3}{2} \quad b = -3$

65. $\dfrac{3}{5}x - y = 4$

$-y = -\dfrac{3}{5}x + 4$

$\dfrac{-y}{-1} = \dfrac{-\frac{3}{5}x}{-1} + \dfrac{4}{-1}$

$y = \dfrac{3}{5}x - 4$

$m = \dfrac{3}{5} \quad b = -4$

67. $3y = 5$

$\dfrac{3y}{3} = \dfrac{5}{3}$

$y = \dfrac{5}{3}$

$m = 0 \qquad b = \dfrac{5}{3}$

69. $m = 3 \quad b = -2$

$y = mx + b$

$y = 3x - 2$

71. $m = \dfrac{2}{1} = 2 \quad b = -2$

$y = mx + b$

$y = 2x - 2$

73. parallel to $x + y = 4$

$y = -x + 4$

$m = (-1), \text{ parallel } m = -1$

$y - y_1 = m(x - x_1) \quad \text{point } (2, 5)$

$y - 5 = -1(x - 2)$

$y - 5 = -1x + 2$

$y = -1x + 2 + 5$

$y = -1x + 7$

standard form: $\quad y = -1x + 7$

$x + y = 7$

75. parallel to $2y = x - 3$

$$\frac{2y}{2} = \frac{x}{2} - \frac{3}{2}$$

$$y = \frac{1}{2}x - \frac{3}{2}$$

$$m = \frac{1}{2}, \text{ parallel } m = \frac{1}{2}$$

$$y - y_1 = m(x - x_1) \quad \text{point } (2, -3)$$

$$y - (-3) = \frac{1}{2}(x - 2)$$

$$y + 3 = \frac{1}{2}x - 1$$

$$y = \frac{1}{2}x - 1 - 3$$

$$y = \frac{1}{2}x - 4$$

standard form : $$y = \frac{1}{2}x - 4$$

$$(2)y = (2)\frac{1}{2}x - (2)4$$

$$2y = x - 8$$

$$-x + 2y = -8$$

$$x - 2y = 8$$

77. parallel to $x - 3y = 5$

$$-3y = -x + 5$$

$$\frac{-3y}{-3} = \frac{-x}{-3} + \frac{5}{-3}$$

$$y = \frac{1}{3}x - \frac{5}{3}$$

$$m = \frac{1}{3}, \text{ parallel } m = \frac{1}{3}$$

$$y - y_1 = m(x - x_1) \quad \text{point } (5, -5)$$

$$y - (-5) = \frac{1}{3}(x - 5)$$

$$y + 5 = \frac{1}{3}x - \frac{5}{3}$$

$$y = \frac{1}{3}x - \frac{5}{3} - 5$$

$$y = \frac{1}{3}x - \frac{5}{3} - \frac{15}{3}$$

$$y = \frac{1}{3}x - \frac{20}{3}$$

standard form: $$y = \frac{1}{3}x - \frac{20}{3}$$

$$(3)y = (3)\frac{1}{3}x - (3)\frac{20}{3}$$

$$3y = x - 20$$

$$-x + 3y = -20$$

$$x - 3y = 20$$

79. parallel to $x + 3y = 6$

$$3y = -x + 6$$

$$\frac{3y}{3} = \frac{-x}{3} + \frac{6}{3}$$

$$y = \frac{-1}{3}x + 2$$

$$m = \frac{-1}{3}, \text{ parallel } m = \frac{-1}{3}$$

$$y - y_1 = m(x - x_1) \quad \text{point } (-4, -2)$$

$$y - (-2) = \frac{-1}{3}(x - (-4))$$

$$y + 2 = \frac{-1}{3}x - \frac{4}{3}$$

$$y = \frac{-1}{3}x - \frac{4}{3} - \frac{6}{3}$$

$$y = \frac{-1}{3}x - \frac{10}{3}$$

standard form: $$(3)y = (3)\frac{1}{3}x - (3)\frac{10}{3}$$

$$3y = -x - 10$$

$$x + 3y = -10$$

81. parallel to $3x - 4y = 0$

$$-4y = -3x$$

$$\frac{-4y}{-4} = \frac{-3x}{-4}$$

$$y = \frac{3}{4}x$$

$$m = \frac{3}{4}, \text{ parallel } m = \frac{3}{4}$$

$$y - y_1 = m(x - x_1) \qquad \text{point}\left(\frac{1}{3}, 2\right)$$

$$y - 2 = \frac{3}{4}\left(x - \frac{1}{3}\right)$$

$$y - 2 = \frac{3}{4}x - \frac{1}{4}$$

$$y = \frac{3}{4}x - \frac{1}{4} + 2$$

$$y = \frac{3}{4}x - \frac{1}{4} + \frac{8}{4}$$

$$y = \frac{3}{4}x + \frac{7}{4}$$

standard form : $(4)y = (\cancel{4})\dfrac{3}{\cancel{4}}x + (\cancel{4})\dfrac{7}{\cancel{4}}$

$$4y = 3x + 7$$

$$-3x + 4y = 7$$

$$3x - 4y = -7$$

83.

$$C(x) = 0.03x + 10$$

The competitor charges 0.03 per minute.

Let m = monthly charge

$$\$46.85 = 0.03(395) + m$$

$$\$46.85 = 11.85 + m$$

$$46.85 - 11.85 = m$$

$$35 = m$$

Competitor cost function: $C(x) = 0.03x + 35$

85. perpendicular to $x + y = 4$

$$y = -x + 4$$

$$m = -1, \text{ perpendicular } m = 1$$

$$y - y_1 = m(x - x_1) \qquad \text{point } (-3, 1)$$

$$y - 1 = 1(x - (-3))$$

$$y - 1 = 1x + 3$$

$$y = 1x + 3 + 1$$

$$y = x + 4$$

standard form: $\qquad y = x + 4$

$$-x + y = 4$$

$$x - y = -4$$

87. perpendicular to $x + 2y = 5$

$$2y = -x + 5$$

$$\frac{2y}{2} = \frac{-x}{2} + \frac{5}{2}$$

$$y = \frac{-1}{2}x + \frac{5}{2}$$

$$m = \frac{-1}{2}, \text{ perpendicular } m = +2$$

$$y - y_1 = m(x - x_1) \qquad \text{point } (-2, 0)$$

$$y - 0 = 2(x - (-2))$$

$$y = 2x + 4$$

standard form: $\qquad y = 2x + 4$

$$-2x + y = 4$$

$$2x - y = -4$$

89. perpendicular to $5x + y = 8$

$$y = -5x + 8$$

$$m = -5, \text{ perpendicular } m = +\frac{1}{5}$$

$$y - y_1 = m(x - x_1) \qquad \text{point } (-1, 2)$$

$$y - 2 = \frac{1}{5}(x - (-1))$$

$$y - 2 = \frac{1}{5}x + \frac{1}{5}$$

$$y = \frac{1}{5}x + \frac{1}{5} + 2$$

$$y = \frac{1}{5}x + \frac{1}{5} + \frac{10}{5}$$

$$y = \frac{1}{5}x + \frac{11}{5}$$

standard form: $\qquad (5)y = (\cancel{5})\dfrac{1}{\cancel{5}}x - (\cancel{5})\dfrac{11}{\cancel{5}}$

$$5y = x + 11$$

$$-x + 5y = 11$$

$$x - 5y = -11$$

91.   perpendicular to $5x - y = 10$

$$-y = -5x + 10$$

$$\frac{-y}{-1} = \frac{-5x}{-1} + \frac{10}{-1}$$

$$y = 5x - 10$$

$m = 5$, perpendicular $m = \frac{-1}{5}$

$$y - y_1 = m(x - x_1) \quad \text{point} \left(\frac{1}{2}, 3\right)$$

$$y - 3 = \frac{-1}{5}\left(x - \frac{1}{2}\right)$$

$$y - 3 = \frac{-1}{5}x + \frac{1}{10}$$

$$y = \frac{-1}{5}x + \frac{1}{10} + 3$$

$$y = \frac{-1}{5}x + \frac{1}{10} + \frac{30}{10}$$

$$y = \frac{-1}{5}x + \frac{31}{10}$$

standard form: $y = \frac{-1}{5}x + \frac{31}{10}$

$$(10)y = (10)\frac{-1}{5}x + (10)\frac{31}{10}$$

$$10y = -2x + 31$$

$$2x + 10y = 31$$

93.   perpendicular to $4x - y = 8$

$$-y = -4x + 8$$

$$\frac{-y}{-1} = \frac{-4x}{-1} + \frac{8}{-1}$$

$$y = 4x - 8$$

$m = 4$, perpendicular $m = \frac{-1}{4}$

$$y - y_1 = m(x - x_1) \quad \text{point} \left(4, -\frac{1}{2}\right)$$

$$y - \frac{-1}{2} = \frac{-1}{4}(x - 4)$$

$$y + \frac{1}{2} = \frac{-1}{4}x + 1$$

$$y = \frac{-1}{4}x + 1 - \frac{1}{2}$$

$$y = \frac{-1}{4}x + \frac{2}{2} - \frac{1}{2}$$

$$y = \frac{-1}{4}x + \frac{1}{2}$$

standard form: $y = \frac{-1}{4}x + \frac{1}{2}$

$$(4)y = (4)\frac{-1}{4}x + (4)\frac{1}{2}$$

$$4y = -x + 2$$

$$x + 4y = 2$$

95. $(3, 6)$ and $(-1, 4)$

$$d = \sqrt{(x_2 - x_1)^2 + (y_2 - y_1)^2}$$

$$d = \sqrt{(-1 - 3)^2 + (4 - 6)^2}$$

$$d = \sqrt{(-4)^2 + (-2)^2}$$

$$d = \sqrt{16 + 4}$$

$$d = \sqrt{20}$$

$$d = 4.472$$

97. $(3, -3)$ and $(0, 7)$

$d = \sqrt{(x_2 - x_1)^2 + (y_2 - y_1)^2}$

$d = \sqrt{(0-3)^2 + (7-(-3))^2}$

$d = \sqrt{(-3)^2 + 10^2}$

$d = \sqrt{9 + 100}$

$d = \sqrt{109}$

$d = 10.440$

99. $(0, 0)$ and $(-3, 5)$

$d = \sqrt{(x_2 - x_1)^2 + (y_2 - y_1)^2}$

$d = \sqrt{(-3-0)^2 + (5-0)^2}$

$d = \sqrt{(-3)^2 + 5^2}$

$d = \sqrt{9 + 25}$

$d = \sqrt{34}$

$d = 5.831$

101. $(5, 2)$ and $(-3, -3)$

$d = \sqrt{(x_2 - x_1)^2 + (y_2 - y_1)^2}$

$d = \sqrt{(-3-5)^2 + (-3-2)^2}$

$d = \sqrt{(-8)^2 + (-5)^2}$

$d = \sqrt{64 + 25}$

$d = \sqrt{89}$

$d = 9.434$

103. $(-5, -4)$ and $(2, -2)$

$d = \sqrt{(x_2 - x_1)^2 + (y_2 - y_1)^2}$

$d = \sqrt{(2-(-5))^2 + (-2-(-4))^2}$

$d = \sqrt{7^2 + 2^2}$

$d = \sqrt{49 + 4}$

$d = \sqrt{53}$

$d = 7.280$

105. $(3, 6)$ and $(-1, 4)$

$\text{midpoint} = \left(\dfrac{x_1 + x_2}{2}, \dfrac{y_1 + y_2}{2} \right)$

$= \left(\dfrac{3 + (-1)}{2}, \dfrac{6 + 4}{2} \right)$

$= \left(\dfrac{2}{2}, \dfrac{10}{2} \right)$

$\text{midpoint} = (1, 5)$

107. $(3, -3)$ and $(0, 7)$

$\text{midpoint} = \left(\dfrac{x_1 + x_2}{2}, \dfrac{y_1 + y_2}{2} \right)$

$= \left(\dfrac{3 + 0}{2}, \dfrac{-3 + 7}{2} \right)$

$= \left(\dfrac{3}{2}, \dfrac{4}{2} \right)$

$\text{midpoint} = \left(1\dfrac{1}{2}, 2 \right)$

109. $(0, 0)$ and $(-3, 5)$

$\text{midpoint} = \left(\dfrac{x_1 + x_2}{2}, \dfrac{y_1 + y_2}{2} \right)$

$= \left(\dfrac{0 + (-3)}{2}, \dfrac{0 + 5}{2} \right)$

$= \left(\dfrac{-3}{2}, \dfrac{5}{2} \right)$

$\text{midpoint} = \left(-1\dfrac{1}{2}, 2\dfrac{1}{2} \right)$

111. $(5, 2)$ and $(-3, -3)$

$\text{midpoint} = \left(\dfrac{x_1 + x_2}{2}, \dfrac{y_1 + y_2}{2} \right)$

$= \left(\dfrac{5 + (-3)}{2}, \dfrac{2 + (-3)}{2} \right)$

$= \left(\dfrac{2}{2}, -\dfrac{1}{2} \right)$

$\text{midpoint} = \left(1, -\dfrac{1}{2} \right)$

113. $(-5, -4)$ and $(2, -2)$

$$\text{midpoint} = \left(\frac{x_1 + x_2}{2}, \frac{y_1 + y_2}{2} \right)$$

$$= \left(\frac{-5 + 2}{2}, \frac{-4 + (-2)}{2} \right)$$

$$= \left(\frac{-3}{2}, \frac{-6}{2} \right)$$

$$\text{midpoint} = \left(-1\frac{1}{2}, -3 \right)$$

115. (a)

Lipsticks	Cost
x	y
0	5,000
100	5,453
1,000	9,530
2,000	14,060

$4.53(0) + 5,000 = 5,000$

$4.53(100) + 5,000 = 453 + 5,000 = 5,453$

$4.53(1,000) + 5,000 = 4,530 + 5,000 = 9,530$

$4.53(2,000) + 5,000 = 9,060 + 5,000 = 14,060$

117.

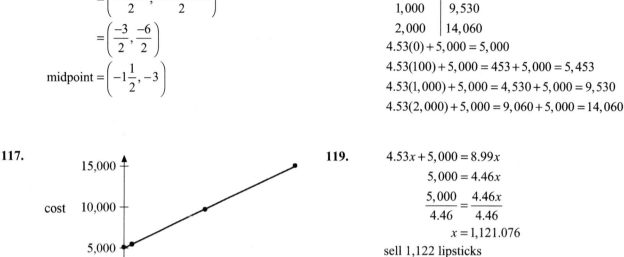

119.

$$4.53x + 5,000 = 8.99x$$

$$5,000 = 4.46x$$

$$\frac{5,000}{4.46} = \frac{4.46x}{4.46}$$

$$x = 1,121.076$$

sell 1,122 lipsticks

Chapter 19 Trial Test

1. $(-3, 6)$ and $(3, 2)$

$$m = \frac{y_2 - y_1}{x_2 - x_1} = \frac{2 - 6}{3 - (-3)} = \frac{-4}{6} = -\frac{2}{3}$$

3. $(1, -5)$ and $(3, 0)$

$$m = \frac{y_2 - y_1}{x_2 - x_1} = \frac{0 - (-5)}{3 - 1} = \frac{5}{2}$$

5. $(-1, -1)$ and $(2, 2)$

$$m = \frac{y_2 - y_1}{x_2 - x_1} = \frac{2 - (-1)}{2 - (-1)} = \frac{3}{3} = 1$$

7. $(1,000, 5,230)$ $(20,000, 9,600)$

$$m = \frac{y_2 - y_1}{x_2 - x_1} = \frac{9,600 - 5,230}{20,000 - 1,000} = \frac{4,370}{19,000} = 0.23$$

Variable cost = \$0.23

9. $(3, -5) \quad m = \dfrac{2}{3}$

$$y - y_1 = m(x - x_1)$$

$$y - (-5) = \frac{2}{3}(x - 3)$$

$$y + 5 = \frac{2}{3}x - 2$$

$$y = \frac{2}{3}x - 2 - 5$$

$$y = \frac{2}{3}x - 7$$

11. $(1, 3) \ \text{and} \ (4, 5)$

$$m = \frac{y_2 - y_1}{x_2 - x_1} = \frac{5 - 3}{4 - 1} = \frac{2}{3}$$

$$y - y_1 = m(x - x_1)$$

$$y - 3 = \frac{2}{3}(x - 1)$$

$$y - 3 = \frac{2}{3}x - \frac{2}{3}$$

$$y = \frac{2}{3}x - \frac{2}{3} + 3$$

$$y = \frac{2}{3}x - \frac{2}{3} + \frac{9}{3}$$

$$y = \frac{2}{3}x + \frac{7}{3}$$

13. $(5, 2) \ \text{and} \ (-1, 2)$

$$m = \frac{y_2 - y_1}{x_2 - x_1} = \frac{2 - 2}{-1 - 5} = \frac{0}{-6} = 0$$

horizontal line
$y = 2$

15. $y = 3x - 22$

slope $\quad m = 3$

y-intercept $\quad b = -22$

17. $C(x) = 9.7x + 50$

fixed cost: $b = \$50$

unit cost: $m = \$9.70$

19. $-2x + y = 34$

$y = 2x + 34$

$m = 2; \ b = 34$

21. $x = 4y$

$4y = x$

$$\frac{4y}{4} = \frac{x}{4}$$

$$y = \frac{1}{4}x$$

$$m = \frac{1}{4} \quad b = 0$$

23. $\dfrac{1}{3}y + 2x = 1$

$(3)\dfrac{1}{3}y + (3)2x = (3)1$

$y + 6x = 3$

$y = -6x + 3$

$m = -6 \quad b = 3$

25. $m = \dfrac{3}{2} \quad b = 3$

$y = mx + b$

$$y = \frac{3}{2}x + 3$$

27. parallel to $2x + y = 4$

$y = -2x + 4$

$m = -2$, parallel $m = -2$

$y - y_1 = m(x - x_1) \qquad$ point $(4, -3)$

$y - (-3) = -2(x - 4)$

$y + 3 = -2(x - 4)$

$y + 3 = -2x + 8$

$y = -2x + 8 - 3$

$y = -2x + 5$

standard form: $\qquad y = -2x + 5$

$2x + y = 5$

29.   perpendicular to $2x + y = 4$

$$y = -2x + 4$$

$$m = -2, \text{ perpendicular } m = \frac{1}{2}$$

$$y - y_1 = m(x - x_1) \quad \text{point } (4, -3)$$

$$y - (-3) = \frac{1}{2}(x - 4)$$

$$y + 3 = \frac{1}{2}x - 2$$

$$y = \frac{1}{2}x - 2 - 3$$

$$y = \frac{1}{2}x - 5$$

standard form: $y = \frac{1}{2}x - 5$

$$(2)y = (2)\frac{1}{2}x - (2)5$$

$$2y = x - 10$$

$$-x + 2y = -10$$

$$x - 2y = 10$$

31. $(-2, 1)$ and $(3, 3)$

$$d = \sqrt{(x_2 - x_1)^2 + (y_2 - y_1)^2} \qquad \text{midpoint} = \left(\frac{x_1 + x_2}{2}, \frac{y_1 + y_2}{2} \right)$$

$$d = \sqrt{(3 - (-2))^2 + (3 - 1)^2} \qquad = \left(\frac{-2 + 3}{2}, \frac{1 + 3}{2} \right)$$

$$d = \sqrt{5^2 + 2^2}$$

$$d = \sqrt{25 + 4} \qquad\qquad\qquad = \left(\frac{1}{2}, \frac{4}{2} \right)$$

$$d = \sqrt{29}$$

$$d = 5.385 \qquad\qquad \text{midpoint} = \left(\frac{1}{2}, 2 \right)$$

chapter 20

Systems of Linear Equations and Inequalities

ASSIGNMENT EXERCISES

1.

$x + y = 8$

$x - y = 2$

$x + y = 8$

$y = -x + 8$

$m = \dfrac{-1}{1}$ $b = 8$

Solution $(5, 3)$

$x - y = 2$

$-y = -x + 2$

$\dfrac{-y}{-1} = \dfrac{-x}{-1} + \dfrac{2}{-1}$

$y = x - 2$

$m = \dfrac{1}{1}$ $b = -2$

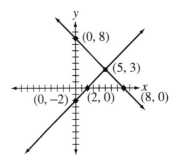

3.

$2x + 2y = 10$

$3x + 3y = 15$

$2x + 2y = 10$

$2y = -2x + 10$

$\dfrac{2y}{2} = \dfrac{-2x}{2} + \dfrac{10}{2}$

$y = -1x + 5$

$m = \dfrac{-1}{1}$ $b = 5$

MANY SOLUTIONS;
dependent; lines coincide

$3x + 3y = 15$

$3y = -3x + 15$

$\dfrac{3y}{3} = \dfrac{-3x}{3} + \dfrac{15}{3}$

$y = -1x + 5$

$y = \dfrac{-1}{1}$ $b = 5$

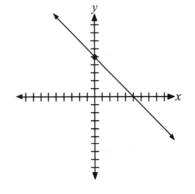

5. $2x - y = 5$
          $4x - 2y = 2$

NO SOLUTION;
inconsistent;
lines are parallel

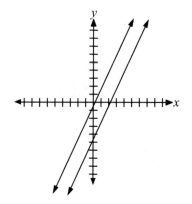

$2x - y = 5$
   $-y = -2x + 5$
   $\dfrac{-y}{-1} = \dfrac{-2x}{-1} + \dfrac{5}{-1}$
     $y = 2x - 5$
$m = \dfrac{2}{1}$ $b = -5$

$4x - 2y = 2$
   $-2y = -4x + 2$
   $\dfrac{-2y}{-2} = \dfrac{-4x}{-2} + \dfrac{2}{-2}$
     $y = 2x - 1$
$m = \dfrac{2}{1}$ $b = -1$

7. $2x + y < 6$
          and
          $x - y < 1$

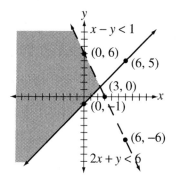

$2x + y < 6$
   $y < -2x + 6$
$m = \dfrac{-2}{1}$ $b = 6$
dotted line
test: $(0, 0)$
$2(0) + 0 < 6$
  $0 + 0 < 6$
    $0 < 6$ true
      shade!
test: $(5, 0)$
$2(5) + 0 < 6$
  $10 + 0 < 6$
    $10 < 6$ false

$x - y < 1$
  $-y < -x + 1$
  $\dfrac{-y}{-1} < \dfrac{-x}{-1} + \dfrac{1}{-1}$
   $y > x - 1$
$m = \dfrac{1}{1}$ $b = -1$
dotted line
test: $(0, 0)$
$0 - 0 < 1$
  $0 < 1$ true
    shade!
test: $(5, 0)$
$5 - 0 < 1$
  $5 < 1$ false

9. $2x + y > 3$
          and
          $x - y \le 1$

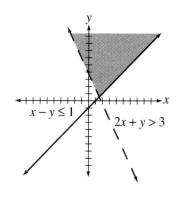

$2x + y > 3$
   $y > -2x + 3$
$m = \dfrac{-2}{1}$ $b = 3$
dotted line
test: $(0, 0)$
$2(0) + 0 > 3$
  $0 + 0 > 3$
    $0 > 3$ false

$x - y \le 1$
  $-y \le -x + 1$
  $\dfrac{-y}{-1} \le \dfrac{-x}{-1} + \dfrac{1}{-1}$
   $y \ge x - 1$
$m = \dfrac{1}{1}$ $b = -1$
solid line
test: $(0, 0)$
$0 - 0 \le 1$
  $0 \le 1$ true
    shade!

(continued)

9. *(continued)*

test: $(5, 0)$	test: $(5, 0)$
$2(5) + 0 > 3$	$5 - 0 \le 1$
$10 + 0 > 3$	$5 \le 1$ false
$10 > 3$ true	
shade!	

11.

$$3x + y = 9$$
$$2x - y = 6$$
$$3x + y = 9$$
$$\underline{2x - y = 6}$$
$$5x \quad = 15$$
$$\frac{5x}{5} = \frac{15}{5}$$
$$x = 3$$

$$3x + y = 9$$
$$3(3) + y = 9$$
$$9 + y = 9$$
$$y = 9 - 9$$
$$y = 0$$
$$x = 3, \, y = 0$$
$$(3, 0)$$

13.

$$Q = 2P + 8$$
$$2Q + 3P = 2$$

$$-2(Q - 2P = 8)$$
$$2Q + 3P = 2$$

$$-2\cancel{Q} + 4P = -16$$
$$\cancel{2Q} + 3P = 2$$
$$\overline{}$$
$$7P = -14$$
$$P = -2$$

$$Q = 2P + 8$$
$$Q = 2(-2) + 8$$
$$Q = -4 + 8$$
$$Q = 4$$
$$P = -2, \, Q = 4$$
$$(-2, 4)$$

15.

$$r = 2y + 6$$
$$2r + y = 2$$

$$r - 2y = 6$$
$$2(2r + y = 2)$$

$$r - 2\cancel{y} = 6$$
$$4r \cancel{+} 2y = 4$$
$$\overline{}$$
$$5r \quad = 10$$
$$r = 2$$

$$r = 2y + 6$$
$$2 = 2y + 6$$
$$-4 = 2y$$
$$-2 = y$$
$$r = 2, \, y = -2$$
$$(2, -2)$$

17.

$$c = 2y$$
$$2c + 3y = 21$$

$$-2(c - 2y = 0)$$
$$2c + 3y = 21$$

$$-2\cancel{c} + 4y = 0$$
$$\cancel{2c} + 3y = 21$$
$$\overline{}$$
$$7y = 21$$
$$y = 3$$

$$c = 2y$$
$$c = 2(3)$$
$$c = 6$$
$$c = 6, \, y = 3$$
$$(6, 3)$$

19. $3R - 2S = 7$

$-14 = -6R + 4S$

$-2(3R - 2S = 7)$ $-6R + 4S = -14$

$\quad\quad 6R - 4S = 14$ $\quad\;\; 6R - 4S = 14$

$\qquad\qquad\qquad\qquad\quad\quad\quad 0 = 0 \;\; \text{true}$

Dependent

MANY SOLUTIONS

21. $c = 2 + 3d$

$3c - 14 = d$

$-3(c - 3d = 2)$ $-3c + 9d = -6$ $c = 2 + 3d$

$\quad\quad 3c - d = 14$ $\quad\; 3c - d = 14$ $c = 2 + 3(1)$

$\qquad\qquad\qquad\qquad\quad\quad\;\; 8d = 8$ $c = 2 + 3$

$\qquad\qquad\qquad\qquad\quad\quad\;\;\; d = 1$ $c = 5$

$\qquad\qquad\qquad\qquad\qquad\qquad\qquad\quad\;\; c = 5, \; d = 1$

$\qquad\qquad\qquad\qquad\qquad\qquad\qquad\quad\;\; (5, 1)$

23. $x - 18 = -6y$

$4x - 0 = 3y$

$x + 6y = 18$ $x + 6y = 18$ $x - 18 = -6y$

$2(4x - 3y = 0)$ $8x - 6y = 0$ $2 - 18 = -6y$

$\qquad\qquad\qquad\qquad\quad 9x \quad\;\; = 18$ $-16 = -6y$

$\qquad\qquad\qquad\qquad\quad\quad x = 2$ $\dfrac{-16}{-6} = \dfrac{-6y}{-6}$

$\qquad\qquad\qquad\qquad\qquad\qquad\qquad\qquad \dfrac{8}{3} = y$

$\qquad\qquad\qquad\qquad\qquad\qquad\qquad x = 2, \; y = \dfrac{8}{3}$

$\qquad\qquad\qquad\qquad\qquad\qquad\qquad \left(2, \dfrac{8}{3}\right)$

25. $3a - 2b = 6$

$6a - 12 = b$

$3a - 2b = 6$ $3a - 2b = 6$ $3a - 2b = 6$

$-2(6a - b = 12)$ $-12a + 2b = -24$ $3(2) - 2b = 6$

$\qquad\qquad\qquad\qquad -9a \quad\quad = -18$ $6 - 2b = 6$

$\qquad\qquad\qquad\qquad\quad\quad a = 2$ $-2b = 0$

$\qquad\qquad\qquad\qquad\qquad\qquad\qquad\qquad\quad b = 0$

$\qquad\qquad\qquad\qquad\qquad\qquad\quad a = 2, \; b = 0$

$\qquad\qquad\qquad\qquad\qquad\qquad\quad (2, 0)$

27. $x + 2y = 7$
$x - y = 1$

$x + 2y = 7$
$2(x - y = 1)$

$x + 2y = 7$
$2x - 2y = 2$
$\overline{\qquad\qquad}$
$3x \quad\;\; = 9$
$x = 3$

$x + 2y = 7$
$3 + 2y = 7$
$2y = 4$
$y = 2$
$x = 3,\; y = 2$
$(3, 2)$

29. $x + 2r = 5.5$
$2x = 1.5r$

$-2(x + 2r = 5.5)$
$2x - 1.5r = 0$

$-2x - 4r = -11$
$2x - 1.5r = 0$
$\overline{\qquad\qquad}$
$-5.5r = -11$
$r = 2$

$x + 2r = 5.5$
$x + 2(2) = 5.5$
$x + 4 = 5.5$
$x = 1.5$
$r = 2,\; x = 1.5$
$(1.5, 2)$

31. $a + 7b = 32$
$3a - b = 8$

$a + 7b = 32$
$a = 32 - 7b$

$3a - b = 8$
$3(32 - 7b) - b = 8$
$96 - 21b - b = 8$
$96 - 22b = 8$
$-22b = -88$
$b = 4$

$a + 7b = 32$
$a + 7(4) = 32$
$a + 28 = 32$
$a = 4$
$a = 4,\; b = 4$
$(4, 4)$

33. $c - d = 2$
$c = 12 - d$

$c - d = 2$
$(12 - d) - d = 2$
$12 - d - d = 2$
$12 - 2d = 2$
$-2d = -10$
$d = 5$

$c = 12 - d$
$c = 12 - 5$
$c = 7$
$c = 7,\; d = 5$
$(7, 5)$

35. $7x - 4 = -4y$
$3x + y = 6$

$3x + y = 6$
$y = 6 - 3x$

$7x - 4 = -4y$
$7x - 4 = -4(6 - 3x)$
$7x - 4 = -24 + 12x$
$-5x = -20$
$x = 4$

$7x - 4 = -4y$
$7(4) - 4 = -4y$
$28 - 4 = -4y$
$24 = -4y$
$-6 = y$
$x = 4,\; y = -6$
$(4, -6)$

37. $a = 2b + 11$

$3a + 11 = -5b$

$3a + 11 = -5b$	$a = 2b + 11$
$3(2b + 11) + 11 = -5b$	$a = 2(-4) + 11$
$6b + 33 + 11 = -5b$	$a = -8 + 11$
$44 = -11b$	$a = 3$
$-4 = b$	$a = 3,\ b = -4$
	$(3, -4)$

39. $c = 2q$

$2c + q = 2$

$2c + q = 2$	$c = 2q$
$2(2q) + q = 2$	$c = 2\left(\dfrac{2}{5}\right)$
$4q + q = 2$	
$5q = 2$	$c = \dfrac{4}{5}$
$q = \dfrac{2}{5}$	$c = \dfrac{4}{5},\ q = \dfrac{2}{5}$
	$\left(\dfrac{4}{5}, \dfrac{2}{5}\right)$

41. $4x - 2.5y = 2$

$2x - 1.5y = -10$

$2x - 1.5y = -10$	$4x - 2.5y = 2$	$4x - 2.5y = 2$
$2x = 1.5y - 10$	$4(0.75y - 5) - 2.5y = 2$	$4x - 2.5(44) = 2$
$\dfrac{2x}{2} = \dfrac{1.5y}{2} - \dfrac{10}{2}$	$3y - 20 - 2.5y = 2$	$4x - 110 = 2$
$x = 0.75y - 5$	$0.5y = 22$	$4x = 112$
	$y = 44$	$x = 28$
		$x = 28,\ y = 44$
		$(28, 44)$

43. $4d - 7 = -c$

$3c - 6 = -6d$

$4d - 7 = -c$	$3c - 6 = -6d$	$4d - 7 = -c$
$\dfrac{4d}{-1} - \dfrac{7}{-1} = \dfrac{-c}{-1}$	$3(-4d + 7) - 6 = -6d$	$4\left(\dfrac{5}{2}\right) - 7 = -c$
$-4d + 7 = c$	$-12d + 21 - 6 = -6d$	$10 - 7 = -c$
	$-12d + 15 = -6d$	$3 = -c$
	$15 = 6d$	$c = -3$
	$\dfrac{15}{6} = d$	$c = -3,\ d = \dfrac{5}{2}$
	$d = \dfrac{5}{2}$	$\left(-3, \dfrac{5}{2}\right)$

45.
$$3.5a + 2b = 2$$
$$0.5b = 3 - 1.5a$$

$$3.5a + 2b = 2$$
$$2b = -3.5a + 2$$
$$\frac{2b}{2} = \frac{-3.5a}{2} + \frac{2}{2}$$
$$b = -1.75a + 1$$

$$0.5b = 3 - 1.5a$$
$$0.5(-1.75a + 1) = 3 - 1.5a$$
$$-0.875a + 0.5 = 3 - 1.5a$$
$$0.625a = 2.5$$
$$a = 4$$

$$3.5a + 2b = 2$$
$$3.5(4) + 2b = 2$$
$$14 + 2b = 2$$
$$2b = -12$$
$$b = -6$$
$$a = 4, \; b = -6$$
$$(4, -6)$$

47.
$$x + 4y = 20$$
$$4x + 5y = 58$$

$$x + 4y = 20$$
$$x = 20 - 4y$$

$$4x + 5y = 58$$
$$4(20 - 4y) + 5y = 58$$
$$80 - 16y + 5y = 58$$
$$80 - 11y = 58$$
$$-11y = -22$$
$$y = 2$$

$$x + 4y = 20$$
$$x + 4(2) = 20$$
$$x + 8 = 20$$
$$x = 12$$
$$x = 12, \; y = 2$$
$$(12, 2)$$

49.
$$3a + 1 = -2b$$
$$4b + 23 = 15a$$

$$3a + 1 = -2b$$
$$\frac{3a}{-2} + \frac{1}{-2} = \frac{-2b}{-2}$$
$$\frac{-3}{2}a - \frac{1}{2} = b$$

$$4b + 23 = 15a$$
$$4\left(\frac{-3}{2}a - \frac{1}{2}\right) + 23 = 15a$$
$$-6a - 2 + 23 = 15a$$
$$-6a + 21 = 15a$$
$$21 = 21a$$
$$1 = a$$
$$a = 1$$

$$3a + 1 = -2b$$
$$3(1) + 1 = -2b$$
$$3 + 1 = -2b$$
$$4 = -2b$$
$$-2 = b$$
$$b = -2$$
$$a = 1, \; b = -2$$
$$(1, -2)$$

51.
let x = pay per electrician
y = pay per apprentice

$$3x + 4y = 365$$
$$x + 2y = 145$$

$$3x + 4y = 365$$
$$-3(x + 2y = 145)$$

$$3x + 4y = 365$$
$$-3x - 6y = -435$$
$$\overline{-2y = -70}$$
$$y = 35$$

$$x + 2y = 145$$
$$x + 2(35) = 145$$
$$x + 70 = 145$$
$$x = 75$$
electrician pay = \$75
apprentice pay = \$35

53. let x = cost of each quart of shellac

$\quad\quad y$ = cost of each quart of thinner

$2x + 5y = 22.50$

$3x + 2y = 14.50$

$3(2x + 5y = 22.50)$ $6x + 15y = 67.50$ $2x + 5y = 22.50$
$-2(3x + 2y = 14.50)$ $-6x - 4y = -29.00$ $2x + 5(3.50) = 22.50$

$\quad\quad\quad\quad\quad\quad\quad\quad\quad\quad 11y = 38.50$ $2x + 17.50 = 22.50$

$\quad\quad\quad\quad\quad\quad\quad\quad\quad\quad\quad y = 3.50$ $2x = 5.00$

$\quad\quad\quad\quad\quad\quad\quad\quad\quad\quad\quad\quad\quad\quad\quad\quad\quad x = 2.50$

$\quad\quad\quad\quad\quad\quad\quad\quad\quad\quad\quad\quad\quad\quad$ cost of shellac = \$2.50

$\quad\quad\quad\quad\quad\quad\quad\quad\quad\quad\quad\quad\quad\quad$ cost of thinner = \$3.50

55. let x = angle

$\quad\quad y$ = angle

$x + y = 175$

$x - y = 63$

$x + y = 175$ $x + y = 175$
$x - y = 63$ $119 + y = 175$

$2x \quad = 238$ $y = 56$

$\quad x = 119$ larger angle = $119°$

$\quad\quad\quad\quad\quad\quad\quad$ smaller angle = $56°$

57. let x = investment at 5%

$\quad\quad y$ = investment at 6%

$\quad\quad x + y = 5,000$

$0.05x + 0.06y = 280$

$x + y = 5,000$ $0.05x + 0.06y = 280$ $x + y = 5,000$
$\quad x = 5,000 - y$ $0.05(5,000 - y) + 0.06y = 280$ $x + 3,000 = 5,000$

$\quad\quad\quad\quad\quad\quad\quad\quad 250 - 0.05y + 0.06y = 280$ $x = 2,000$

$\quad\quad\quad\quad\quad\quad\quad\quad\quad\quad\quad\quad 0.01y = 30$ amount at 5% = \$2,000

$\quad\quad\quad\quad\quad\quad\quad\quad\quad\quad\quad\quad y = 3,000$ amount at 6% = \$3,000

59. let x = cost per pound of Colombian coffee

$\quad\quad y$ = cost per pound of blended coffee

$30x + 10y = 190$

$20x + 5y = 120$

$30x + 10y = 190$ $30x + 10y = 190$ $30x + 10y = 190$
$-2(20x + 5y = 120)$ $-40x - 10y = -240$ $30(5) + 10y = 190$

$\quad\quad\quad\quad\quad\quad\quad\quad -10x \quad\quad = -50$ $150 + 10y = 190$

$\quad\quad\quad\quad\quad\quad\quad\quad\quad\quad x = 5$ $10y = 40$

$\quad\quad\quad\quad\quad\quad\quad\quad\quad\quad\quad\quad\quad\quad\quad y = 4$

$\quad\quad\quad\quad\quad\quad\quad\quad\quad\quad\quad\quad\quad\quad$ cost of Colombian coffee = \$5

$\quad\quad\quad\quad\quad\quad\quad\quad\quad\quad\quad\quad\quad\quad$ cost of blended coffee = \$4

61.   let x = cost of Ohio map

   y = cost of Alaska map

$25x + 8y = 65.55$

$20x + 5y = 49.50$

$-5(25x + 8y = 65.55)$

$8(20x + 5y = 49.50)$

$-125x - 40y = -327.75$

$160x + 40y = 396.00$

$\overline{35x = 68.25}$

$x = 1.95$

$25(1.95) + 8y = 65.55$

$48.75 + 8y = 65.55$

$8y = 16.80$

$y = 2.10$

cost of Ohio map = \$1.95

cost of Alaska map = \$2.10

63.   let x = name brand suit cost

   y = generic label suit cost

$-1(20x + 35y = 12,525)$

$30x + 35y = 15,725$

$-20x - 35y = -12,525$

$30x + 35y = 15,725$

$\overline{10x = 3,200}$

$x = 320$

$20(320) + 35y = 12,525$

$6,400 + 35y = 12,525$

$35y = 6,125$

$y = 175$

name brand suit cost = \$320

generic label suit cost = \$175

65.   let x = telephone sales

   y = show room sales

$x + y = 40,000$

$0.05x + 0.06y = 2,250$

$-5(x + y = 40,000)$

$100(0.05x + 0.06y = 2,250)$

$-5x - 5y = -200,000$

$5x + 6y = 225,000$

$\overline{y = 25,000}$ showroom sales

$x + y = 40,000$

$x + 25,000 = 40,000$

$x = 15,000$ telephone sales

telephone sales = \$15,000

show room sales = \$25,000

67.   let x = gallons of 75% fertilizer

   y = gallons of 25% fertilizer

$x + y = 8$

$0.75x + 0.25y = 4$ (50% of 8 gallons = 4)

$x + y = 8$

$-4(0.75x + 0.25y = 4)$

$x + y = 8$

$-3x - y = -16$

$\overline{-2x = -8}$

$x = 4$ gal of 75% fertilizer

$x + y = 8$

$4 + y = 8$

$y = 4$ gal of 25% fertilizer

4 gallons of each fertilizer is needed.

69.   Solve by addition: $2c + 3d = 9$ and $3c + d = 10$

$2c + 3d = 9$

$3c + d = 10$ (multiply by -3)

$$2c + 3d = 9$$
$$\underline{-9c - 3d = -30}$$
$$-7c = -21$$
$$c = 3$$

$$2c + 3d = 9$$
$$2(3) + 3d = 9$$
$$6 + 3d = 9$$
$$3d = 3$$
$$d = 1$$

check: $2c + 3d = 9$

$2(3) + 3(1) = 9$

$6 + 3 = 9$

$9 = 9$

$3c + d = 10$

$3(3) + (1) = 10$

$9 + 1 = 10$

$10 = 10$ $(3, 1)$

71.   Answers will vary.

Three boxes of golf balls and five boxes of tees cost \$28. The difference in the price of the box of golf balls and the box of tees is \$4. Find the cost of each.

$3x + 5y = 28$

$5(x - y = 4)$

$$3x + 5y = 28$$
$$\underline{5x - 5y = 20}$$
$$8x = 48$$
$$x = 6$$

$$3(6) + 5y = 28$$
$$18 + 5y = 28$$
$$5y = 10$$
$$y = 2 \quad (6, 2)$$

check: $x - y = 4$

$6 - 2 = 4$

$4 = 4$

Chapter 20 Trial Test

1. $2a + b = 10$

$a - b = 5$

$2a + b = 10$

$b = -2a + 10$

$m = \dfrac{-2}{1}$ $y\text{-intercept} = 10$

$a - b = 5$

$-b = -a + 5$

$\dfrac{-b}{-1} = \dfrac{-a}{-1} + \dfrac{5}{-1}$

$b = a - 5$

$m = \dfrac{1}{1}$ $y\text{-intercept} = -5$

$(5, 0)$

3. $3x + 4y = 6$

$x + y = 5$

$3x + 4y = 6$

$4y = -3x + 6$

$\dfrac{4y}{4} = \dfrac{-3x}{4} + \dfrac{6}{4}$

$y = \dfrac{-3}{4}x + \dfrac{3}{2}$

$m = \dfrac{-3}{4} \quad b = 1\dfrac{1}{2}$

$(14, -9)$

$x + y = 5$

$y = -x + 5$

$m = -1 \quad b = 5$

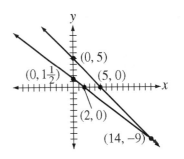

5. $2c - 3d = 6$

$c - 12 = 3d$

$2c - 3d = 6$

$-3d = -2c + 6$

$\dfrac{-3d}{-3} = \dfrac{-2c}{-3} + \dfrac{6}{-3}$

$d = \dfrac{2}{3}c - 2$

$m = \dfrac{2}{3} \quad b = -2$

$c - 12 = 3d$

$3d = c - 12$

$\dfrac{3d}{3} = \dfrac{c}{3} - \dfrac{12}{3}$

$d = \dfrac{1}{3}c - 4$

$m = \dfrac{1}{3} \quad b = -4$

$(-6, -6)$

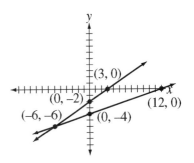

7. $x + y < 4$

and

$y > 3x + 2$

$x + y < 4$

$y < -x + 4$

$m = -1 \quad b = 4$

dotted line

test: $(0, 0)$

$0 + 0 < 4$

$0 < 4$ true

shade!

test: $(5, 0)$

$5 + 0 < 4$

$5 < 4$ false

$y > 3x + 2$

$m = 3 \quad b = 2$

dotted line

test: $(0, 0)$

$0 > 3(0) + 2$

$0 > 0 + 2$

$0 > 2$ false

test: $(-5, 0)$

$0 > 3(-5) + 2$

$0 > -15 + 2$

$0 > -13$

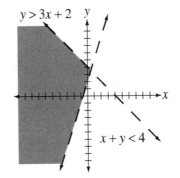

9. $p + 2m = 0$
$2p = -m$

$-2(p + 2m = 0)$ $-2p - 4m = 0$ $p + 2m = 0$
$\quad\quad 2p + m = 0$ $\quad\;\; 2p + \;\; m = 0$ $p + 2(0) = 0$
$\rule{4cm}{0.4pt}$ $p + 0 = 0$
$-3m = 0$ $p = 0$
$m = 0$ $p = 0,\, m = 0$
$(0, 0)$

11. $3x + y = 5$
$2x - y = 0$

$3x + y = 5$ $3x + y = 5$
$2x - y = 0$ $3(1) + y = 5$
$\rule{3cm}{0.4pt}$ $3 + y = 5$
$5x \quad\;\; = 5$ $y = 2$
$x = 1$ $x = 1,\, y = 2$
$(1, 2)$

13. $4x + 3y = 14$
$x - y = 0$

$x - y = 0$ $4x + 3y = 14$ $x - y = 0$
$x = y$ $4(y) + 3y = 14$ $x - 2 = 0$
$4y + 3y = 14$ $x = 2$
$7y = 14$ $x = 2,\, y = 2$
$y = 2$ $(2, 2)$

15. $7p + r = -6$
$3p + r = 6$

$7p + r = -6$ $3p + r = 6$ $7p + r = -6$
$\quad\quad r = -6 - 7p$ $3p + (-6 - 7p) = 6$ $7(-3) + r = -6$
$-4p - 6 = 6$ $-21 + r = -6$
$-4p = 12$ $r = 15$
$p = -3$ $p = -3,\, r = 15$
$(-3, 15)$

17. $38 + d = -3a$
$5a + 1 = 4d$

$4(3a + d = -38)$ $12a + 4d = -152$ $38 + d = -3a$
$\quad\quad 5a - 4d = -1$ $\quad\;\; 5a - 4d = -1$ $38 + d = -3(-9)$
$\rule{4cm}{0.4pt}$ $38 + d = 27$
$17a \quad\quad = -153$ $d = -11$
$a = -9$ $a = -9,\, d = -11$
$(-9, -11)$

19.   let x = current

y = current

$x + y = 35$

$x - y = 5$

$x + \cancel{y} = 35$

$x \cancel{-} y = 5$

—————

$2x \quad = 40$

$\qquad x = 20$

$x + y = 35$

$20 + y = 35$

$y = 15$

larger current = 20 A

smaller current = 15 A

21.   let x = length

y = width

$x = 1.5y$

$x - y = 17$

$x - y = 17$

$(1.5y) - y = 17$

$0.5y = 17$

$y = 34$

$x = 1.5y$

$x = 1.5(34)$

$x = 51$

length = 51 in.

width = 34 in.

23.   let x = 3.5% investment

y = 4.0% investment

$x + y = 25,000$ Equation 1

$0.035x + 0.04y = 900$ Equation 2

$-35(x + y) = 25,000(-35)$ Equation 1

$1000(0.035x + 0.04y) = 900(1000)$ Equation 2

$-35x - 35y = -875,000$ Equation 1

$35x + 40y = 900,000$ Equation 2

$5y = 25,000$ Sum of Equations 1 and 2

$y = 5,000$

$x + y = 25,000$

$x + 5,000 = 25,000$

$x = 25,000 - 5,000$

$x = 20,000$

$20,000 invested at 3.5%

$5,000 invested at 4%

25.   let x = capacitance = 0.000215 F

y = capacitance = 0.000055 F

$x + y = 0.00027$

$x - y = 0.00016$

$x + \cancel{y} = 0.00027$

$x \cancel{-} y = 0.00016$

—————

$2x \quad = 0.00043$

$\qquad x = 0.000215$

$x + y = 0.00027$

$0.000215 + y = 0.00027$

$y = 0.000055$

ASSIGNMENT EXERCISES

1. Line AB

$\overleftrightarrow{AB}$

3. Ray AB

$\overrightarrow{AB}$

5. $\overrightarrow{NO}$

7. $\overline{MN}$ is *not* the same as $\overline{MO}$ because one of the endpoints of the segment is different.

9. $\overrightarrow{NO}$ is *not* the same as $\overrightarrow{NM}$ because their directions are different.

11. $\overleftrightarrow{AB} \parallel \overleftrightarrow{CD}$

13. $\overleftrightarrow{GH}$ intersects $\overleftrightarrow{EF}$

15. Yes, $\overleftrightarrow{IJ}$ *is* the same as $\overleftrightarrow{KJ}$.

17. $\angle b \cong \angle EDF$
or
$\angle FDE$

19. $\angle a \cong \angle P$

21. $\angle c \cong \angle M$

23. $90°$ right

25. $18°$ acute

27. $180°$ straight

29. $179°$ obtuse

31. $63° + 37° = 100°$; neither

33. $135° + 45° = 180°$; supplementary

35. $21° + 79° = 100°$; neither

37. Congruent angles have *equal* measures.

39. Perpendicular lines are formed when a *horizontal* and a *vertical* line intersect.

41.
$$
\begin{array}{r}
115°\,34'\,29'' \\
-\;\;84°\,26'\,18'' \\
\hline
31°\;\;\;8'\,11''
\end{array}
$$

43.
$$
\begin{array}{r}
64°\,15'\,37'' \\
-\;29°\,37'\,41''
\end{array}
$$

$$
\begin{array}{r}
14'\;\;97'' \\
64°\;\cancel{15}'\;\cancel{37}'' \\
-\;29°\;\;37'\;\;41'' \\
\hline
56''
\end{array}
\longrightarrow
\begin{array}{r}
74' \\
63°\;\cancel{14}'\;97'' \\
\cancel{64}°\;\cancel{15}'\;\cancel{37}'' \\
-\;29°\;\;37'\;\;41'' \\
\hline
34°\;37'\;56''
\end{array}
$$

45.
$$
\begin{array}{r}
74° \\
-\;13°\,19'\,42''
\end{array}
$$

$$
\begin{array}{r}
59'\;\;60'' \\
73°\;\;\cancel{60}' \\
\cancel{74}° \\
-13°\;\;19'\;\;42'' \\
\hline
60°\;\;40'\;\;18''
\end{array}
$$

47. 29′ to decimal degree, ten-thousandth

$$29' = \frac{29°}{60} = 0.4833°$$

49. 7′34″

$$7'34'' = 7' + \frac{34'}{60} = 7.5667'$$

$$= \frac{7.5667°}{60} = 0.1261°$$

51. 0.75° minutes and seconds

$$0.75° = 0.75(60)' = 45'$$

53. 0.2176° minutes and seconds

$$0.2176° = 0.2176(60)' = 13.056'$$

$$= 13' + 0.056(60)''$$

$$= 13'3''$$

55.

$$\begin{array}{r} 23° \quad\; 20' \\ 6\overline{|140°} \\ \underline{138°} \\ 2° \to 120' \\ \underline{120'} \\ 0' \end{array}$$

57.

$$\begin{array}{r} 18° \quad 39' \quad 50.5'' \\ 2\overline{|37°\quad 19'\quad 41''} \\ \underline{36°} \\ 1° \to \underline{60'} \\ 79' \\ \underline{78'} \\ 1' \to \underline{60''} \\ 101'' \\ \underline{100''} \\ 1'' \end{array}$$

59. isosceles

61. largest angle is 80°, thus longest side is $\overline{ST}$

smallest angle is 42°, thus shortest side is $\overline{RS}$

63. order of sides: 15, 13, 7.5

thus angles: ∠C, ∠B, ∠A

65. ∠B ≅ ∠E

∠C ≅ ∠D

BC = DE or ED

67. ∠J ≅ ∠M

JL = MP

JK = MN

69. RT = 15 cm (hyp)

$$\text{leg} = \frac{\text{hyp}\sqrt{2}}{2}$$

$$\text{leg} = \frac{15\sqrt{2}}{2}$$

$$\text{leg} = 10.607$$

$$RS = ST = 10.607 \text{ cm}$$

71. RT = $9\sqrt{2}$ hm (hyp)

$$\text{leg} = \frac{\text{hyp}\sqrt{2}}{2}$$

$$\text{leg} = \frac{9\sqrt{2} \cdot \sqrt{2}}{2} = \frac{9 \cdot 2}{2} = 9$$

$$RS = ST = 9 \text{ hm}$$

73. AC = 12 dm   (side opposite 60°)

(side opp. 60°) = (side opp. 30°) × $\sqrt{3}$

12 = (side opp. 30°) × $\sqrt{3}$

$$\frac{12}{\sqrt{3}} = \text{side opp. } 30° = BC$$

6.928 = side opp. 30° = BC

AB = hyp = (side opp. 30°)(2)

AB = hyp = 6.928(2)

AB = hyp = 13.856

$\qquad$ AB = 13.856 dm

$\qquad$ BC = 6.928 dm

75.   BC = 10 in.   (30° side)

AB = hyp = (30° side) × 2   AC = (60° side) = (30° side) × $\sqrt{3}$

AB = hyp = 10 × 2   AC = (60° side) = 10 × $\sqrt{3}$

AB = hyp = 20 in.   AC = (60° side) = 17.321

AB = 20 in.   AC = 17.321 in.

77.   AC = 40 ft 7 in. = $40\frac{7}{12}$ ft or $\frac{487}{12}$ ft   (60° side)

(60° side) = (30° side) × $\sqrt{3}$ AB = hyp = (30° side) × 2

$\frac{487}{12}$ = (30° side) × $\sqrt{3}$ AB = hyp = 23.43079842 × 2

$\frac{487}{12\sqrt{3}}$ = 30° side = BC   AB = hyp = 46.86159685

23.43079842 = 30° side = BC $\left(\dfrac{487\sqrt{3}}{18}\right)$

23.431 = 30° side = BC   AB = hyp = 46 ft 10 in.

23 ft 5 in. = 30° side = BC   AB = 46 ft 10 in.

79.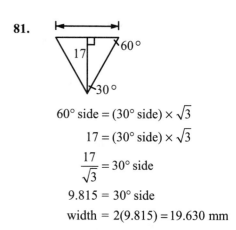

hyp = (30° side) × 2

hyp = 14 × 2

hyp = 28 in.   (BC)

AB + BC + CD

(AB + CD) + BC   60° side = (30° side)$\left(\sqrt{3}\right)$

71.751 in. + 28 in.   60° side = 14$\sqrt{3}$

99.751 in.   60° side = 24.249 in.   (BE)

100 in.

8 ft 4 in.

XY − BE = (AB + CD)

8 ft − 24.249 in. = (AB + CD)

96 in. − 24.249 in. = (AB + CD)

71.751 in. = (AB + CD)

total length of conduit ABCD is 100 in. or 8 ft 4 in.

81.

60° side = (30° side) × $\sqrt{3}$

17 = (30° side) × $\sqrt{3}$

$\frac{17}{\sqrt{3}}$ = 30° side

9.815 = 30° side

width = 2(9.815) = 19.630 mm

83. $p = 5(23) = 115$ in.

Area of $\Delta = \dfrac{1}{2} bh$

Area of $\Delta = \dfrac{1}{2} (23)(15.8)$

Area of $\Delta = 181.7$ in^2

5Δ Area $= 5(181.7) = 908.5$ in^2

85.   regular pentagon

degrees of
each angle
$= \dfrac{180(n-2)}{n}$ where n is number of sides

$= \dfrac{180(5-2)}{5}$

$= \dfrac{180(3)}{5}$

$= 108°$

87. $P = 28 + 12 + 12 + 13 + 40 + 25$

$P = 130$ ft

89. $A = (5\text{ ft }6\text{ in.} \times 9\text{ ft }6\text{ in.}) + (7\text{ ft} \times 4\text{ ft }4\text{ in.})$

$A = (5.5\text{ ft} \times 9.5\text{ ft}) + (7\text{ ft} \times 4.333\text{ ft})$

$A = 52.25 + 30.331$

$A = 82.581$ ft$^2 \approx 83$ ft^2

12 ft 6 in.

−5 ft 6 in.

7 ft

91. $A = (10 \times 8) + (10 \times 16) + (10 \times 24) + (10 \times 32)$

$A = 80 + 160 + 240 + 320$

$A = 800$ in^2

$\dfrac{800\ \text{in}^2}{1} \left(\dfrac{1\ \text{ft}^2}{144\ \text{in}^2} \right) = 6\ \text{ft}^2$

$\dfrac{6\ \text{ft}^2}{1} \left(\dfrac{6\ \text{bricks}}{1\ \text{ft}^2} \right) = 36\ \text{bricks}$

36 bricks $\times$ 2 sides = 72 bricks total

93. $\angle = 45°9' = 45 + \dfrac{9°}{60} = 45.15°$

$r = 2.58$ cm

$A = \dfrac{\theta}{360} \pi r^2$

$A = \dfrac{45.15}{360} \pi (2.58)^2$

$A = 2.62$ cm^2

95. $\angle = 15°15' = 15 + \dfrac{15°}{60} = 15.25°$

$r = 110$ mm

$A = \dfrac{\theta}{360} \pi r^2$

$A = \dfrac{15.25}{360} \pi (110)^2$

$A = 1{,}610.28$ mm^2

97. $\angle = 40°$

$r = 2\dfrac{1}{2}$ ft = 2.5 ft

$A = \dfrac{\theta}{360}\pi r^2$

$A = \dfrac{40}{360}\pi (2.5)^2$

$A = 2.18$ ft^2

99. $\angle = 45°$

$r = 14$ mm

$h = 12.9$ mm

$b = 10.9$ mm

$A = \dfrac{\theta}{360}\pi r^2 - \dfrac{1}{2}bh$

$A = \dfrac{45}{360}\pi (14)^2 - \dfrac{1}{2}(10.9)(12.9)$

$A = 76.97 - 70.31$

$A = 6.66$ mm^2

101. $\angle = 30°$

$r = 24$ cm

$h = 23.2$ cm

$b = 12.4$ cm

$A = \dfrac{\theta}{360}\pi r^2 - \dfrac{1}{2}bh$

$A = \dfrac{30}{360}\pi (24)^2 - \dfrac{1}{2}(12.4)(23.2)$

$A = 150.80 - 143.84$

$A = 6.96$ cm^2

103. $A = \dfrac{\theta}{360}\pi r^2 - \dfrac{1}{2}bh$

$A = \dfrac{137}{360}\pi (14.5)^2 - \dfrac{1}{2}(27)(5.29)$

$A = 251.3645005 - 71.415$

$A = 179.9495005$ mm^2 or 179.9 mm^2

Area of lens $= \pi r^2 - 179.9495005$

$\qquad\qquad = \pi (14.5)^2 - 179.9495005$

$\qquad\qquad = 660.5198554 - 179.9495005$

$\qquad\qquad = 480.5703549$ mm^2

$\qquad\qquad = 480.57$ mm^2

105.   Area of rounded corner

$A = \dfrac{\theta}{360}\pi r^2$

$A = \dfrac{90}{360}\pi (6)^2$

$A = 28.27$ ft^2

Area of rectangle

$A = lw$

$A = 20(12) = 240$ ft^2

$A_{corner} = 6(6) = 36$ ft^2

240 ft$^2 - 36$ ft$^2 = 204$ ft^2

$A = 204$ ft$^2 + 28.27$ ft^2

$A = 232.27$ ft^2

107. $A = \dfrac{\theta}{360}\pi r^2 - \dfrac{1}{2}bh$

$A = \dfrac{106}{360}\pi (10)^2 - \dfrac{1}{2}(16)(6)$

$A = 92.50 - 48$

$A = 44.50$ in^2

109. $\angle = 180°$

$r = 10$ in.

$s = \dfrac{\theta}{360}(2\pi r)$

$s = \dfrac{180}{360}(2)\pi (10)$

$s = 31.42$ in.

111. $\angle - 70°10' = 70 + \dfrac{10}{60}° = 70.17°$

$r = 30$ mm

$s = \dfrac{\theta}{360}(2\pi r)$

$s = \dfrac{70.17}{360}(2)\pi (30)$

$s = 36.74$ mm

113. $AB = 10, \ AE = ?$

$$AE = \frac{1}{2}AB = \frac{1}{2}(10)$$

$$AE = 5$$

115. $\angle GJO = \frac{1}{2}\angle GJI$

$$\angle GJO = \frac{1}{2}(90°)$$

$$\angle GJO = 45°$$

117. $KO = 10, \ IJ = ?$

$$KO = \frac{1}{2} \ \text{side}$$

$$10 = \frac{1}{2} \ \text{side}$$

$$2(10) = 2\left(\frac{1}{2} \ \text{side}\right)$$

$$20 = \text{side}$$

$$IJ = 20$$

119. $\angle MOP = ?$

$$\text{each angle} = \frac{180(n-2)}{n} = \frac{180(6-2)}{6}$$

$$\text{each angle} = \frac{180(4)}{6}$$

$$\text{each angle} = 120°$$

$$\angle LMN = 120°$$

$$\angle OMN = \frac{1}{2}\angle LMN = \frac{1}{2}(120°) = 60°$$

$$\angle OPM = 90°$$

$$\angle MOP = 30°$$

121. $d = 20 \ \text{mm}$, thus $r = 10 \ \text{mm}$

$$r = \frac{2}{3}h$$

$$10 = \frac{2}{3}h$$

$$(3)10 = (3)\frac{2}{3}h$$

$$30 = 2h$$

$$15 = h$$

height of Δ is 15 mm

$$r = \frac{1}{3}h$$

$$r = \frac{1}{3}(15)$$

$$r = 5 \ \text{mm}$$

123.

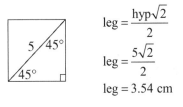

$$\text{leg} = \frac{\text{hyp}\sqrt{2}}{2}$$

$$\text{leg} = \frac{5\sqrt{2}}{2}$$

$$\text{leg} = 3.54 \ \text{cm}$$

125. $A_{\text{square}} = (7.07)^2 = 50 \ \text{cm}^2$

$$A_{\text{circle}} = \pi(5)^2 = 78.54 \ \text{cm}^2$$

The area will be *between* the area of the pentagon of the inscribed square, 50 cm², and the area of the circle, 78.54 cm².

$$A_{\text{hexagon}} = 6(0.5)(5)(4.33) = 64.95 \ \text{cm}^2$$
$$A_{\text{circle}} = \pi(5)^2 = 78.54 \ \text{cm}^2$$

The area of the inscribed regular octagon will be *between* the area of an inscribed hexagon, 64.95 cm², and the area of the circle, 78.54 cm².

Chapter 21 Trial Test

1. $\overline{BC}$ **3.** 42°
acute

5. parallel   **7.** perpendicular
(and intersecting)

9.
$$3\overline{\smash{\big)}47°\;16'\;28''} \quad \begin{array}{ccc} 15° & 45' & 29'' \end{array}$$
$$\underline{3}$$
$$17$$
$$\underline{15}$$
$$2 \;\rightarrow\; \underline{120'}$$
$$136'$$
$$\underline{135'}$$
$$1' \rightarrow \underline{60''}$$
$$88''$$
$$\underline{87''}$$
$$1''$$

11.
$$0.3125° = 0.3125(60)'$$
$$= 18.75'$$
$$= 18' + 0.75(60'')$$
$$= 18'45''$$

13. largest $\angle A$
smallest $\angle B$

15.

$$\text{hyp} = \text{leg}\sqrt{2}$$
$$\text{hyp} = 4\sqrt{2}$$
$$\text{hyp} = 5.657 \text{ cm} = BC$$

$$ABEK = AB + BE + EK = 12$$
$$\text{if } BE = 4$$
$$\text{then } AB + EK = 8$$
$$\text{and } CD = EK$$
$$\text{thus } AB + CD = 8$$
$$ABCD = AB + BC + CD$$
$$ABCD = (AB + CD) + BC$$
$$ABCD = 8 + 5.657$$
$$ABCD = 13.657 \text{ cm}$$

17.

$$p = \begin{array}{rr} 22 \text{ ft} & 6 \text{ in.} \\ 15 \text{ ft} & 6 \text{ in.} \\ 23 \text{ ft} & 0 \text{ in.} \\ 16 \text{ ft} & 6 \text{ in.} \\ 4 \text{ ft} & 0 \text{ in.} \\ 2 \text{ ft} & 0 \text{ in.} \\ 41 \text{ ft} & 6 \text{ in.} \\ +\; 30 \text{ ft} & 0 \text{ in.} \\ \hline 153 \text{ ft} & 24 \text{ in.} \\ +\; 2 \text{ ft} & -24 \text{ in.} \\ \hline 155 \text{ ft} & \end{array}$$

19.
$$\text{degrees} = 180°(8 - 2)$$
$$\text{degrees} = 180°(6)$$
$$\text{degrees} = 1,080°$$
$$\left(\frac{\text{each}}{\text{angle}} = \frac{1,080°}{8} = 135° \right)$$

21.
$$s = \frac{\theta}{360}(2\pi r)$$
$$s = \frac{55}{360}(2)\pi(45)$$
$$s = 43.20 \text{ mm}$$

23.
$$r = \frac{1}{3}h \qquad C = 2\pi r$$
$$\qquad\qquad C = 2\pi(4)$$
$$r = \frac{1}{3}(12) \qquad C = 25.13 \text{ in.}$$
$$r = 4 \text{ in.}$$

25.
$$d = \frac{1}{2} \text{ in.}$$
$$r = \frac{1}{4} \text{ in.} = 0.25 \text{ in.}$$
$$C = 2\pi r$$
$$C = 2\pi(0.25)$$
$$C = 1.57 \text{ in.}$$

Introduction to Trigonometry

ASSIGNMENT EXERCISES

1. $60° = 60°\left(\dfrac{\pi \text{ rad}}{180°}\right) = \dfrac{\pi}{3}\text{rad}$

or

$= 1.05 \text{ rad}$

3. $300° = 300°\left(\dfrac{\pi \text{ rad}}{180°}\right) = \dfrac{5\pi}{3}\text{rad}$

$= 5.24 \text{ rad}$

5. $99°45' = 99 + \dfrac{45°}{60} = 99.75°$

$99.75° = 99.75°\left(\dfrac{\pi \text{ rad}}{180°}\right) = 1.74 \text{ rad}$

7. $\dfrac{5\pi}{6}\text{ rad}$

$\dfrac{5\pi}{6}\left(\dfrac{180°}{\pi}\right) = 150°$

9. 1.7 rad

$1.7\left(\dfrac{180°}{\pi}\right) = 97.4028°$

11. $\dfrac{3\pi}{8}\text{ rad}$

$\dfrac{3\pi}{8}\left(\dfrac{180°}{\pi}\right) = \dfrac{135}{2} = 67.5°$

$67.5° = 67°(0.5 \times 60)'$

$= 67°30'$

13. $\theta = 0.7 \text{ rad}$ $s = \theta r$

$r = 2.3 \text{ cm}$ $s = (0.7)(2.3)$

$s = 1.61 \text{ cm}$

15. $\theta = 2.1 \text{ rad}$ $s = \theta r$

$s = 3.6 \text{ ft}$ $3.6 = 2.1r$

$1.7143 = r$

$r = 1.71 \text{ ft}$

17. $\theta = 4.2 \text{ rad}$

$A = 24 \text{ in}^2$

$A = \dfrac{1}{2}\theta r^2$

$24 = \dfrac{1}{2}(4.2)r^2$

$(2)24 = (2)\dfrac{1}{2}(4.2)r^2$

$48 = 4.2r^2$

$r^2 = 11.4286$

$r = \sqrt{11.4286}$

$r = 3.38 \text{ in.}$

19. $s = \theta r$

$s = (0.35)(6)$

$s = 2.10 \text{ in.}$

21. $r = 4.6$ cm

$A = \dfrac{1}{2}\theta r^2$

$A = \dfrac{1}{2}(1.48)(4.6)^2$

$A = (0.5)(1.48)(21.16)$

$A = 15.66$ cm^2

23.
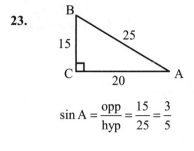

$\sin A = \dfrac{\text{opp}}{\text{hyp}} = \dfrac{15}{25} = \dfrac{3}{5}$

25.
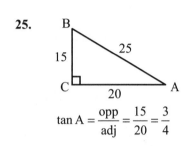

$\tan A = \dfrac{\text{opp}}{\text{adj}} = \dfrac{15}{20} = \dfrac{3}{4}$

27.
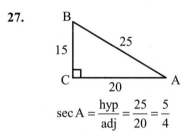

$\sec A = \dfrac{\text{hyp}}{\text{adj}} = \dfrac{25}{20} = \dfrac{5}{4}$

29.
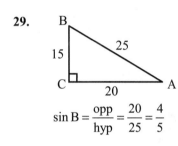

$\sin B = \dfrac{\text{opp}}{\text{hyp}} = \dfrac{20}{25} = \dfrac{4}{5}$

31.
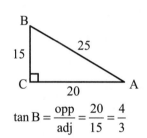

$\tan B = \dfrac{\text{opp}}{\text{adj}} = \dfrac{20}{15} = \dfrac{4}{3}$

33.
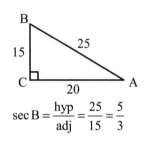

$\sec B = \dfrac{\text{hyp}}{\text{adj}} = \dfrac{25}{15} = \dfrac{5}{3}$

35.

10 in. $= \dfrac{10}{12}$ ft $= \dfrac{5}{6}$ ft   or

2 ft 2 in. $= 2 + \dfrac{2}{12}$ ft

$= 2\dfrac{1}{6}$ ft

2 ft 2 in. $= 2 \cdot 12 + 2$ in.

$= 26$ in.

$\sin A = \dfrac{\text{opp}}{\text{hyp}} = \dfrac{2}{2\dfrac{1}{6}}$

$= \dfrac{2}{1} \cdot \dfrac{6}{13} = \dfrac{12}{13}$

$\sin A = \dfrac{24}{26} = \dfrac{12}{13}$

37.

10 in. $= \dfrac{10}{12}$ ft $= \dfrac{5}{6}$ ft   or in inches

2 ft 2 in. $= 2 + \dfrac{2}{12}$ ft

$= 2\dfrac{1}{6}$ ft

$\cot B = \dfrac{\text{adj}}{\text{opp}} = \dfrac{2}{\dfrac{5}{6}}$

$= \dfrac{2}{1} \cdot \dfrac{6}{5} = \dfrac{12}{5}$

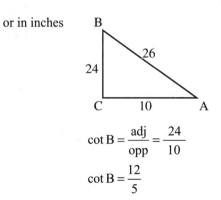

$\cot B = \dfrac{\text{adj}}{\text{opp}} = \dfrac{24}{10}$

$\cot B = \dfrac{12}{5}$

39.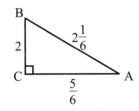

$$10 \text{ in.} = \frac{10}{12} \text{ ft} = \frac{5}{6} \text{ ft}$$

$$2 \text{ ft } 2 \text{ in.} = 2 + \frac{2}{12} \text{ ft}$$

$$= 2\frac{1}{6} \text{ ft}$$

$$\tan B = \frac{\text{opp}}{\text{adj}} = \frac{\frac{5}{6}}{2}$$

$$= \frac{5}{6} \cdot \frac{1}{2} = \frac{5}{12}$$

or in inches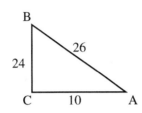

$$\tan B = \frac{\text{opp}}{\text{adj}} = \frac{10}{24} = \frac{5}{12}$$

41.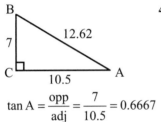

$$\cos B = \frac{\text{adj}}{\text{hyp}} = \frac{7}{12.62} = 0.5547$$

43.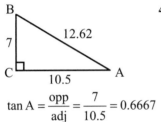

$$\tan A = \frac{\text{opp}}{\text{adj}} = \frac{7}{10.5} = 0.6667$$

45.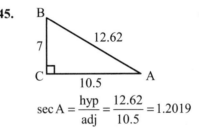

$$\sec A = \frac{\text{hyp}}{\text{adj}} = \frac{12.62}{10.5} = 1.2019$$

47.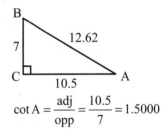

$$\cot A = \frac{\text{adj}}{\text{opp}} = \frac{10.5}{7} = 1.5000$$

49. $\sin 0.4712 = 0.4540$

51. $\cot 73° = \dfrac{1}{\tan 73°} = 0.3057$

53. $\tan 47° = 1.0724$

55. $\sin 0.8610 = 0.7585$

57. $\cos 32°50' = \cos\left(32 + \dfrac{50}{60}\right)^{\circ}$
$= \cos 32.8333°$
$= 0.8403$

59. $\cos 80°10' = \cos\left(80 + \dfrac{10}{60}\right)^{\circ}$
$= \cos 80.1667°$
$= 0.1708$

61. $\cos\theta = 0.6088$
$\theta = \cos^{-1}(0.6088)$
$\theta = 52.5°$

63. $\cot\theta = 0.9884$
$\tan\theta = \dfrac{1}{0.9884}$
$\tan\theta = 1.0117$
$\theta = \tan^{-1}(1.0117)$
$\theta = 45.3°$

65. $\cot\theta = 3.340$
$\tan\theta = \dfrac{1}{3.340}$
$\tan\theta = 0.2994$
$\theta = \tan^{-1}(0.2994)$
$\theta = 16.7°$

67. $\tan \theta = 2.723$

$\theta = \tan^{-1}(2.723)$

$\theta = 1.2188 \text{ rad}$

69. $\cot \theta = 0.3772$

$\tan \theta = \dfrac{1}{0.3772}$

$\tan \theta = 2.6511$

$\theta = \tan^{-1}(2.6511)$

$\theta = 1.2101 \text{ rad}$

71. $\tan \theta = 0.3440$

$\theta = \tan^{-1}(0.3440)$

$\theta = 0.3313 \text{ rad}$

73. $\csc 71° = \dfrac{1}{\sin 71°} = 1.0576$

75. $\csc 1.0821 = \dfrac{1}{\sin 1.0821} = 1.1326$

77. $\csc 0.4829 = \dfrac{1}{\sin 0.4829} = 2.1536$

79. $\csc 82°20' = \dfrac{1}{\sin 82°20'} = \dfrac{1}{\sin 82.3333} = 1.0090$

81. $\csc 1.235 = \dfrac{1}{\sin 1.235} = 1.0592$

83. $\sec 4.23 = \dfrac{1}{\cos 4.23} = -2.1557$

85.

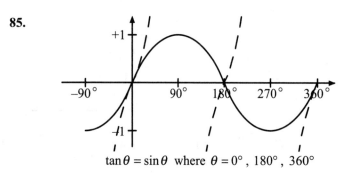

$\tan \theta = \sin \theta$ where $\theta = 0°,\ 180°,\ 360°$

Chapter 22 Trial Test

1. $35° = 35°\left(\dfrac{\pi \text{ rad}}{180°}\right) = \dfrac{7\pi}{36} \text{ rad}$

or

$= 0.61 \text{ rad}$

3. $315° = 315°\left(\dfrac{\pi \text{ rad}}{180°}\right) = \dfrac{7\pi}{4} \text{ rad}$

$= 5.50 \text{ rad}$

5. $15°25' = \left(15 + \dfrac{25}{60}\right)^{\circ}$

$= 15.4167°$

$= 15.4167°\left(\dfrac{\pi \text{ rad}}{180°}\right)$

$= 0.27 \text{ rad}$

7. $16°12' = \left(16 + \dfrac{12}{60}\right)^{\circ}$

$= 16.2°$

$= 16.2°\left(\dfrac{\pi \text{ rad}}{180°}\right)$

$= 0.28 \text{ rad}$

9. $\dfrac{5\pi}{8} \text{ rad} = \dfrac{5\cancel{\pi}}{8}\left(\dfrac{180°}{\cancel{\pi}}\right)$

$= 112.5°$

11. $1.2 \text{ rad} = 1.2\left(\dfrac{180°}{\pi}\right)$

$= 68.75493542°$

$= 68°(0.75493542 \times 60)'$

$= 68°45.29612494'$

$= 68°45' + 0.296149419''$

$= 68°45'17.7674952''$

$= 68°45'18''$

13. $\theta = 0.5$ $s = \theta r$

     $r = 2$ in. $s = 0.5(2)$

               $s = 1$ in.

15. $\theta = 1.7$ $s = \theta r$

     $s = 2.9$ m $2.9 = 1.7r$

               $\dfrac{2.9}{1.7} = r$

               $r = 1.71$ m

17.

$$\sin A = \frac{\text{opp}}{\text{hyp}} = \frac{10}{26} = \frac{5}{13}$$

19.

$$\csc A = \frac{\text{hyp}}{\text{opp}} = \frac{26}{10} = \frac{13}{5}$$

21.

$$\cos A = \frac{\text{adj}}{\text{hyp}} = \frac{11.5}{12.54} = 0.9171$$

23. $\sin 53° = 0.7986$

25. $\sin 1.1519 = 0.9135$

27. $\sin \theta = 0.2756$

       $\theta = \sin^{-1}(0.2756)$

       $\theta = 16.0°$

29. $\cos \theta = 0.9426$

       $\theta = \cos^{-1}(0.9426)$

       $\theta = 19.5°$

31. $\sin \theta = 0.7660$

       $\theta = \sin^{-1}(0.7660)$

       $\theta = 0.8726$

33. $\tan \theta = 0.3259$

       $\theta = \tan^{-1}(0.3259)$

       $\theta = 0.3150$

35. $\csc 47° = \dfrac{1}{\sin 47°} = 1.3673$

chapter 23   Right-Triangle Trigonometry

ASSIGNMENT EXERCISES

1.

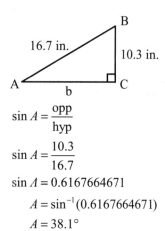

$$\sin A = \frac{\text{opp}}{\text{hyp}}$$

$$\sin A = \frac{10.3}{16.7}$$

$$\sin A = 0.6167664671$$

$$A = \sin^{-1}(0.6167664671)$$

$$A = 38.1°$$

3.

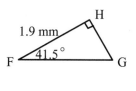

$$\cos F = \frac{\text{adj}}{\text{hyp}}$$

$$\cos 41.5 = \frac{1.9}{h}$$

$$0.7489557208 = \frac{1.9}{h}$$

$$(h)\ 0.7489557208 = \not{h}\left(\frac{1.9}{\not{h}}\right)$$

$$0.7489557208\ h = 1.9$$

$$h = \frac{1.9}{0.7489557208}$$

$$h = 2.537 \text{ mm}$$

5.

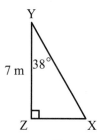

$$\tan Y = \frac{y}{x}$$

$$\tan 38 = \frac{y}{7}$$

$$y = 7\tan 38$$

$$y = 7(0.7812856265)$$

$$y = 5.468999386$$

$$y = 5.47 \text{ m}$$

7.

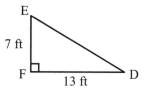

$$a^2 + b^2 = c^2$$

$$7^2 + 13^2 = c^2$$

$$49 + 169 = c^2$$

$$218 = c^2$$

$$\sqrt{218} = c$$

$$14.76 \text{ ft} = c$$

$$\tan D = \frac{\text{opp}}{\text{adj}}$$

$$\tan D = \frac{7}{13}$$

$$\tan D = 0.5384615385$$

$$D = \tan^{-1}(0.5384615385)$$

$$D = 28.3°$$

$$D + E = 90°$$

$$28.3° + E = 90°$$

$$E = 61.7°$$

9.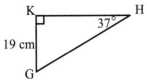

$$H + G = 90°$$
$$37° + G = 90°$$
$$G = 53°$$

$$\sin H = \frac{\text{opp}}{\text{hyp}}$$

$$\sin 37° = \frac{19}{k}$$

$$0.6018150232 = \frac{19}{h}$$

$$(k)(0.6018150232) = k\left(\frac{19}{k}\right)$$

$$0.6018150232\ k = 19$$

$$k = \frac{19}{0.6018150232}$$

$$k = 31.57 \text{ mm}$$

$$a^2 + b^2 = c^2$$
$$19^2 + g^2 = 31.57^2$$
$$361 + g^2 = 996.6649$$
$$g^2 = 635.6649$$
$$g = \sqrt{635.6649}$$
$$g = 25.21 \text{ cm}$$

11. Find A

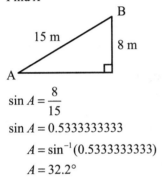

$$\sin A = \frac{8}{15}$$
$$\sin A = 0.5333333333$$
$$A = \sin^{-1}(0.5333333333)$$
$$A = 32.2°$$

13. Find a

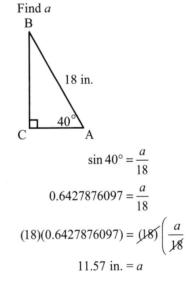

$$\sin 40° = \frac{a}{18}$$

$$0.6427876097 = \frac{a}{18}$$

$$(18)(0.6427876097) = (18)\left(\frac{a}{18}\right)$$

$$11.57 \text{ in.} = a$$

15.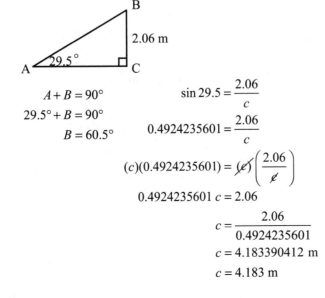

$$A + B = 90°$$
$$29.5° + B = 90°$$
$$B = 60.5°$$

$$\sin 29.5 = \frac{2.06}{c}$$

$$0.4924235601 = \frac{2.06}{c}$$

$$(c)(0.4924235601) = (c)\left(\frac{2.06}{c}\right)$$

$$0.4924235601\ c = 2.06$$

$$c = \frac{2.06}{0.4924235601}$$

$$c = 4.183390412 \text{ m}$$

$$c = 4.183 \text{ m}$$

$$a^2 + b^2 = c^2$$
$$(2.06)^2 + b^2 = (4.183390412)^2$$
$$4.244 + b^2 = 17.50075534$$
$$b^2 = 13.25675534$$
$$b = \sqrt{13.26}$$
$$b = 3.640982744$$
$$b = 3.641 \text{ m}$$

17.

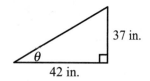

$$\tan\theta = \frac{37}{42}$$

$$\tan\theta = 0.880952381$$

$$\theta = \tan^{-1}(0.880952381)$$

$$\theta = 41.3785153°$$

$$\theta = 41.4°$$

two acute angles: 41.4°, 48.6°

$$90° - 41.4° = 48.6°$$

19.

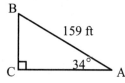

$$A + B = 90°$$

$$34° + B = 90°$$

$$B = 56°$$

$$\sin 34° = \frac{a}{159}$$

$$0.559129035 = \frac{a}{159}$$

$$(159)(0.559129035) = (159)\left(\frac{a}{159}\right)$$

$$88.91167165 = a$$

$$88.91 \text{ ft} = a$$

$$a^2 + b^2 = c^2$$

$$(88.91167165)^2 + b^2 = 159^2$$

$$7905.285356 + b^2 = 25,281$$

$$b^2 = 17,375.71464$$

$$b = \sqrt{17,376}$$

$$b = 131.816974$$

$$b = 131.8 \text{ ft}$$

21.

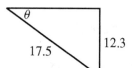

$$\sin\theta = \frac{\text{opp}}{\text{hyp}}$$

$$\sin\theta = \frac{12.3}{17.5}$$

$$\sin\theta = 0.7028571429$$

$$\theta = \sin^{-1}(0.7028571429)$$

$$\theta = 44.65668483°$$

$$\theta = 44.7°$$

23.

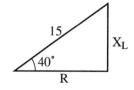

$$\sin 40° = \frac{\text{opp}}{\text{hyp}}$$

$$\sin 40° = \frac{X_L}{15}$$

$$15(\sin 40°) = X_L$$

$$X_L = 15(0.6427876097)$$

$$X_L = 9.641814145$$

$$X_L = 9.64 \ \Omega$$

$$\cos 40° = \frac{\text{adj}}{\text{hyp}}$$

$$\cos 40° = \frac{R}{15}$$

$$R = 15\cos 40°$$

$$R = 15(0.7660444431)$$

$$R = 11.49066665$$

$$R = 11.49 \ \Omega$$

25.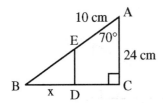

let $BE = y$

$\angle B = 20°$ $(A + B = 90°, A = 70°)$

$$\sin 20° = \frac{24}{y+10}$$

$$0.3420201433 = \frac{24}{y+10}$$

$$0.3420201433(y+10) = 24$$

$$0.3420201433y + 3.420201433 = 24$$

$$0.3420201433y = 20.57979857$$

$$y = \frac{20.57979857}{0.3420201433}$$

$$y = 60.17130561$$

$$y = 60.17 \text{ cm}$$

using smaller triangle:

$$\cos 20° = \frac{x}{60.17130561}$$

$$0.9396926208 = \frac{x}{60.17130561}$$

$$(60.17130561)(0.9396926208) = \cancel{(60.17130561)}\left(\frac{x}{\cancel{60.17130561}}\right)$$

$$56.54253186 \text{ cm} = x$$

$$BD = 56.54 \text{ cm}$$

Chapter 23 Trial Test

1. Find A

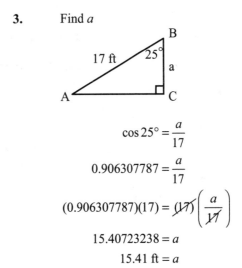

$$\tan A = \frac{16}{14}$$

$$\tan A = 1.142857143$$

$$A = \tan^{-1}(1.142857143)$$

$$A = 48.81407483°$$

$$A = 48.8°$$

3. Find a

$$\cos 25° = \frac{a}{17}$$

$$0.906307787 = \frac{a}{17}$$

$$(0.906307787)(17) = \cancel{(17)}\left(\frac{a}{\cancel{17}}\right)$$

$$15.40723238 = a$$

$$15.41 \text{ ft} = a$$

5.   Find A

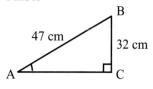

$$\sin A = \frac{32}{47}$$

$$\sin A = 0.6808510638$$

$$A = \sin^{-1}(0.6808510638)$$

$$A = 42.91018402$$

$$A = 42.9°$$

7.   Find a

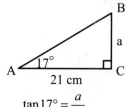

$$\tan 17° = \frac{a}{21}$$

$$0.3057306815 = \frac{a}{21}$$

$$(21)0.3057306815 = \cancel{(21)}\frac{a}{\cancel{21}}$$

$$6.420344311 = a$$

$$6.420 \text{ cm} = a$$

9.   Find A

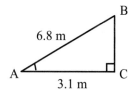

$$\cos A = \frac{3.1}{6.8}$$

$$\cos A = 0.4558823529$$

$$A = \cos^{-1}(0.4558823529)$$

$$A = 62.87827925$$

$$A = 62.9°$$

11.

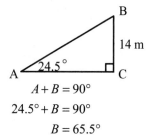

$$A + B = 90°$$

$$24.5° + B = 90°$$

$$B = 65.5°$$

$$\sin 24.5° = \frac{14}{c}$$

$$0.4146932427 = \frac{14}{c}$$

$$0.4146932427c = 14$$

$$c = \frac{14}{0.4146932427}$$

$$c = 33.75989421$$

$$c = 33.76 \text{ m}$$

$$a^2 + b^2 = c^2$$

$$14^2 + b^2 = 33.76^2$$

$$196 + b^2 = 1139.7376$$

$$b^2 = 943.7376$$

$$b = \sqrt{943.7376}$$

$$b = 30.7203125$$

$$b = 30.72 \text{ m}$$

13.

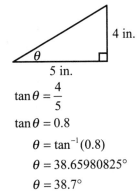

$$\tan\theta = \frac{4}{5}$$

$$\tan\theta = 0.8$$

$$\theta = \tan^{-1}(0.8)$$

$$\theta = 38.65980825°$$

$$\theta = 38.7°$$

15.

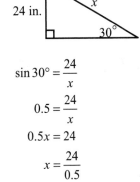

$$\sin 30° = \frac{24}{x}$$

$$0.5 = \frac{24}{x}$$

$$0.5x = 24$$

$$x = \frac{24}{0.5}$$

$$x = 48 \text{ in.}$$

17.

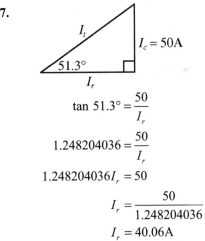

$$\tan 51.3° = \frac{50}{I_r}$$

$$1.248204036 = \frac{50}{I_r}$$

$$1.248204036 I_r = 50$$

$$I_r = \frac{50}{1.248204036}$$

$$I_r = 40.06\text{A}$$

19.

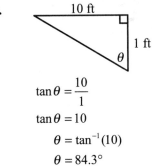

$$\tan\theta = \frac{10}{1}$$

$$\tan\theta = 10$$

$$\theta = \tan^{-1}(10)$$

$$\theta = 84.3°$$

Oblique Triangles

ASSIGNMENT EXERCISES

1. (4, 6)

magnitude	direction
$p^2 = x^2 + y^2$	$\tan\theta = \dfrac{y}{x}$
$p^2 = 4^2 + 6^2$	
$p^2 = 16 + 36$	$\tan\theta = \dfrac{6}{4}$
$p^2 = 52$	$\tan\theta = 1.5$
$p = \sqrt{52}$	$\theta = \tan^{-1}(1.5)$
$p = 7.211$	$\theta = 56.3°$

3. (6, 1)

magnitude	direction
$p^2 = x^2 + y^2$	$\tan\theta = \dfrac{y}{x}$
$p^2 = 6^2 + 1^2$	
$p^2 = 36 + 1$	$\tan\theta = \dfrac{1}{6}$
$p^2 = 37$	$\tan\theta = 0.1666666667$
$p = \sqrt{37}$	$\theta = \tan^{-1}(0.1666666667)$
$p = 6.083$	$\theta = 9.5°$

5. $(1 + 4i) + (6 + 8i) = 7 + 12i$

magnitude	direction
$p^2 = x^2 + y^2$	$\tan\theta = \dfrac{y}{x}$
$p^2 = 7^2 + 12^2$	
$p^2 = 49 + 144$	$\tan\theta = \dfrac{12}{7}$
$p^2 = 193$	$\tan\theta = 1.714285714$
$p = \sqrt{193}$	$\theta = \tan^{-1}(1.714285714)$
$p = 13.89$	$\theta = 59.7°$

7. related angle of 3.04 rad

3.04 rad

$\begin{array}{r} 3.1415926540 \text{ rad } (180°) \\ -3.0400000000 \text{ rad} \\ \hline 0.1015926536 \text{ rad} \end{array}$

9. related angle of 221°

$\begin{array}{r} 221° \\ -180° \\ \hline 41° \end{array}$

11. related angle of 5.4 rad

$\begin{array}{r} 6.283185307 \text{ rad } (2\pi) \\ -5.400000000 \text{ rad} \\ \hline 0.8831853072 \text{ rad} \end{array}$

13. related angle of 212°15′10″

$\begin{array}{r} 212°15′10″ \\ -180° \\ \hline 32°15′10″ \end{array}$

15. $\sin 2.1 = 0.8632$

196

17. $\sin 340° = -0.3420$

19. $\cos 290° = 0.3420$

21. $\tan \dfrac{5\pi}{4} = 1.000$

23. $(-2, 2)$

magnitude

$p^2 = x^2 + y^2$

$p^2 = (-2)^2 + (2)^2$

$p^2 = 4 + 4$

$p^2 = 8$

$p = \sqrt{8}$

$p = 2.83$

direction

$\tan \theta = \dfrac{y}{x}$

$\tan \theta = \dfrac{2}{-2}$

$\tan \theta = -1$

$\theta = \tan^{-1}(-1)$

$\theta = -0.7853981634$ rad   Reference angle must be in Quad II.

π rad $- 0.7853981634 = 2.35619449$ rad or 2.36 rad

25. $B = 120°, \ C = 20°, \ a = 8$

$A + B + C = 180°$

$A + 120° + 20° = 180°$

$A + 140° = 180°$

$A = 40°$

$\dfrac{a}{\sin A} = \dfrac{b}{\sin B}$

$\dfrac{8}{\sin 40°} = \dfrac{b}{\sin 120°}$

$\dfrac{8}{0.6427876097} = \dfrac{b}{0.8660254038}$

$0.6427876097b = 6.92820323$

$b = \dfrac{6.92820323}{0.6427876097}$

$b = 10.77837084$

$b = 10.8$

$\dfrac{a}{\sin A} = \dfrac{c}{\sin C}$

$\dfrac{8}{\sin 40°} = \dfrac{c}{\sin 20°}$

$\dfrac{8}{0.6427876097} = \dfrac{c}{0.3420201433}$

$0.6427876097c = 2.736161147$

$c = \dfrac{2.736161147}{0.6427876097}$

$c = 4.25671109$

$c = 4.3$

27. $a = 5, \ c = 7, \ C = 45°$

$\dfrac{a}{\sin A} = \dfrac{c}{\sin C}$

$\dfrac{5}{\sin A} = \dfrac{7}{\sin 45°}$

$\dfrac{5}{\sin A} = \dfrac{7}{0.7071067812}$

$7 \sin A = 3.535533906$

$\sin A = 0.5050762723$

$A = \sin^{-1}(0.5050762723)$

$A = 30.33641562°$

$A = 30.3°$

$A + B + C = 180°$

$30.3° + B + 45° = 180°$

$B + 75.3° = 180°$

$B = 104.7°$

$\dfrac{b}{\sin B} = \dfrac{c}{\sin C}$

$\dfrac{b}{\sin 104.7} = \dfrac{7}{\sin 45°}$

$\dfrac{b}{0.9672677528} = \dfrac{7}{0.7071067812}$

$0.7071067812b = 6.770874269$

$b = \dfrac{6.770874269}{0.7071067812}$

$b = 9.575462221$

$b = 9.6$

29.   Since we are given a, b, and B, and because $b < a$, there may be 2 solutions.

$a = 9.2$, $b = 6.8$, $B = 28°$

$$\frac{a}{\sin A} = \frac{b}{\sin B}$$

$$\frac{9.2}{\sin A} = \frac{6.8}{\sin 28°}$$

$$\frac{9.2}{\sin A} = \frac{6.8}{0.4694715628}$$

$$6.8 \sin A = 4.319138378$$

$$\sin A = 0.6351674085$$

$$A = \sin^{-1}(0.6351674085)$$

$$A = 39.43240195°$$

$$A = 39.4°$$

or

$$A = 180° - 39.4° = 140.6°$$

$$A + B + C = 180°$$

$$39.4° + 28° + C = 180°$$

$$C + 67.4° = 180°$$

$$C = 112.6°$$

$$\frac{b}{\sin B} = \frac{c}{\sin C}$$

$$\frac{6.8}{\sin 28°} = \frac{c}{\sin 112.6°}$$

$$\frac{6.8}{0.4694715628} = \frac{c}{0.9232102171}$$

$$0.4694715628c = 6.277829476$$

$$c = 13.37211873$$

$$c = 13.4$$

$$\boxed{\begin{array}{l} A = 39.4° \\ C = 112.6° \\ c = 13.4 \end{array}}$$

$$A + B + C = 180°$$

$$140.6° + 28° + C = 180°$$

$$C + 168.6° = 180°$$

$$C = 11.4°$$

$$\frac{b}{\sin B} = \frac{c}{\sin C}$$

$$\frac{6.8}{\sin 28°} = \frac{c}{\sin 11.4°}$$

$$\frac{6.8}{0.4694715628} = \frac{c}{0.1976573404}$$

$$0.4694715628c = 1.344069915$$

$$c = 2.862942127$$

$$c = 2.9$$

$$\boxed{\begin{array}{l} A = 140.6° \\ C = 11.4° \\ c = 2.9 \end{array}}$$

31.   Find RS

$$T + S + R = 180°$$

$$T + 38° + 25.1° = 180°$$

$$T + 63.1° = 180°$$

$$T = 116.9°$$

$$\frac{r}{\sin R} = \frac{s}{\sin S}$$

$$\frac{20}{\sin R} = \frac{29}{\sin 38°}$$

$$\frac{20}{\sin R} = \frac{29}{0.6156614753}$$

$$29 \sin R = 12.31322951$$

$$\sin R = 0.4245941209$$

$$R = \sin^{-1}(0.4245941209)$$

$$R = 25.1249753°$$

$$R = 25.1°$$

(continued)

31. *(continued)*

let $t = RS$

$$\frac{t}{\sin T} = \frac{s}{\sin S}$$

$$\frac{t}{\sin 116.9°} = \frac{29}{\sin 38°}$$

$$\frac{t}{0.8917975296} = \frac{29}{0.6156614753}$$

$$0.6156614753t = 25.86212036$$

$$t = 42.00704673 \text{ ft}$$

$$RS = t = 42.0 \text{ ft}$$

33.

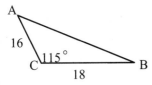

$$c^2 = a^2 + b^2 - 2ab\cos C$$

$$c^2 = 18^2 + 16^2 - 2(18)(16)\cos 115°$$

$$c^2 = 324 + 256 - 576(-0.4226182617)$$

$$c^2 = 324 + 256 + 243.4281188$$

$$c^2 = 823.4281188$$

$$c = \sqrt{823.4281188}$$

$$c = 28.69543725$$

$$c = 28.70$$

$$\frac{a}{\sin A} = \frac{c}{\sin C}$$

$$\frac{18}{\sin A} = \frac{28.69543725}{\sin 115°}$$

$$\frac{18}{\sin A} = \frac{28.69543725}{0.906307787}$$

$$\sin A = 0.5685064153$$

$$A = \sin^{-1}(0.5685064153)$$

$$A = 34.64613909$$

$$A = 34.6°$$

$$A + B + C = 180°$$

$$34.6 + B + 115° = 180°$$

$$B + 149.6° = 180°$$

$$B = 30.4°$$

35.

$$a^2 = b^2 + c^2 - 2bc\cos A$$

$$a^2 = 27^2 + 27^2 - 2(27)(27)\cos 34°$$

$$a^2 = 729 + 729 - 1,458(0.8290375726)$$

$$a^2 = 729 + 729 - 1,208.7360781$$

$$a^2 = 249.2632192$$

$$a = \sqrt{249.2632192}$$

$$a = 15.78807206$$

$$a = 15.79$$

$B = C$ since the triangle is isosceles

$$A + B + C = 180°$$

$$34° + 2B = 180°$$

$$2B = 146°$$

$$C = B = 73°$$

37.

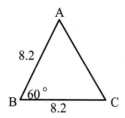

equilateral triangle, thus $A = C$

$$A + B + C = 180°$$
$$A + 60° + C = 180°$$
$$A + C = 120°$$
$$2A = 120°$$
$$A = 60° = C$$

therefore, equilateral triangle
so $b = 8.2$

39.

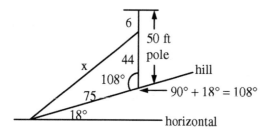

$$a^2 = b^2 + c^2 - 2bc \cos A$$
$$x^2 = 44^2 + 75^2 - 2(44)(75)\cos 108°$$
$$x^2 = 1,936 + 5,625 - 6,600(-0.3090169944)$$
$$x^2 = 1,936 + 5,625 + 2,039.512163$$
$$x^2 = 9,600.512163$$
$$x = \sqrt{9,600.5120163}$$
$$x = 97.9822033$$
$$x = 97.98 \text{ ft}$$

41. Find x and y

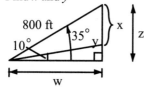

large right triangle

$$\sin 35° = \frac{z}{800}$$
$$0.5735764364 = \frac{z}{800}$$
$$z = 458.8611491$$
$$z = 458.9 \text{ ft}$$
$$a^2 + b^2 = c^2$$
$$a^2 + 458.8611491^2 = 800^2$$
$$w^2 + 210,553.5541 = 640,000$$
$$w^2 = 429,446.4459$$
$$w = \sqrt{429,446.4459}$$
$$w = 655.3216354$$
$$w = 655.3 \text{ ft}$$

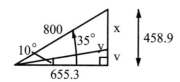

small right triangle

$$\tan 10° = \frac{v}{655.3216354}$$
$$0.1763269807 = \frac{v}{655.3216354}$$
$$v = 115.5508854$$
$$v = 115.6$$
$$x = 458.9 - 115.6$$
$$x = 343.3 \text{ ft vertical feet to be removed}$$

$$a^2 + b^2 = c^2$$
$$655.3^2 + 115.5508854^2 = y^2$$
$$429,418.09 + 13,352.00712 = y^2$$
$$442,770.0971 = y^2$$
$$\sqrt{442,770.0971} = y$$
$$y = 655.4097212$$
$$y = 665.4 \text{ ft}$$

distance from bottom to top of road bed

43.

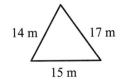

14 m   17 m

15 m

$a^2 = b^2 + c^2 - 2bc \cos A$

$\cos A = \dfrac{b^2 + c^2 - a^2}{2bc}$

$\cos A = \dfrac{(14)^2 + (15)^2 - (17)^2}{2(14)(15)}$

$\cos A = \dfrac{196 + 225 - 289}{420}$

$\cos A = \dfrac{132}{420}$

$\cos A = 0.3142857143$

$A = \cos^{-1} 0.3142857143$

$A = 71.68230159°$

$A = 71.7°$

Area $= \frac{1}{2} bc \sin A$

Area $= \frac{1}{2}(14)(15)\sin 71.68230159$

Area $= 99.67948636$

Area $= 99.68 \text{ m}^2$

45.

36 cm   110°   42 cm

$A = \dfrac{1}{2} ab \sin C$

$A = \dfrac{1}{2}(36)(42)\sin 110°$

$A = \dfrac{1}{2}(36)(42)(0.9396926208)$

$A = 710.4 \text{ cm}^2$

47.

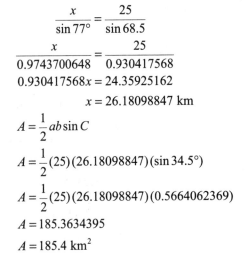

68.5°   x

y   34.5°

25 km

$68.5° + 34.5° + y = 180°$

$103° + y = 180°$

$y = 77°$

$\dfrac{x}{\sin 77°} = \dfrac{25}{\sin 68.5}$

$\dfrac{x}{0.9743700648} = \dfrac{25}{0.930417568}$

$0.930417568x = 24.35925162$

$x = 26.18098847 \text{ km}$

$A = \dfrac{1}{2} ab \sin C$

$A = \dfrac{1}{2}(25)(26.18098847)(\sin 34.5°)$

$A = \dfrac{1}{2}(25)(26.18098847)(0.5664062369)$

$A = 185.3634395$

$A = 185.4 \text{ km}^2$

49.

8 ft   8 ft

8 ft

Equilateral triangle so
$A = B = C = 60°$

$A = \frac{1}{2}(8)(8) \sin 60°$

$A = \frac{1}{2}(8)(8)(0.8660254038)$

$A = 27.71281292 \text{ ft}^2$

$A = 27.71 \text{ ft}^2$

51.

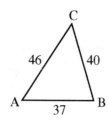

$$a^2 = b^2 + c^2 - 2bc \cos A$$

$$\cos A = \frac{b^2 + c^2 - a^2}{2bc}$$

$$\cos A = \frac{46^2 + 37^2 - 40}{2(46)(37)}$$

$$\cos A = \frac{1885}{3404}$$

$$\cos A = 0.553760282$$

$$A = \cos^{-1} 0.553760282$$

$$A = 56.37463153°$$

$$A = 56.4°$$

$$\text{Area} = \frac{1}{2} bc \sin A$$

$$\text{Area} = \frac{1}{2} (46)(37) \sin 56.37463153°$$

$$\text{Area} = 708.6073931$$

$$\text{Area} = 708.6 \text{ in}^2$$

53.

$$A = \frac{1}{2} xy \sin 108$$

$$A = \frac{1}{2} (115)(114.1653258) \sin 108°$$

$$A = 6,243.216428$$

$$c^2 = a^2 + b^2 - 2ab \cos C$$

$$c^2 = 130^2 + 95^2 - 2(130)(95) \cos 110°$$

$$c = 185.3992922$$

$$\frac{115}{\sin \theta} = \frac{185.3992922}{\sin 108°}$$

$$\theta = 36.151618°$$

$$108° + 36.151618° + \alpha = 180°$$

$$\alpha = 35.8°$$

$$\frac{x}{\sin 35.848382°} = \frac{185.3992922}{\sin 108°}$$

$$x = 114.1653258$$

$$A = \frac{1}{2} ab \sin C$$

$$A = \frac{1}{2} (130)(95) \sin 110°$$

$$A = 5,802.601933$$

Total area:

$$A = 6,243.216428 + 5,802.601933$$

$$A = 12,045.81836$$

$$A_{\text{total}} = 12,046 \text{ ft}^2 \text{ or } 12,050$$

Chapter 24 Trial Test

1. $\sin 125° = 0.8192$

3. $\cos 160° = -0.9397$

5. $(-8, 8)$

$\tan \theta = \dfrac{y}{x}$

$\tan \theta = \dfrac{8}{-8}$

$\tan \theta = -1$

    $\theta = \tan^{-1}(-1)$

    $\theta = -45°$

related angle is $45°$
quadrant II
$180° - 45° = 135°$

7.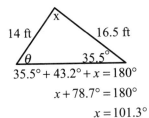

$35.5° + 43.2° + x = 180°$

    $x + 78.7° = 180°$

        $x = 101.3°$

$\dfrac{14}{\sin 35.5°} = \dfrac{16.5}{\sin \theta}$

$\dfrac{14}{0.5807029557} = \dfrac{16.5}{\sin \theta}$

$14 \sin \theta = 9.581598769$

    $\sin \theta = 0.6843999121$

       $\theta = \sin^{-1}(0.6843999121)$

       $\theta = 43.18843189$

       $\theta = 43.2°$

9.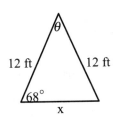

isosceles triangle
$68°$

$68° + 68° + \theta = 180°$

    $\theta + 136° = 180°$

        $\theta = 44°$

$\dfrac{x}{\sin 44°} = \dfrac{12}{\sin 68°}$

$\dfrac{x}{0.6946583705} = \dfrac{12}{0.9271838546}$

$0.9271838546x = 8.335900446$

       $x = 8.990558242$ ft

       $x = 8.991$ ft

11.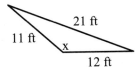

$21^2 = 11^2 + 12^2 - 2(11)(12)\cos x$

$441 = 121 + 144 - 264 \cos x$

$176 = -264 \cos x$

$-0.6666666667 = \cos x$

       $x = \cos^{-1}(0.6666666667)$

       $x = 131.8103149°$

       $x = 131.8°$

13.

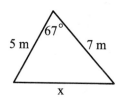

$$x^2 = 5^2 + 7^2 - 2(5)(7)\cos 67°$$
$$x^2 = 25 + 49 - 70(0.3907311285)$$
$$x^2 = 74 - 27.351017899$$
$$x^2 = 46.64882101$$
$$x = 6.829994217 \text{ m}$$
$$x = 6.830 \text{ m}$$

15.

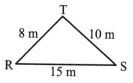

$$r^2 = s^2 + t^2 - 2st \cos R$$
$$\cos R = \frac{s^2 + t^2 - r^2}{2 st}$$
$$\cos R = \frac{8^2 + 15^2 - 10^2}{2(8)(15)}$$
$$\cos R = \frac{8^2 + 15^2 - 10^2}{240}$$
$$\cos R = \frac{64 + 225 - 100}{240}$$
$$\cos R = \frac{189}{240} = 0.7875$$
$$R = \cos^{-1} 0.7875$$
$$R = 38.04750745°$$
$$R = 38.0°$$

$$\text{Area} = \tfrac{1}{2} st \sin R$$
$$\text{Area} = \tfrac{1}{2}(8)(15)\sin 38°$$
$$\text{Area} = 36.97887911$$
$$\text{Area} = 36.98 \text{ m}^2$$

17.
$$a^2 = 76^2 + 110^2 - 2(76)(110)\cos 107°$$
$$a^2 = 5,776 + 12,100 - 16,720(-0.2923717047)$$
$$a^2 = 5,776 + 12,100 + 4,888.454903$$
$$a^2 = 22,764.4549$$
$$a = 150.8789412 \text{ ft}$$
$$a = 150.9 \text{ ft}$$

19.
$$A = \frac{1}{2}(12)(15)\sin 48°$$
$$A = \frac{1}{2}(12)(15)(0.7431448255)$$
$$A = 66.88 \text{ ft}^2$$

21.

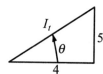

$$I_t^2 = 4^2 + 5^2$$
$$I_t^2 = 16 + 25$$
$$I_t^2 = 41$$
$$I_t = 6.4 \text{ milliamps}$$

23.

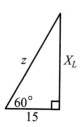

$$\cos 60° = \frac{15}{z}$$
$$0.5 = \frac{15}{z}$$
$$0.5z = 15$$
$$z = 30 \text{ ohms}$$